For my mother and father,
who would have liked the picture

How to
Make a
Jewish
Movie

How to
Make a
Jewish
Movie

by

Melville Shavelson

W. H. Allen

LONDON & NEW YORK

1971

Unless otherwise credited, all photos by Bob Penn for United Artists

How to Make a Jewish Movie by Melville Shavelson

Copyright © 1971 by Melville Shavelson

First British Edition, 1971.
Printed in the United States of
America for the publishers
W. H. Allen & Co. Ltd.,
Essex Street, London WC2R 3JG

ISBN 0 491 00156 8

ISRAEL is a country so small there is hardly room in it for a difference of opinion.

But they manage.

For instance, in Israel there are three sides to everything: Right, Wrong, and *Aha!*

I had barely informed some of my Israeli friends of the title of this forthcoming work when the debate began: Would it be better to call the book, "How *Not* To Make A Jewish Movie," or "How To Make A Bad Jewish Movie"? There was no doubt in their minds, though, that the book *should* be written. Anyone who had managed to make a motion picture with Kirk Douglas, John Wayne, Frank Sinatra, Yul Brynner, Angie Dickinson, and Senta Berger that had not even earned back its negative cost obviously had some important message for the world.

Aha!

They found great amusement in the fact that the late Colonel David "Mickey" Marcus, the forceful Jewish hero of this monumental flop, was distantly related to me through marriage. (After seeing the picture, the family decided it wasn't distant enough.) No one in Israel would ever make a movie about a relation, distant or close, unless he were putting up the money, a highly unlikely arrangement.

It reminded me of George Kaufman's celebrated remark that the only thing wrong with incest is that you have to do it with relatives.

The only thing wrong with making a picture in Israel is that you have to do it with friends.

The debate over whether this book should be written at all having been settled, en masse, by this group of friends, I took up the task with considerable misgivings. There is an old saying in Israel—let's face it, there are no *new* sayings in Israel—that a camel is a horse that was designed by a committee.

Dear reader, here comes your horse. It can go thirty days without water.

How to

Make a

Jewish

Movie

A Jewish boy becomes a man the day he turns thirteen. That is, everyone *tells* him he has become a man and gives him a fountain pen. But he is not allowed to sign checks with it. He is not allowed to smoke, drink—except for an occasional nip of sacramental wine on Biblical occasions—vote, get drafted, or have sexual intercourse with beautiful women. I'm not certain this last is written into the Torah, but that's how it worked out with me.

One thing he *is* allowed to do: he is allowed to make a *minyan*. Since I have a wife who is half Presbyterian, half Jewish and half Pennsylvania (who says it has to add up?), I am used to explaining authoritatively many Jewish customs I don't understand myself. At any rate a *minyan* consists of ten Jewish men who, when they are together, are only then allowed to pray to God. Why God doesn't accept prayers from less than ten I have never comprehended, but have usually passed it off as something akin to getting a charter rate on an airline. Anyway, nine old Jews, they could pray together for a hundred years and God would never hear them. But *ten* Jews, immediately God is notified someone is calling long distance, and He pays attention.

The morning after I had been plied with honey cake, wine, and fountain pens on the occasion of my thirteenth birthday, I was strolling along the Old Nyack Turnpike in my hometown of Spring Valley, New York, a sleepy community full of trees, grass, cows, and hotels displaying signs, "Dietary Laws Obeyed," that has now been encased in concrete and renamed the New York State Thruway. After a while, I became acutely aware of my changed status in life. Not that the cows along my route regarded me any less threateningly or the girls any more adoringly; no, it was our beloved rabbi, standing on the

1

steps of our little Temple in the wildwood, calling out to me in sugary tones.

"Look at the man!" he said. "How big he has grown! How clever! How handsome! Come here, my son, let me shake your hand!"

Never had he deigned to notice me before, except once during Hebrew class when I had attempted to slip out the window and he had slammed it on my fingers. Now, apparently, I was a distinguished and revered member of the community; therefore, I couldn't bring myself to hurt his feelings, in my newfound eminence, by refusing to be kind to him.

So I shook his hand.

Quick as a flash, he applied an arm lock and attempted to drag me into the little Temple, explaining that they had been waiting all morning for a tenth man to make their prayers legal, and God Himself must have sent me down that road, thirteen years and one day old!

For an old rabbi who was always complaining the community didn't supply him with enough money to eat properly, he was exceedingly muscular, and also had a working knowledge of jiu jitsu that was an essential part of his job every morning and evening, which consisted of standing on the steps of the Temple, peering up and down the road, *minyan*-hunting.

What he didn't know was that I had a tendency to run over the heels of my shoes, and my mother always had the shoemaker install steel plates in them to prevent me from wearing them out too rapidly and walking at a forty-five degree angle until we could afford a new pair. I brought one of my armored heels down sharply on the rabbi's renowned sore toe, and half a second later was running up the road, the beloved rabbi in hot, though limping, pursuit.

He made a pretty good race of it for the first furlong or so, and then class began to tell. All those years of drinking hot tea with lemon out of a glass, those countless hundreds of indigestible *kreplach* he had to consume at the home of the wife of the president of the congregation, had finally taken their toll. He began to falter, his breath became labored, his eye clouded, and as I reached the top of the hill, he came to a halt, shook his fist at me, and predicted I would come to no good and would marry a *shiksa*.

It all came true.

I have, since that time, been in flight from my heritage. I have never entered a synagogue of my own free will, except for the ceremonies attendant on birth, death, or marriage. My own children have been brought up free of any organized religion, and allowed to make their own choice or nonchoice, as they wished. And while I like to ascribe this to my liberal, free-thinking outlook on life, I know it's not true.

I was, quite simply, and not uniquely, ashamed of my Jewishness, of my father's and my mother's and my aunts' and my uncles' and even of the rabbi's. I can remember to this day coming back from a childhood visit to my mother's relations in London and telling a friend in the sixth grade all about it, only to be startled when he began to laugh.

"Gee, that must be funny," he said, not at all unkindly, "*English Jews!*"

I don't think I ever spoke to him again, him with his straight nose and his blonde hair and his bacon and tomato sandwiches.

When the opportunity came to make a picture in Israel, I suppose I felt I could dissipate the vague feelings of guilt I had nourished since leaving the panting *minyan*-hunter at the bottom of the hill by "doing something" for that "brave little country" of my forefathers.

I believed much of what happened after that could be entitled "The Rabbi's Revenge." He must be laughing now, wherever he is, especially if he's seen the grosses of the picture.

But I'm not laughing, not any more, about my father's habit of reading a newspaper that he opened from the back, and not because he was looking for the sports section; or my mother putting a napkin on her head before lighting the Friday candles and serving the world's toughest matzo balls; or the way they managed to send me ten dollars every week during the depths of the depression so I could go to college, for in education lay survival.

And that's what it's all about. Take it from one who just barely managed. That's what I found out, after shooting three hundred thousand feet of motion picture film in Israel—enough to span that sovereign state five times at its narrowest point. That's what it's all about.

Survival.

Don't think I rushed into all this with the enthusiasm of ignorance. I had been well trained in the disasters attendant on the writing, directing, and/or producing of motion pictures away from the comfortable—and fast-disappearing—womb of Hollywood. I have directed pictures at Cinecitta in Rome, Boreham Wood in England, and some studio in Paris whose name escapes me but you can see the Eiffel Tower through holes in the roof.

It was in Italy that I first decided to combine a pleasant European vacation at Paramount Pictures' expense with the leisurely shooting of a technicolor bonbon entitled (by someone who insisted on remaining anonymous) *It Started In Naples.*

The scene: *Ext. Naples Railway Station, Day.* Characters: Clark Gable, Vittorio De Sica. CAMERA PULLS BACK ahead of them as they cross through the throng outside the station, uttering brilliant dialogue by Jack Rose and your humble servant. BANG. CRASH. THUMP. A huge crane with a tremendous iron ball at the end of a steel cable is destroying the railway station immediately behind the camera where I am attempting to direct the actors. It seems that, almost twenty years after the end of World War II, the station has been declared unsafe because of bomb damage and is to be torn down. *Today.* CRASH. SMASH. THUD.

Of course, the workmen will stop the destruction while we shoot the scene—for a consideration in the neighborhood of half a million lire. As the iron ball swings closer and closer, I roughly calculate the dialogue remaining to be shot, the possibility of getting it in one take, the proximity of the steel ball, and the fact that my life insurance has lapsed. To Gable and De Sica I suggest they pick up the tempo just a bit—we don't want it to drag, do we?—and as the camera starts to roll, the Naples railway terminal disintegrates behind us, faster and faster, until the shot is completed in just under fifty seconds, everyone leaps out of the way, and we leave for our next location— and more *tsouris*—on the island of Capri.

One month later, returning from Capri, I visited the station again. The iron ball was still suspended in mid-air. Not one stone of the building had been touched since the moment I shouted, "Cut!" and ran for cover. For all I know the Naples railway station still stands, waiting shakily for World War III, intact except for a collapsed portion reaching from forty feet behind the camera position to the point where The King had uttered the last line of the brilliant dialogue.

We should have been forewarned. Before the company made its hegira from Rome to Naples, an Italian friend had inquired, Who was our Company Thief? While we felt there were several in our employ we didn't think they cared to be identified by title; but our friend complained we didn't understand. *Every* motion picture company going to Naples hires a Company Thief. He saves incalculable shooting time. Obviously, in Naples our equipment was going to be stolen, and since the Naples thieves' market is moved constantly to avoid the *carabinieri,* only a bonafide Thief in good standing would know exactly where it was every minute. Thus he could quickly buy back, at quite reasonable rates, our lenses, cameras, and whatever else of our equipment had disappeared during the balmy Neapolitan night, thereby reducing delays and costs to a minimum.

Obviously, we needed someone fast, efficient, and reliable, and our friend could heartily recommend a Thief with excellent references from both MGM and Warner Brothers. (NOTE: I hasten to mention that, although in subsequent years both MGM and Warner Brothers have been in considerable financial difficulties, these difficulties had nothing to do with *our* Thief. Right is right.) We hired him on the spot.

I must say he proved invaluable. There was never any delay in getting back any of our equipment that had mysteriously disappeared, and on several occasions he returned equipment to us that hadn't even been stolen. He did such an excellent job that at the end of shooting I presented him with my watch, although I wasn't aware of it until later.

One final trauma to complete this Italian opera. I have mentioned the late Clark Gable without thinking it necessary to repeat what everyone who ever worked with him knows: that he was one of the finest and most considerate of men at all times, not only to the little people, which gets you publicity, but also to the director, which sometimes gets you nothing but contempt from your brother actors. However, he did have in his contract a clause which declared his working day finished at 5:00 P.M., whether we were out of film or not.

I had been shooting a courtroom sequence with Gable, Sophia Loren,

De Sica, and four actors playing the judges—an Italian court has four judges and no jury, a kind of spread-the-work-among-us-lawyers idea. On the second day of shooting, an assistant director informed me that the chief judge hadn't shown up. When I inquired why, he told me, quite simply, that the actor had found a better job.

Five minutes later, when they pulled me down from the catwalk where I had gone for a short stroll, the assistant tried to calm me by explaining that there was no reason to get upset, since the actor had sent his brother to take his place.

It was then that Bob Surtees, the Academy Award-winning cameraman—but not for *our* picture, I must sadly add—endeared himself to all of us for all time.

"I wonder," he mused softly, "if Gable has a brother who'll work after 5?"

Let us shift the scene, mercifully, to England and the White Cliffs of Dover. This was the location unit for *On the Double,* starring Danny Kaye, on which a British crew and cameraman were employed. The White Cliffs, incidentally, are three tedious hours' drive from London, where we were based. We finally arrived one chilly morning, unbussed, and began to set up the equipment. This took an hour or so, and by this time the light was just about right for the shot we needed. But I noticed an unusual amount of commotion around the camera. The British, usually so reserved and self-contained, were muttering epithets at each other in a strange tongue—English—and several of them almost came to blows, which is not as dangerous as it may sound, since the last Briton of any note to hold the World's Heavyweight Championship was Henry VIII, and he won it by outpointing his wives.

The problem was simply that this was one of the first Panavision pictures to be shot in England, and the first Panavision lens, which had been imported to London from the Colonies, was a curious-looking monster that didn't seem to belong on the standard Mitchell motion picture camera we were using.

So they had left the lens in London, not being certain what it was.

But never fear, mate—they had already phoned the studio, the lens had been loaded into a speedy British sportscar, and at that very moment the sleek Jaguar XK140 was racing toward its garage with fuel pump trouble.

Eight hours later, just before the sun set on the British Empire, we got the lens and the shot. And the bill for the Jaguar.

Paris. The start of the *Tour de France.* We were shooting location shots for *A New Kind Of Love,* starring Paul Newman and Joanne Woodward, who had wisely remained in Hollywood while we employed doubles for their roles in France. Wisely, because I had not finished writing the script. I'm not certain I ever did.

We had hired an extra camera crew to cover the start of the race since our schedule was tight and our regular crew was busy on another location. The new crew was French, but—*mon dieu, certainement* they were familiar with our Mitchell camera!

Mais alors, more lens trouble. We only had one Panavision lens of the proper focal length, for the two companies. By that time it was getting late. We contacted our first unit and had the lens rushed over by a Paris taxi. The cab driver got out just as the starting gun for the race went off, and he almost dropped the lens.

There was no time for him to go around to the entrance—we were set up in a fenced area—so he ran to the fence and *threw* the $40,000 lens over the fence to the camera loader, who caught it with the hand that wasn't rolling a cigarette.

And only then did the trouble begin.

The lens went on the camera all right. But the camera itself would not close. The cameraman assured me it was because the film reels were too large for this *bête americaine.*

But the race had started!

I happened to be wearing a black overcoat, perhaps in mourning for my future. I threw it over both camera and camera operator to keep the light from getting into the open camera and ruining the film. The camera and operator looked like those early photographs of D. W. Griffith making *Birth of a Nation.* But we made the shot.

The crew and I waited all the next day for the laboratory reports. Had the film become light-struck? Was the day's work ruined?

The reports came in: exposure perfect!

We could hardly wait to see the rushes.

They were excellent. What we saw on the screen was a beautifully exposed shot of the rump of the 200th bicyclist as he disappeared around a corner a block from the camera.

When the lights came on, the camera operator informed me, happily, that he had finally learned how to close an American Mitchell camera. It is this little knob, *n'est-ce pas?*

I invoked the rabbi's curse, but I don't think it took.

Well, then. This is only a brief glimpse of the trials I had endured up to this point in a haphazard career. You must understand, of course, that in spite of it all, I have a deep and abiding affection for Italy and its people, the English and their courage and tradition, and the French and their Coca Cola.

But it was hardly sufficient preparation for making a picture in *Eretz Yisrael.* What I say now is meant in deepest kindness, but it is meant.

The Israelis are impossible.

Moreover, they *know* they are impossible, and they want it that way, and now that I've grown to know them a little better, I understand. It doesen't make it easier to shoot movies in their country, but where in the Ten Commandments does it say, "Thou shalt not take advantage of American directors"?

It can best be summed up by a joke that made the rounds in Israel recently. The fact that the joke has already made the rounds of America, England, Siam, and Outer Mongolia doesn't mean a thing. Until a joke arrives in Israel, it hasn't lived. This one has various versions. In the latest, President Nixon said to Golda Meir at their last meeting, "It will be difficult for you to understand my problems, since your country only has two million inhabitants, while I am the President of a country of 200 million citizens!"

And Mrs. Meir answered, "Mr. President, you don't understand *my* problem. I am the President of two million *presidents!*"

Had I heard, and understood, that story before I left for Israel, I might have never made the journey.

Who would blithely attempt to be the director of two million *directors?*

CHAPTER II

I had a friend—at least, I considered her one at the time—who was in charge of the story department at Metro-Goldwyn-Mayer, an astute, knowledgeable, and highly perceptive woman named Marjorie Thorsen. She called me one day to tell me that MGM had just dropped its option on one of the most exciting books she had ever read—Ted Berkman's biography of Colonel David "Mickey" Marcus—and why didn't I see if I could pick it up and make a *wonderful* movie?

At the time it never occurred to me that Marge didn't mention *why* her studio had dropped its option. Or why she was letting the opposition —I was under contract to Paramount Pictures—in on this certain Academy Award winner. I just looked on it as a nice, friendly gesture.

It also never occurred to me that this was the first nice, friendly gesture I had encountered since my arrival in Hollywood some twenty years earlier. Further, Miss Thorsen was a practicing Protestant. It never crossed my mind that the rabbi's curse could include *WASPs.*

Little, I assure you, did I know.

After reading Ted Berkman's book I knew I had to make that picture if it killed me. Did I hear a throaty, otherworldly, rabbinical chuckle? I literally ran to Paramount's front office and pantingly laid this hot project on the desk of the head man. Would Paramount buy it for me?

He was kindly, intelligent, shrewd, and went to Temple regularly every Rosh Hashonah. Who, he asked me, would want to see a picture about a Jewish general?

Since, at the moment—and ever since—I couldn't think of an answer, I decided to buy the rights to the book myself.

I phoned the kindly, intelligent, shrewd, young Italian Catholic agent who handled the property, explained how close this story was to my heart, and after only fourteen weeks of continuous haggling he let me outbid the eight other frantic buyers who were calling him night and day . . . about another story, I have since learned.

So there I was, the proud owner of a book which would make me immortal. But to become immortal there is one little thing you have to do first: you have to drop dead.

Which I was invited to do by the first half-dozen studio executives I brought my "project" to. The consensus seemed to be that they had already given to the United Jewish Appeal.

I was turned down by every studio in Hollywood, one in England, and twice by United Artists, which is in New York. The United Nations could use a little of that kind of unanimity.

This was not as discouraging as the meeting I had with the Israeli Consul in Los Angeles, who complimented me on my courage—my what?—and told me something my friend Miss Thorsen hadn't bothered to mention. Israeli Intelligence had informed him that the reason MGM had dropped the project was because agents of the Egyptian government had threatened to expropriate all MGM theaters in the Arab world if they made the picture.

I was never able to determine if this were rumor or fact; but in Hollywood rumors carry much more weight than fact, anyway, and besides, everyone I went to with the book *also* knew what Israeli Intelligence had told the Consul. The best way to spread information is to entrust it to a Jewish Secret Service.

So there I was, out of pocket a not inconsiderable sum, and trying to interest Hollywood in making a movie that might close 90 percent of its theaters in the Middle East.

Allah be praised.

Having failed in my first attempt to talk my way past the Egyptian propaganda barrier, I decided to write a screen treatment of Ted Berkman's book. A "treatment" is just that; it is akin to a massage, an effortless way to keep fit by having someone do all the work for you. It is, in essence, a condensation of lengthy material that no executive has the time or patience to absorb in its unprocessed state, and at the same time a bending of that material into a form that suits the story-telling abilities of the camera; further, it is a means of subtly pointing out why *this* picture absolutely cannot lose money.

Since the executive, even if he likes what he reads, cannot get the money for the production until he calls the executives in New York, and since in New York they have even less time to read than they do in Hollywood—it has something to do with the time differential, I think—all he has to explain to them is this last point.

Now, you would think an author with any brains would go directly to New York and explain it in person, but you are wrong. While this would eliminate telephone bills, it would also eliminate Hollywood. Reduced to its simplest terms, this is exactly what is happening to Hollywood today, except that now the studios are moving their New York offices to California, an action akin to inviting a boa constrictor to have dinner with you. But, in 1964, Hollywood was still reading.

So, somewhat reluctantly I wrote. Reluctantly, because my motion picture experience had been entirely with comedy, and I had firmly intended that the screenplay of this monumental epic would be written by a writer with a track record for writing monumental epics. But since such writers also commanded monumental salaries, and my Italian Catholic agent friend had relieved me of most of my ready cash, the cheapest writer I could find for this entirely preliminary and thankless job was myself.

I wrote the following thankless "treatment":

CAST A GIANT SHADOW
An Approach for the Screen to the Story of Mickey Marcus, Who Died to Save Jerusalem

> This is the great adventure story of our time, a revolt in the desert against incredible odds, and an American of the heroic proportions of Lawrence of Arabia,* but with a robust sense of humor, a heart, and the ability to love.**

* "Lawrence of Arabia," on its way to several Academy Awards at the time, was grossing $20,000,000.
** Translation, "Sex."

It is a story which all of the world that loves freedom*
can thank God is fact, not fiction. And all of the world
that roots for the underdog** can take heart in the
knowledge that the impossible, sometimes, can be accomplished through courage, and daring, and the unquenchable
human spirit.

This is an adventure for everyone.***

And it all took place in less than six unbelievable months;
the time it took for Colonel Mickey Marcus to find his
own personal River Kwai**** on the banks of the Jordan,
and to face the Guns of Navarone***** on the road to
Jerusalem.

His tanks were only trucks armored with gravel, and his
heavy artillery was a loudspeaker on a jeep;****** his air
force was a joke, and some of his army didn't have pants;
and 10 percent of his infantry were women.******* But they
fought a well-trained, well-equipped enemy to a standstill,
and earned the respect and admiration of a world that
had disowned them.

Mickey Marcus was an American, first, last, and always.
He had the inbred American hatred for injustice; he would,
probably, have fought this fight for any underdog who came
to him and asked, as this unborn nation asked, for his
help.********

    * **That is, everyplace where they don't expropriate your
theaters for making pictures about Jewish generals.**

    ** **In those days, this meant all of the United States, the largest
motion picture market in the world. But the underdog has gone somewhat out of style since Vietnam.**

    *** **Top *that* for an audience.**

    **** **Grossed $25,000,000.**

    ***** **Grossed $30,000,000.**

    ****** **Think of the savings in the budget.**

    ******* **The implication here is, maybe *they* didn't have pants,
either. Go to the movie and see.**

    ******** **So this is not *really* a Jewish story. Mickey would have
done the same thing if the country were, say, Saudi Arabia. Is it my
fault no little country was in trouble at the time except Israel? Is it
my fault that Israel is *always* in trouble? When God chose the Jews, who
would have guessed it was because He was anti-Semitic?**

It all began in December of 1947 when Mickey, a successful lawyer in Brooklyn, was tapped on the shoulder by a man he didn't know, and asked to join in the search for a general to help lead a lost army out of the wilderness.

The search was fruitless; there was no general willing to undertake the task; but its purpose was accomplished. By the time the search was over, the man who tapped Mickey on the shoulder knew he had found the only soldier willing and able to attempt the impossible. And to tell the truth, he had known it all the time.

And Mickey had to go home, and tell the wife* he loved he was breaking his promise to her; he was going back to war. When she had heard the facts she told him to go; there was no other choice.

But he promised he'd be home by June.

It wouldn't be the first fight; Mickey had been fighting since he was born, from the East Side of New York to West Point, and at West Point to the Intercollegiate Welterweight Championship, and to the respect of the entire Military Academy. That perhaps, was the toughest fight of all. But the friends he made at The Point are still the friends of his memory today, right up to the Chief of Staff of the United States Army, General Maxwell D. Taylor.**

It was at West Point, too, that his lifelong romance with Emma Chaison began. He married her, in uniform, after

---

* Emma Marcus, still lovely today, has not spoken to me since the premiere of the picture about her husband. The fact that I invented another woman in Mickey's life may have had something to do with it. The fact that she was not completely a fiction may have had something more. The fact that I made a not-very-good movie may have had the most.

** Intended to provoke visions of endless free tanks, free heavy bombers, free aircraft carriers. Where to put them in a story about Israel was another question. But who could resist the opportunity for such a bargain? Everybody, it turned out.

graduation; but no one in her family or his had ever married a soldier, so, while stationed on Governor's Island in New York, Mickey went to night school and made himself a lawyer, like every Jewish husband should be. For Emma he resigned his commission in the army.

(NOTE: I no longer want to interrupt with editorial comment. Colonel David Marcus was an authentic, larger than life hero, and for the countless millions who never saw the motion picture—and the few who did—I feel his story should be told, for once, without embellishment.)

There was still action: Fiorello La Guardia, then Mayor of New York, appointed him Deputy Commissioner of Correction, and Mickey, with his bare fists, walked into a New York City prison and cleaned up a mess of graft and corruption. They made a movie about him then; it was called *Blackwell's Island,* and John Garfield played the lead.

But in 1940 Mickey saw the handwriting on the wall; he rejoined the United States Army. By the time we were in the war, Mickey was Commandant of the tough Ranger Training School in Hawaii; more than that, he was the originator of many of its techniques for jungle warfare, and the author of its training manuals.

But he was too valuable a man to be left in Hawaii, so he was called to the staff of the Judge Advocate General in Washington, where his battle against a desk job began.

Mickey Marcus, under personal assignment from General George Marshall, drew up the terms of surrender for Italy. Later, he was to have the unique pleasure of drafting the terms of unconditional surrender for Nazi Germany, and to be at Roosevelt's side at Cairo, Teheran, Quebec, and Yalta. But in the meantime he wangled a trip to England at the precisely correct moment, and talked his friends in the 101st Airborne into giving him a free ride.

Mickey was in the first wave to be parachuted into Normandy on D-Day. It was his first parachute jump.

He was fighting his way through to the coast at the head
of a company when orders arrived from General Walter
Bedell Smith to kidnap him.

He was the only American officer who had to be captured
by his own army and returned to Washington.

But he managed to get back to the fighting when it reached
Germany. General George Patton appointed him liaison
officer with the survivors of the concentration camps as they
were being liberated. He talked Patton out of blankets,
trucks, first aid and medical supplies, which Patton's army
needed, but the victims of the camps needed more.

When the war was over, Colonel Marcus was made second
in command to General Lucius Clay in occupied Berlin,
partly because of his iron-clad stomach. Mickey, trained in
the night clubs of New York, could drink almost any man
under the table, including Russian General Zhukov; after
that, the negotiating would begin.

It was Mickey who organized the setting up of the
Nuremberg trials and later the Japanese War Crimes trials.

And then, it was over, and he returned to Brooklyn, and
to Emma, and made his promise to her that they would
never again be separated. There were no worlds left for him
to conquer—until the tap on the shoulder, and a world he
had never dreamed of, the new world being born in the
Middle East.

When he knew he was going to Palestine, Mickey sat
down and memorized every pertinent U. S. Army Training
Manual, many of which he had written himself. He knew
his baggage would be searched. When he arrived in the
Promised Land, then still under British Mandate, one of
his first acts was to transcribe, from memory, the books that
became the New Testament of the land which gave birth to
the Old.

Mickey arrived with the private blessings of the Pentagon,
but his identity was secret and he was known only as
"Colonel Stone." He was to be an "advisor;" but he wasn't
cut out for the job. Mickey couldn't advise a taffy pull
without turning it into a riot.

When he first saw the "army" he was to help, he almost

collapsed with laughter; it took a sense of humor even to contemplate it.

Here was the cockamamie fighting force of all time, a rag-tag collection of men and materiel. And this tin-can force had to be put in shape in a matter of weeks to face the armies of six countries outnumbering unborn Israel's population by sixty to one, whose Arab leaders had openly promised to murder them all as soon as the British army withdrew.

Mickey joined the military leaders of the invisible underground state and went to work. Tanks were created from trucks, armored with gravel and steel; bullets were shipped from Turkey, hidden inside bananas; guns were manufactured in factories supposedly producing false teeth. When war came, Mickey's credo was attack and attack, throw the enemy off balance, move over the desert so quickly at night they thought the little army had doubled or tripled in size.

In the words of *The New York Times,* "He blended ... underground experience with American techniques. He injected into the night-fighting Palmach—Israel's crack but unruly partisan-style raiders—the vital virtues of discipline. ... He persuaded the civilian chiefs that shoes and clothing were as important to soldiers as guns, the military chiefs that a brigade was more effective than battalions and a division more mobile than brigades. He preached successfully the doctrines of concentrated attack—the 'striking fist'—and of surprise harassment, helping thus to confuse and halt the armored Egyptian advance in the Negev. He had a major hand in planning three offensives against Jordanian-held Latrun, the key to Jerusalem.

"A measure of the Israelis' esteem was that in their time of sharpest peril they entrusted to this foreigner the unifying supreme command over all elements on their central front."

Mickey Marcus was made General of the Armies of Israel—the first in two thousand years.

In the middle of the most hectic preparations, Mickey flew back to Washington to beg for equipment. It was then that he was called to the White House, there to be presented, ironically, with the Order of Knight Commander of the British Empire by the British Ambassador, for his help in World War II. As he pinned it on him, the Ambassador said, "Don't wear this out in the sun, Mickey." And Mickey smiled at him, knowing. And returned to the sun, and the desert.

Throughout all the fighting, the bloodshed, and the danger, Mickey never lost his sense of humor. It was, perhaps, his most valuable weapon.

When his troops complained about their lack of firepower, he reminded them: "David did it with a slingshot, didn't he?"

And when Jerusalem was under terrible siege, and Mickey decided to build a secret road through the desert at night under the very guns of the Arab Legion fortress at Latrun, he was told it was impossible.

"But this ought to be easy," he protested, "After all, we made it across the Red Sea."

When the battle to build the road to Jerusalem had been won, the lifting of the siege assured, and a truce about to be declared, Mickey's job was all but finished and he knew it was time to go back home.

At three o'clock in the morning, camped in the hills above Jerusalem in preparation for a triumphal entry, Mickey found it difficult to sleep. He went out into the night, possibly to look down upon the Biblical city in the distance; more prosaically, and more probably, to answer the call of nature.

There was a sentry, a boy of eighteen, one of the refugees he had been fighting for, who challenged him. He spoke no language that Mickey understood, and Mickey thought he was joking, and joked back.

Mickey Marcus was shot through the head at 3:50 A.M. on the eleventh of June, 1948, six hours and ten minutes before the guns were silent—the last casualty before the truce on the Israeli side.

Mickey came home in June, as he had promised.

He was interred with full military honors in the place
he loved, the only American soldier buried at West Point
who fell while fighting under a foreign flag.

His headstone bears the quiet legend, "Colonel David
Marcus—A Soldier for All Humanity."

David Ben Gurion said, simply, "He was the best man
we had."

This little "treatment" trudged the rounds of Hollywood and wound
up bludgeoned, blackjacked, or ignored by every front office and story
department in town. Who wants to see a picture about a Jewish
general?

It dawned on me that a majority of the executives who were reject-
ing my "project" had once been small boys, running up some distant
hill, pursued by a rabbi in quest of an elusive *minyan*. They were still
running.

Obviously, I had to persuade them that this story of a tough Jewish
soldier who helped save the cradle of Judea by teaching a Jewish army
how to fight a Jewish war had nothing to do with Jews. It would be
like persuading them that *I Am Curious, Yellow* grossed $22 million
because audiences were interested in its philosophical stance against the
Vietnam war.

Now, there is a game played in Hollywood every time an actor
called Richard Carlton or Buck Sherman or an executive named Harri-
son Wilson becomes successful; it is called, "I wonder what his name
was before?" The implication is, always, that it was Schwartz.

But there is one actor in Hollywood about whom the canard of
Schwartzism is absolutely unthinkable. His name stands for the Fourth
of July and sourdough bread and bulldogging steers and George Washington and pork chops.

John Wayne.

If God set out to print a million photographs of Jewishness, he
would use John Wayne as the negative.

If I could persuade this Rock of Gibralter of Gentile culture to agree
to appear in Mickey's movie, it would be equivalent to circumcizing
the entire Israeli army. The major drawback to making the picture,
conscious and subconscious, on the part of the wary executives, would

have vanished. And in its place would come the assurance of that vast audience that goes to see every John Wayne movie, no matter what it is about.

That it is always about the same thing didn't occur to me at the time. Or if it did, I brushed it under the rug.

How to bring forth this miracle? I had once co-written a picture for "Duke"—everyone calls him that whether they know him or not; but everyone seems to know him. I worked on it in collaboration with Jack Rose, and it was entitled *Trouble Along the Way*. Believe me, it was. Wayne played an alcoholic football coach who was running away from a broken marriage and wound up coaching a tiny Catholic college. There was a difference of opinion between Wayne and the authors as to how the story line should run, and since this was the first picture on which I functioned as a "producer," I decided to Produce. Wayne was given one version of the script; on the days that he was not shooting, we prepared another version, to film with subsidiary characters, that changed the plot line to *our* liking.

Only one thing went wrong; Duke showed up on the set on a day he wasn't supposed to be there, and found out what was going on.

Ordinarily, he is one of the kindest and most level-headed of men. But when crossed, and particularly when double-crossed, he can make an underground nuclear explosion seem like a baby's sigh.

Wayne outweighed me by a hundred and five pounds. By the end of our confrontation—which was, fortunately, purely verbal—he outweighed me by a hundred and seven.

We finished the picture—*his* way—shortly afterward, and went our separate paths, his mainly on horseback.

But Duke is truly a big man, in many ways. I was startled one day to find in my mail a letter from him, signed in that distinguished scrawl, telling me how much he had liked and admired one of my recent pictures. I wrote him how much I had liked and admired one of *his* recent pictures.

Now, in Hollywood, you can phone a friend and tell him you *loved* his last horribly inept masterpiece and both of you know you are lying. But to put it in *writing* to an *enemy*—that, my friends, is known as Sincere. And I was certain this was.

There is something else of which I am certain. While John Wayne has the deserved reputation of being—in the stock phrase—several miles to the right of Louis XIV, he is there because he honestly believes it is best for America. Any man who will invest—and lose—over a million dollars of his own money to bring the story of *The Alamo* to the screen is not merely paying lip service to an ideal. For John Wayne, the Alamo is here, today, and he is inside it.

To Duke, it is immaterial whether a man is Jewish or not; what matters is, how does he stand on the Boston Tea Party?

So I called him, a little hesitantly, and told him I wanted to tell him a story. Immediately, he invited me to the offices of his company, Batjac, on the second floor of the Cecil B. DeMille building on the Paramount lot.

There was no time to find out if the stairway had been booby-trapped. I climbed it, opened the door, and stood face to face with the American monument who, on our last meeting, had called me names my rabbi couldn't even pronounce.

CHAPTER III

D uke shook my hand warmly and offered me a chair. As soon as the circulation came back into my right arm, I took it.

And then I told him Mickey's story, as briefly and simply as I could. When I finished, I read him this telegram which was received by the Israeli mission in New York City, June 11, 1948:

PLEASE INFORM MRS. DAVID MARCUS THAT HER HUSBAND FELL LAST NIGHT AT HIS POST IN THE HILLS OF JERUSALEM STOP THE GOVERNMENT OF ISRAEL THE JEWISH ARMY AND ENTIRE JEWISH PEOPLE OF PALESTINE SEND HER EXPRESSION OF DEEPEST SYMPATHY IN HER GRIEF STOP AS A MAN AND A COMMANDER HE ENDEARED HIMSELF TO ALL THOSE WHO CAME INTO PERSONAL CONTACT WITH HIM AND HIS FAME SPREAD THROUGH ALL RANKS OF OUR ARMED FORCES STOP HE WAS RECENTLY APPOINTED AS SUPREME COMMANDER OF OUR FORCES AT THE JERUSALEM FRONT AND BECAME IMMEDI-ATELY THE MOVING SPIRIT OF THAT CAMPAIGN THE MOST DIFFICULT AND FAR REACHINGLY IMPORTANT OF ALL THOSE WHICH WE HAVE HAD TO FIGHT SO FAR STOP HIS NAME WILL LIVE FOREVER IN THE ANNALS OF THE JEWISH PEOPLE

DAVID BEN GURION

During all of this, Wayne hadn't moved one expensive muscle. I wondered if I had been wrong; whether, behind that Gibraltarlike stock anti-Semitic façade, lay some *real* anti-Semitism.

21

Duke got to his feet and took six and a half months to light a cigarette. Then he exhaled, and I could see my future disappearing in the tobacco smoke.

"Well," he said, "that's the most *American* story I ever heard."

I wasn't certain I had understood him correctly. Ben Gurion had signed that telegram—not Ben Franklin.

"Everybody's knockin' the United States today," Duke said, pacing the floor and covering half an acre of carpet with each stride. "Claiming we're sendin' in troops all over the world to knock over some little country where we've got no right to be. They've forgotten who we are and what we've done. At a time like this, we *need* to remind them of how we helped the littlest country of all get its independence. How an American army officer gave his life to do it."

"Mickey was Jewish," I insisted on reminding him.

"Don't gimme that crap," said Duke, "Jesus Christ was Jewish, too, and he didn't even go to West Point."

I thought I followed him. I decided to press my advantage.

"Jerusalem," I said. "You could call Jerusalem the Jewish Alamo."

Duke paused and glared at me.

"You out of your mind? That picture lost so much money I can't buy a pack of chewing gum in Texas without a co-signer! Let's not remind anybody."

Then he looked at me.

"That's a good story," he said. "What's your problem?"

I told him of all the executives who had turned me down, either through honest judgment or their own subliminal fear of being caught by the galloping rabbi.

"I dunno how the hell *I* can help you," Wayne rumbled, understanding immediately. "I'm too old to play Marcus and even if I wasn't, a deaf and dumb blind Eskimo wouldn't be convinced I was Jewish—unless he hadn't been to Temple lately."

"All I want you to do," I told him, "is agree to appear somewhere in the picture. It's a ploy. You could call it Gentile by association."

Duke grinned.

"They got any cowboys on those camels down there?" he inquired.

"No," I said, "but one of Mickey's greatest friends, the one who spoke to President Truman for him when the United States and the United Nations were about to abandon Israel, was Major General John H. Hildring. And during World War II, Mickey was very close to General Patton and to General Maxwell Taylor. I want to create the character of a general who would represent the entire Establishment Brass Hat Military Complex, and have him turn all the stereotypes upside down, by acting like a human being."

"How would he do that?"

The Actor was at work now, the Star, trying to visualize a Role, watching me, shrewdly, as the wheels clicked. Behind that Marlboro Country façade resides a sharp, show-business-wise intellect.

"Well," I said, "by doing and saying cockeyed things. Like, 'Jesus Christ was Jewish, too, and he didn't even go to West Point.'"

Duke held out his hand.

"Okay," he said. Laconically is the word, I believe.

I took his hand. Mine had regained a little feeling.

"Okay?" I couldn't believe it.

"It's a deal—if I like the first thirty pages of the screenplay."

I heard that protective clause. Marlboro Country is only skin deep.

I did my best to find a Great Screenwriter to compose those vital words. Someone with the depth of Shakespeare, the fire of Albee, the wit of Shaw, who could write John Wayne dialogue.

All those I approached were unwilling or unavailable. They were also Jewish. And running up that hill.

So I made a fast deal with myself and sat down to write Mickey's story into screenplay form. When I had completed thirty or so pages, I sent them over to the Batjac Corporation offices and called my doctor for an open-end Miltown prescription.

Duke himself was on the phone when it rang the next day.

"I'll make this picture only under one condition," he drawled. I think you can drawl that.

I hesitated, figuring the least he would demand would be that the character of the general be made the hero, and Mickey a Presbyterian minister who had adopted Judaism as a cover for his activities for the CIA. All right, I thought, all great writers have to learn to bend a little. So I asked him, "What condition?"

"That you write the rest of this screenplay yourself," said Wayne, and hung up.

An author doesn't receive many genuine compliments in his life. John Wayne was not Clive Barnes or Judith Crist or Pauline Kael—all of whom have taken occasion to flay me alive—but he was John Wayne and he *looks* three times as honest as they do. When he says, "Good morning," you can *believe* him. I believed him.

Oh, how I believed him! I reveled in his literary approval, and still do. No matter that those thirty pages were the first we cut from the finished script; no matter that the movie later was split down the middle, gutted and sprinkled with salt like a kosher chicken by 90 percent of the critics who reviewed the finished product. John Wayne liked the pages I had written about a Jewish boy who had grown up in a Jewish family, married a Jewish girl, and fought for Israel. And who should know this *milieu* better than Wayne?

This meant that I had made the big leap; not merely the author of light and frivolous entertainments, I was now capable of writing *drama*. Stark, searing, serious—oh, with the occasional leavening of a *bon mot* to show that I could handle anything—but stirring, meaningful prose, with the high purpose of marshaling public opinion to the side of the beleaguered little country that might disappear without my assistance.

If Alexandre Dumas *père* had phoned me and offered to write the remainder of the screenplay merely for the privilege of having me direct his work, I would have inquired when was the last time John Wayne liked anything *he* wrote?

Having made this decision, you might think, if you are unfamiliar with the ways of the cinema, that the next move was for me to lock myself up with my muse and complete the entire script while I was on a hot roll.

Wrong. The next step was to lock myself up with my agent and figure out how to clinch a deal with a studio and get Wayne's signature to a contract before I wrote something he might *not* like.

Which, in my rare lucid moments, I admitted was a possibility.

My agent at that time was a quiet-spoken man named Herman Citron. So, I understand, was Attila the Hun a quiet-spoken man. Mr. Citron's reputation in a cut-throat business passeth belief. For over a quarter of a century, his word has been considered more binding than the Oath of Allegiance; his handshake can be deposited in the Bank of America, where it will draw interest. The clients of his office, Chasin-Park-Citron, include such lights as Jimmy Stewart, Dean Martin, Rock Hudson, Julie Andrews, and Shirley MacLaine, for all of whom he has been known to do battle as fiercely as if they were penniless inmates of a heartless orphanage.

Five minutes after I had signed a contract for him to represent me, he informed me firmly we would undoubtedly be together until one of us died. Consequently, for a long time I was unwilling to terminate our association for any reason whatever. Maybe he didn't mean it that way, but I played it safe.

And there was a certain warm feeling I got when he walked into a meeting of hostile studio brass with me. It was nice to know he was on *my* side.

Herman's strategy this time was summed up in three words: Mirisch. Meaning Harold, Walter, and Marvin, collectively the world's largest independent producer of films. I pointed out that their company released through United Artists, who had already turned Mickey's story down.

"When *you* go to United Artists," said Herman, "and when Harold Mirisch goes, it's two different things. First of all, he's making a lot of money for them."

"And, secondly?" I asked.

"Who cares?" Herman answered, reasonably.

Then he laid out the plan, like a football coach before the big game. We would walk in together. He would mention casually that John Wayne had approved the first thirty pages of the screenplay. Then I would tell the story.

Tell? But what about the magnificent treatment I had written? Couldn't the Mirisches read?

Of course they could read. They could read so well, they could afford to hire people to read *for* them. If I gave them the treatment, that would be the end of the meeting. They would send it over to the cold storage division—also known as the Story Department—where it would be read, dehydrated, compressed, and placed on Harold's desk to be used as a paperweight.

Tell the story.

What Herman was implying, I suppose, was that I had developed a style in detailing Mickey's history. There was a quaver in my voice now when I reached each climax, not so much due to my histrionic ability as to the fact that I was reflecting on all the time, effort, and money I had sunk into this impossible project. Desperation, when telling a desperate story, carries its own conviction.

Harold Mirisch was sitting behind his big desk when we walked in, Walter and Marvin lounging nearby. The atmosphere was relaxed, unlike any high-pressure executive suite of my experience. We had all met before. Harold was kindly, wore Harold Lloyd glasses, had a gravelly voice, and during the meeting paid close attention to every word I uttered while placing bets on six football games in various parts of the nation. The fact that in every case I knew he was backing the wrong team made me believe that I had a chance.

By the time I had reached the words of David Ben Gurion at the end of Mickey's odyssey, I had a feeling my luck had changed. Walter and Harold exchanged glances with Marvin, and Herman was looking at the ceiling and frowning, a certain sign he was pleased. It is Herman's rule never to show his real emotions, so you take the one he shows and change its course by 180 degrees, which brings you somewhere near target.

It was then that Harold remarked that he had been informed—secretly, of course—that MGM had dropped the project because of their fears that their theaters would be expropriated. I nodded glumly.

But Harold had a sparkle in his eye. Did I realize that United Artists didn't own any theaters in the Middle East?

I told him, in all fairness, that I had journeyed twice to New York to speak to its executives, and twice had been refused.

"When *you* go to United Artists," said Harold, "and when *I* go, it's two different things."

Herman frowned happily.

Shortly afterward, Harold lost six football games and we were in business together. It is to United Artists' credit that they were the only source of financing willing to take the risk of bringing a major motion picture about Israel to the screen at that time.

When Harold Mirisch died in 1968, *The New York Times* led off its obituary with a description of how he had fought Hollywood's timidity and secured financial backing for *Cast a Giant Shadow,* the story of a Jewish general.

Would I had left him a more profitable epitaph.

CHAPTER IV

Nate Edwards stands six feet two, wears a ten-gallon hat and cowboy boots. And I don't mean casually. I think he wears them to bed. On one occasion, in London, when we were forced to share a hotel room because the cattle show was on—yes, *London*—the two of us were slumbering side by side when I could swear he kicked in his sleep and roweled me. Nate is clear of eye, firm of spirit, and speaks pure Nebraskan. Or Oregonian. At any rate, one of the Gentile states.

If you were looking for a man to negotiate contracts in Tel Aviv with Israeli businessmen and Jewish labor unions in their native tongue, with sidebar conferences in Yiddish, who, of all men, would you choose?

If you were the Mirisches, Honest Nate Edwards. He was their chief production man on all of their pictures. Of course, he had no personal knowledge of the Holy Land. But even God had to learn by experience there.

Nate Edwards was assigned as production manager of *Cast a Giant Shadow,* and in November of 1964 the two of us left for Israel on a preliminary "scouting trip." I was certain Nate would spend most of his time on his hands and knees, sniffing for the spoor of Indian war parties.

It is not generally understood that the two or three hours of carefree mayhem and romance that make up the average motion picture "spectacle" require months, and sometimes years, of painstaking preparation to reduce the actual, expensive "shooting time" in front of the cameras to an economic minimum. My job was to search out the locations we would be photographing, to research the details of Mickey Marcus's participation in Israel's war for the screenplay I was still writing, and to interview personnel for the cast and crew. Nate would participate in most of this, and in addition would be negotiating for housing, transportation, construction, and the thousand-and-one financial details necessary before boy can meet girl, or horse, or, these days, another boy. Seven months were spent in Israel preparing for some eight weeks of photography. The mountain labored and brought forth a Jewish mouse.

Nate Edwards and I arrived at the Dan Hotel in Tel Aviv after a 9,000-mile journey during which Nate had never once removed his ten-gallon hat. When we registered at the desk, the clerk looked at our names and had us figured out in an instant. Nate was a nice Jewish man who had obviously changed his last name for business reasons. And probably his nose. I had obviously changed my *first* name, which was never done and made me an object of suspicion. The ten-gallon hat? Who knew what kind of *yarmulkas* they were wearing in Beverly Hills these days?

I was fearful that the entire production—which was still on delicate ground, because we had not yet secured a leading man—would go under when the two cultures, East and Nate's, met head on.

The kosher laws would probably drive him up the walls. This bewildering array of dietary admonitions keeps Orthodox Jews thumbing through the rule books like uncertain baseball umpires, fearful of committing some inadvertent gastronomic error which might keep them out of Heaven—where, surely, they also keep kosher. The Deborah Hotel, down the street from the Dan, could never be explained to him; here all 130 Talmudic laws are strictly obeyed, with separate restaurants for dairy and meat, and strict regulations against table-hopping; the Deborah has His and Hers *mikvahs,* the ritual baths for spiritual as well as bodily cleanliness; and since no Orthodox Jew is permitted to do work of any kind on the Sabbath, which extends from sundown Friday to sundown Saturday, the staff of the Deborah spends Friday morning tearing the toilet tissue into usable pieces for the guests. I could just see Nate, at the Deborah, charging out of his bathroom shouting, "Some dumb sumbitch tore all my toilet paper into confetti! Who the hell's birthday is it?"

The confusion of the kosher laws turned many of the Tribes of Israel into vegetarians out of sheer frustration. Tel Aviv is dotted with vegetarian restaurants, where you can get anything you want to eat:

chopped liver (soybeans), roast beef (soybeans), broiled lobster (soybeans), and Canadian bacon (soybeans). The fact that it all tastes like soybeans doesn't seem to bother anyone. After all, when a Jewish mother cooks an honest-to-goodness roast beef, it *still* tastes like soybeans.

As it turned out, Nate Edwards spent forty-eight hours trying to get ham and eggs at the Dan Hotel, and finally succumbed to the pangs of hunger and went into the vegetarian restaurant. He loved it. On his ranch in Oregon, he *grows* soybeans. Every bite was making him richer.

Thus fortified, Nate plunged into a round of meetings to arrange preliminary deals for housing, transportation, and equipment. He didn't understand anything in the Hebrew language except the numbers, but that was all he needed. In his mind, he interpolated for the number "shtaim" three head of cattle, and so on. By the end of a business conference, he owned the ranch.

But it was all "if" money. I once fantasized for myself the ideal racetrack: it would be run on the honor system. After every race, you would go up to the payoff window and tell the mutuel clerk which horse you had been *thinking* of betting on and how much, and he, being a gentleman, would immediately pay off. Of course, it was also incumbent upon you to tell him when you had lost, but since I was relying on the inherent honesty of the average American horse player, it was inevitable that everyone would get rich. But, alas, no such track exists, or ever will. Neither do such deals as Nate worked out in Israel. The Mirisches, in their infinite wisdom, were not committing any of their cash before a star had been set to play Mickey.

We were all playing games, the Israelis knew it, and enjoyed playing as much as we did. They took great pleasure in pretending to be schnooks. Everyone loves a character part.

While Nate was involved in these mythical negotiations, the Israeli Army entered my life, in the person of Lieutenant Colonel Gershon Rivlin.

The name itself conjures up visions of Paul Newman in *Exodus,* or at least General Moshe Dayan in the Sinai. But instead of an eye-patch, Gershon wears bifocals. His uniform looks as if he laundered it himself, which is possibly true. He is neither brawny nor tall nor bloodthirsty. It seems impossible that this friendly, soft-spoken, lovable man spent twenty years fighting the British Occupying Forces as one of the leading members of the Underground, and then fought through the War of Independence beside all of the new state's legendary heroes.

Gershon himself has never been looked upon as a legendary hero because he never insisted. He probably said, "You should excuse me," before he pressed the trigger of his tommy gun. He contented himself with writing down the exploits of others and ignoring his own. He is the Official Historian of the Israeli Army, which means that he gets into more arguments than anyone else in Israel—no mean achievement.

Gershon appeared at my hotel one morning in his faded uniform. He wore no tie. I never met anyone in the Israeli Army who wore a tie. Come to think of it, before the advent of air conditioning, I never met an Israeli who wore anything around his neck, unless it was a prayer shawl. The tie is the mark of the tourist, a badge as visible as if someone had lettered on his forehead the legend "Shlemiel."

In my brief encounter with the American military mind during several months' service in the ROTC, we spent most of our drill time learning to tie our ties. And to polish our shoes. And shine our buttons. Gershon's shoes, I noted, were not polished. One of them, in fact, was not tied. One button hung slightly loose. Thus, the mystery of the invincibility of the Israeli Army was immediately solved. While the other side is tying its ties and shining its shoes and polishing its buttons, the Israeli Army is shooting at them.

Gershon—Lieutenant Colonel Rivlin, in case you, like me, keep forgetting his rank—was apologetic because we couldn't go to see Ben Gurion immediately. The Grand Old Man of the State of Israel, then in his late seventies, was busy on his *kibbutz* near the Negev desert, digging holes for palm trees or pouring concrete. He, of course, had been Mickey Marcus's mentor, his advocate, and, sadly, his eulogist.

What Gershon didn't know is that I didn't want to see Ben Gurion. I had included him as a character in the screenplay, under a fictitious name, and I didn't want to have to argue history, drama, and, probably, screenwriting, with the tough old warrior who had fought off the British, the Arabs, and most of his own countrymen in his incredible and successful effort to create an impossible nation. Looking back,

I wish I had let him rewrite. What critic would dare attack *him?* Outside of Israel, of course. Inside, he is attacked every day. In fact, during my time there, Ben Gurion was expelled from his own party, every member of which still has to carry a membership card with the old man's picture on it.

Instead, Gershon arranged for me to meet the entire roster of heroes who had fought beside Mickey, which included most of the Israeli Army. It included Gershon, too, but he modestly tried to keep himself in the background, dropping only an occasional hint of his own participation in those terrible but exciting days, which will never come again—except possibly every two or three years.

We would drive in his dusty old jeep with Gershon's nephew, a corporal, at the wheel—Gershon didn't seem to drive a car, ride a horse, or, so far as I knew, roller-skate, but he could *walk* my entire ROTC unit into the ground—while he would drop incidental bits of information that gradually evoked the image of a serio-comic war of extinction, a seemingly contradictory description that seemed perfectly appropriate because this was Israel and the heroes were Israeli. The Jewish people have lost their sense of humor only once in their existence, and that was to a vaudeville Austrian wearing a Charlie Chaplin moustache; it was almost fatal, and the lesson is remembered.

Gershon would feed me details of the humorous side of the war. One day he pointed out the site of Camp Eliyahu, a secret base used in 1947 to train officers of the Palmach, the clandestine Israeli commandos, when the British started to pull out of Palestine just before the end of the Mandate. Nearby was a camp that had been under British control at the time. Sometimes members of the Underground Army—in mufti, of course—would arrive at the British camp by mistake. The British sentry on duty was always considerate.

"Sorry, old chaps," he would explain, "you want the secret Jewish camp—it's half a mile down the road. Can't miss it."

Rivlin also told me of a British sergeant major who became incensed at his own officers for their countenancing of Arab atrocities. To "save the honor of the British Empire," he decided to help the Israelis. Knowing they were short of transport, he contrived to steal the armored car of the British Commander-in-Chief of the Middle East, a vehicle so well known it stood out in Palestine like a pork chop at a B'nai B'rith picnic. He delivered it to a grateful but embarrassed Underground Army headquarters. They had to risk their lives to return it before its discovery could unmask their entire operation.

Gershon also passed along to me the story of May 15, 1948, when Ben Gurion sent a historic and flowery dispatch to all the commanders on the fighting front announcing the creation of the new State of Israel. He got the following communication from one of his harried officers: DON'T BOTHER ME WHEN DO I GET THE TRUCKS YOU PROMISED?

One of the first heroes Gershon took me to visit was a small, wiry man with the unlikely name of Pinhok, the Official Smuggler of the Israeli Army, who lived in one of the few beautiful *kibbutzim* I ever encountered. The hardy socialist pioneers who established most of the early communal farms had little time for beauty or comfort; anything attractive was looked upon with suspicion, including women, who were judged by muscle and the ability to milk a cow dry in three powerful clutches.

Pinhok's *kibbutz*, however, had become quite prosperous over the years, and there were blooming oleander trees and flowering lawns and graceful buildings, giving an unreal Gentile aura to the entire interview, which was unreal enough to begin with. I concluded that anyone with the talent to smuggle arms, airplanes, and money through the treacherous Middle East would have only slightly more difficulty in smuggling beauty into Israel.

Pinhok was open, forthright, and outspoken, the most unsmuggler-like smuggler of my acquaintance—which, come to think of it, was limited to Pinhok himself. When I inquired by what training, what devious preparation, he had acquired the knowledge to become Chief Smuggler for the overmatched little army, he merely shrugged.

"They told me I was a smuggler, so I smuggled," he said.

No, he had had no training. No experience. What's so difficult about smuggling? You can get killed, but what's so difficult? Besides, the entire war was new. The Israelis had officers who had never commanded, pilots who had never flown, a navy that had never fired a shot, and a government that had never been elected.

Pinhok, at least, had been in business. The difference between retailing and smuggling is a matter of filling out forms or not filling out forms. Smuggling actually takes less time, since it is essentially nontaxable.

So he had wandered over Europe, collecting arms and ammunition, but finally had decided it was a waste of time and had come back home. Why should he bother traveling, picking up a few rifles here, some machine guns there, from unwilling suppliers? Everybody in the world was shipping military weapons to the Arabs. England, France, Russia, the United States. The Arabs were, to use Pinhok's succinct phrase, up to their ass in hand grenades. They had more trucks than they could drive, more cannon than they could shoot, more machine guns than they could load. When an Arab has more than he needs to eat or drink or sit on, he opens a bazaar.

"Do you mean to tell me," I inquired, "the Arabs *sold* you their own weapons?"

Again, Pinhok shrugged. Where else would they have found such a good customer? Cash in advance, we pick up, you don't even have to deliver! No returns, no complaint department!

Two weeks before the outbreak of hostilities, Pinhok himself had bought two truckloads of arms and ammunition from King Talal of Jordan—father of the present king. To paraphrase a *bon mot,* when you have an Arab for an enemy, you don't need a friend.

Of course, it wasn't all that simple. Much of the needed supplies were stockpiled in Egypt. In Egypt the most valued commodity at the time was not a gun or a tank or a rifle. It was heroin.

The cheapest supplies of heroin existed in Lebanon. Pinhok organized a force of Arabic-speaking Israelis who traveled to Lebanon by various routes with some of the underground government's meager supply of hard currency and purchased heroin. This was then smuggled into Palestine through normal, everyday heroin-smuggling channels.

"You turned the Israeli government into dope smugglers!" I almost shouted at him.

Pinhok offered me some lemonade made from lemons picked by his own hand on the *kibbutz,* and nodded.

"It was a living," he said, accenting the last word. Survival.

The heroin was divided up and sealed inside small lead capsules. In the south, in the Negev, is a tribe of Bedouin who have led caravans across the vast reaches of the desert for so many thousands of years they regard the Dead Sea Scrolls as the latest Book of the Month.

Incredibly, for twenty years they had been infiltrated by Israelis posing as Arab nomads, who spoke their language and lived among them as their own kind, waiting, always waiting, for the moment when they could be of use.

It was these Jewish Bedouin who were handed the lead-encapsulated heroin. It was their job to shove their arms down the throats of their pack-camels and drop the capsules in. The weight of the lead made it impossible for the camels to cough them up, and carried them into the camels' stomachs where, again because of the weight, they remained.

When the caravans crossed the border into Egypt, no amount of searching ever uncovered the hiding place of the heroin, although one or two camels were occasionally observed cantering sideways across the desert, whistling, "Yellow Submarine" between their snaggly teeth.

Safely inside Egypt, the camels were butchered, the drugs retrieved, and the money from their sale used as bribes to secure the needed war materiel, which was then smuggled back into Palestine on returning caravans shepherded by the same Bedouin tribe.

Shortly after the war began, an Egyptian-piloted fighter plane was shot down over this same desert. It was found to contain, under the floorboards, twenty pounds of pure heroin. This had nothing to do with Pinhok. To the pilot, obviously, the war was secondary. He was in business for himself.

All of this sounded so unreal, I decided against including it in the screenplay. I was having difficulty enough making Mickey's history credible; Pinhok's verged on science fiction. So I told Gershon it was time to move on to the more sober military minds with whom Colonel Marcus had worked during the country's struggle for independence. I hoped, from them, to get an insight into the events and the man, which would help in the construction of the story when I returned to Hollywood.

CHAPTER V

I had never in my life met an authentic hero, except possibly my mother, until Rivlin introduced me to the men who had led the rag-tag Army of Israel to its first victory.

That they were all alive seemed incredible. Incredible, because in the Israeli army, when an officer yells "Charge!" he yells it back over his shoulder. The Jews have the quaint idea that anyone who orders an attack should have enough enthusiasm to *lead* it. In any other country, this would immediately result in a negotiated peace, but in Israel it works. No officer gives an impossible order, because *he* will have to carry it out. And he will have his back to his own troops while he is doing it. This provokes more intensive and intelligent military planning than a bushel basket full of Distinguished Service Medals. Many an Israeli officer, after leading a few such forays, looks forward to being promoted to private.

Among those Rivlin introduced me to were General Chaim Laskov, who had been commander of the armored forces at the age of twenty-three; Vivyan Herzog, who, at about the same ripe old age, had been in charge of intelligence; and General Yigael Yadin, who had been Chief Operations Officer for the Haganah in 1948. All these authentic heroes had one thing in common: despite their comparative youth, not one of them was still in the army. In Israel, as soon as a soldier makes general, he is on his way out. First he is made commander-in-chief, then he is kicked into civilian life. The reason for this is that in the army he has received the best education and training the little country can afford. In the lull between wars, these talents can best be put to use in the business world, which in the end supports the perpetual military effort. No business meeting that does not include two or three former commanders-in-chief and an admiral in the Israeli Navy shouting at each other over a sales chart can be *really* important.

Now, this happens in the United States, also. Our generals and admirals leave the Pentagon in a steady stream to take over positions with large and important business firms, who have been made large and important by the military contracts placed with them by generals and admirals. But this is really an exercise in geriatrics. The officers are retired into affluence only when they are too old to enjoy the money. Their age prohibits their ever returning to the military. It is a large, green pasture they are turned into, and no one really expects them to do anything to help the business. They have already done it.

In Israel, on the contrary, senior officers are retired shortly after they have begun to shave. In wartime, the little country can mobilize a trained, armed force that equals in size the authorized standing army of the United States of America. In peacetime, however, to save money, the Army meets in shifts. Last week's Army may have nobody in it who will be in this week's army. There is little enough opportunity to learn the job of handling large numbers of men, and the Israelis want every officer capable of doing it to have the experience. So a commander-in-chief can only serve five years, then he's a civilian. Thus they get a large number of highly trained officers who have been given top responsibility. In the U.S., this can only happen during a major war. It's like saying a professional quarterback should only report for training during a game. By the time an Israeli general staff officer received training under fire, the war would be over and Gamel Abdel Nasser's successors would be scrubbing themselves in the *mikvah* at the Deborah Hotel.

Also, war is a young man's game. Constant turnover precludes the evolution of a military-industrial complex that maintains old men and old ideas in positions of power. When your life is constantly at stake, you can't afford to fight last year's war.

The Army is Youth, and Youth is the Army. The undergraduates at the Hebrew University in Jerusalem don't have bumper stickers shouting, "Draft beer—not students!" In the first place, the Israeli beer is terrible. In the second place, nobody is *drafted.* The term implies some process of selection, which doesn't exist. In Israel, everybody is or has been in the army, including your mother and your Aunt Becky. You are in the regular army from age eighteen to twenty-one, and *then* everyone is in the Reserve, which is compulsory. I never heard anyone mention the age at which you are out of the Reserve, but I don't think it's official until they light a *yortzeit* candle for you.

Which brings us, in roundabout Israeli fashion, back to the generals. First, Chaim Laskov. *He* looks like a soldier. He is tough and forthright. His civilian job, at the time, was manager of the port of Ashdod, but in five minutes you could imagine him back in uniform without missing a beat.

In the 1948 war, Laskov commanded the little army's one "armored" brigade, consisting of some jeeps and homemade armored cars and half-tracks. This brigade attacked the fortress of Latrun which had closed the Jerusalem road. It was this battle which was to be the highlight of the movie; I had no idea, then, that most of it would not be shot in Israel, or that I would have Italians playing Arabs and Jews, or that I would have to smuggle flamethrowers into Cinecitta, all because our hotel reservations ran out. Wait. *My* war hadn't begun yet.

General Vivyan Herzog had been in the struggle at Latrun, also; but at the time I met him, he was a stockbroker. To demonstrate how universal is his occupation in his country, I will cite only one incident: this was 1964, the Israeli government had just instituted its first capital gains tax, and all the mailmen had promptly gone on strike.

We have experienced a postal strike in the United States, too, but ours was a strike of workers. This was a strike of capitalists. A capital gains tax hits heavily at profits made in the stock market. The mailmen argued, quite reasonably, that no self-respecting Israeli could live decently on the salary paid a mail carrier, so they were all heavily involved in the market and couldn't afford to deliver the mail if the government were going to tax what they earned there.

I believe in the long run the mailmen won their point and the tax was rescinded. I can't be sure, because one of my Israeli friends wrote me about it and mailed the letter on Saturday. A letter mailed on *Shabbat* is considered *trayf* (unclean) and no self-respecting mailman will pick it up. That's the day he goes to *shul* to pray for the local Dow-Jones Index.

General Herzog, of course, never delivered the mail in his life. He is a tall, handsome man with a Scotch bristle moustache and clipped British accent, whose father had been the Chief Rabbi of Jerusalem.

That is like having a father who was Pope, but had been allowed to be sexy. The patriarchs may have considered official abstinence for the Hebrew priesthood, but if so, the women shouted them down. The rabbi's son is the best catch in town for their daughters, and they wanted to be certain he was legitimate.

General Herzog was an officer in the British Army in World War II, as were many of the Israelis, and to some extent he was fighting his buddies in the War of Liberation. But so, come to think of it, was General George Washington. The British Army has trained the best of its enemies, and of that it is justifiably proud.

Yigael Yadin is a Doctor of Philosophy and one of the world's leading archaeologists. Through his hands have recently passed the Dead Sea Scrolls and the hidden treasures of King Herod's castle at Masada. But in 1948, he, too, was at Latrun, as Chief Operations Officer of the Haganah, the underground army which had come above ground to create a history for some Yadin of the future to excavate.

From Yadin and Herzog and Laskov I got complete and typically contradictory descriptions of the war and Mickey's role in it. Professor Yadin—I never could call him "General"—felt Mickey's major contribution had been in just being there. The fact that a professional soldier of his stature could look at their army without laughing inspired a certain amount of confidence in the Haganah command. That he would remain in the country after the war started meant a great deal, since obviously he had no suicidal tendencies. When the inexperienced young officers drew up their battle plans, Mickey had to withdraw his own just to give them confidence. They could afford to argue with him, because he would never allow them to make *too* big a mistake.

His "well done" was a tremendously important compliment. He was their professional conscience. When Mickey returned to the United States in the middle of the war, several colleagues tried to get some money down on the Arabs. Real estate in Tel Aviv immediately dropped in price unless it was under a rock. Then Mickey came back, as he promised, and it was like the second coming of Christ—if Christ had gone to West Point. (I knew that would come in handy *someplace.*) They welcomed him, because Mickey was the only one who could unify the virgin generals. Nobody lost face by *agreeing* with him; he wasn't Israeli and didn't know how to find the other side to everything. And no one could question his motives. He had come back voluntarily into a desperate situation he could easily have avoided.

I never found out if Yadin was speaking for himself as well as for the others. Did he welcome Mickey's return and his advice, or ignore it? Was he Mickey's friend or the opposite? Did the death of an American officer who had been called on in desperation to command their troops remove one small obstacle to Israel's pride in its military accomplishments?

At any rate, after talking to the generals, I still had no precise grasp of the character of the man who was to be the hero of the motion picture. He was a tough soldier, he was a romantic poet, he was faithful, he was unfaithful, he was loved, he was resented. In short, he was a human being, and capturing his essence on the screen would require skill and luck and artistry.

Some day I may have all three when I need them.

But the stories they told me—many of which, as you will see, I incorporated into the motion picture—had the same unreal quality as Pinhok's saga of the turned-on camel caravan. The trouble is that there is nothing real about the continuing state of belligerency in the Middle East. How a tiny people can continue to exist in the face of massed hate, soldiery, and weaponry that by sheer weight of numbers should have overwhelmed them in a day is a puzzle, a feat of legerdemain having nothing to do with military tactics. Clausewitz would have wigged out seeking an explanation.

But there was one. War, as our bearded generation is continually pointing out, is primarily the dirty business of dying. My rabbi, sore toe and all, had the seed of death within him. He had read the Torah, that incomprehensible collection of funny-looking writing that is carried in and out of the Ark of the Congregation on the days when they charge for seats; he knew that he, or any member of his flock, might be called on some day to die for the crime of being different; he didn't like the idea, he didn't look forward to it, he might do his best to escape it, or get a friend to do it for him, but in the end he accepted it. It was the Inevitable. It had happened time and again in the past, and always something better had come of it. Until the final good: Israel. For thousands of years, my rabbi had been dying, spat upon and kicked by the booted feet of the enemy. Now that at last he had something worth dying for, you think he would pass up the opportunity? Shaking his fist, uttering a curse at the stupid *schlemiels* of his own race who had got him into this spot, looking around to see if at least he was dying in a *minyan,* he would die if absolutely necessary.

Hear Ye, O Israel, the Lord is One, So would it have hurt Him to let me live and He would have company? But, *if absolutely necessary . . .*

Take, on the other hand, the Arab *fellahin.* Oppressed by the last feudal governments of the modern world. Born into poverty the depth of which is unknown in our society. A poverty in which women have no standing, education is for the privileged, ideas are suspect, and abject obedience the only entrance to Mecca. Place him in the middle of a twentieth-century world. In the wastes of the Negev desert, the black-robed Bedouin tend their camels amid the sand dunes as they and their ancestors have done since time immemorial; but a strange sound wafts across the endless sands, a strange and wailing sound, from the thousands of tiny transistor radios held to their ears. The twentieth century is leaking into the Sahara, and all King Hussein's horses and all Egypt's men cannot put Abdul Humpty Dumpty together again.

Listen to the shouts of the Arab world, the trumpets of war and hate, the unanimously expressed desire to push Israel into the sea. So who's stopping them from pushing?

But the voices you hear are the voices of literacy. Educated men. Strong and brave. They make the speeches, they lead the highly trained commando raids into Israeli territory. But, if it comes to all-out war, not between commando units but between armies, who must do the dying?

Abdul. His voice is never heard, because he is of the Voiceless. His body wracked with disease, his mind dulled with hashish, he is not as stupid as his rulers would like him to be. Paul McCartney has whispered in his ear. Glen Campbell's Moslem equivalent has told him that Mohammed Made Little Green Apples. With his own eyes he can see. The enemy is not ahead of him, it is behind him. Put a gun in his hand, place him in the belly of a tank, give him the opportunity, and see what happens. By the tens of thousands, he will turn the other way, leaving his shoes behind in the desert.

Some day, when he has something to live for, he will be willing to die. But his masters cannot let him have it, for it will be the end of their way of life. Educate him, cure his fevers, protect his children, give him an automobile, and he will be capable of ruling himself. He will have impossible traffic jams, there will be smog in the Sahara, but he will be ruling his self. The feudal thrones will be gone, and the desert Camelots turned into Albany, New York.

Maybe you like it better the way it is. Abdul doesn't.

During the Six Day War, when Israeli forces captured the Golan Heights, the Syrian radio broadcast the entirely fictitious news that the Israeli army was already advancing on Damascus itself. The Syrian government hoped this lie would be heard by the Russians, who would be forced to come to their defense.

Units of the Syrian Army, hearing the broadcast on their transistor radios, threw down their arms and went home.

The sands of the Sahara are made of the same silicon as a solid state diode. And the winds are starting to blow.

CHAPTER VI

Nate Edwards, Gershon, and I entered the headquarters of the commander-in-chief of the Israeli Army, and everybody saluted Nate. Gershon saluted the commander-in-chief and lost a button off his uniform.

An officer handed me a glass of tea and told me to pass it to Nate. I made a mental resolve to learn to wear a ten-gallon hat. And look Gentile.

The same Yitzhak Rabin who later became Ambassador to the United States sat behind the desk. With some bad news.

The Israeli Army would give us all the cooperation possible—*after* they had read the screenplay.

This is a gambit known as "script approval" which has long served Hollywood stardom as a means of escaping legal obligations. That the Israeli Army knew all about it indicates the efficiency of its intelligence network, the speed in which it adapts to a combat situation, and the basic philosophy of Attack! Attack! Attack! to keep the enemy off balance, which had been carefully taught by Colonel Marcus.

It meant, of course, that if the script I was writing did not please all elements of the General Staff, all bets were off. Since in Israel the possibility of getting everybody to agree on anything (including the fact that the sky is blue), is as remote as marinating a herring without sour cream, I could see my whole "project" disappearing in a puff of smoke.

In the Hollywood version of this situation, a star may sign a contract to make a motion picture at a stipulated price but reserve the right to approve the screenplay. If, before the screenplay is completed, the star's last picture makes money, his literary standards immediately improve. He finds the script lacking in motivation, imagination, and punctuation, until his agreed-upon salary is doubled. Immediately the punctuation looks better and the picture is made.

One of my more memorable encounters with this syndrome involved no less a personage than Mr. Cary Grant, who has often been known to reserve script approval until after the picture is finished. Cary is at once the most charming and most frustrating performer the film world has ever known, to which he will cheerfully agree. He has mellowed in his later years, and apparently decided on self-imposed retirement, but if he doesn't like the way it plays, he may rewrite *that,* too.

On one occasion, Cary invited my then partner, Jack Rose, and myself, to lunch, and showed us a screen story which had been written by *his* then partner, Betsy Drake. We liked its basic premise, and liked it even more when Cary said he would play the title role, and *would give up script approval,* if the studio bought Betsy's story.

However, he wanted Betsy to know that her work was being purchased solely on its literary merit. Therefore, he would not sign anything, including our luncheon check, until after the studio had paid the money. And it would be nice, he thought, if Paramount gave Betsy around exactly $35,000.

The studio was not precisely overjoyed at the prospect of being out on that expensive a limb, especially with as mercurial a personality as Mr. Grant, but we assured them of his sincerity and his desire to encourage his wife's literary talent. Somewhat reluctantly, the Front Office shelled out the full amount without haggling, and then sent Cary a contract for his role in the picture, stipulating his waiver of script approval.

He didn't sign it.

A month passed. Two.

At the Los Angeles International Airport, as Cary was about to embark for Spain, where he was to make *The Pride and the Passion,* a panting studio executive finally trapped him at the door to the plane with the contract and a fountain pen, and Cary smilingly signed, no doubt having enjoyed the game immensely.

Betsy's story was titled, *Houseboat,* and Jack and I set to work writing a screenplay about a typical American couple—Betsy was to play the wife, of course, and Cary the husband, and if you don't consider them a typical American couple, you're out of touch with reality —who settle on a houseboat with their brood of typical American children.

We were typing the last page of the script when we got a call from Cary in Spain. He had met the world's most wonderful actress, the new Garbo, and her name was Sophia Loren. Would it be much of a change to switch the heroine of *Houseboat* to an Italian girl?

"Of course not, Cary," we said, hanging up and tearing the screenplay into tiny bits. I put a fresh sheet of paper in the typewriter and typed, hopefully, "Fade In."

His marriage to Betsy, apparently, was on the rocks. Probably Cary had taken a dislike to her punctuation. Such are the perils of authorship.

Three months and a hundred and twenty-five pages later, Cary returned from Spain. We had another meeting and handed him the new script. He leafed through it idly.

"Why," he said, "the leading lady is an *Italian* girl!"

We nodded happily. He had actually recognized our characterization, involving clever usage of the phrase, "Buon giorno!"

"But that's impossible," Cary said. "Make her something else."

The trouble with mercurial personalities is that, if you look at the mercury closely, they are usually running a temperature. Apparently the one Cary had been running for Sophia had cooled off. We discovered, shortly, that the atmosphere between them was cool enough to liquefy the oxygen in it. Cary informed the studio he would not report for the picture if Miss Loren appeared opposite him.

The studio, having already run through two leading ladies and one author with him, decided to call a halt. He was served legal notice that he had given up script approval and would have to report.

He finally did. What ensued would fill the covers of another book, including the story of how Sophia married Carlo Ponti by proxy in Mexico at the very moment I was directing her screen marriage to Mr. Grant.

Houseboat, incidentally, was a considerable hit, the critics remarking on the air of gaiety and lightness which affected all concerned with its making. No one bothered to weigh the matzo ball that was my heart.

So when General Yitzhak Rabin began to look like Cary Grant to me, I knew I was in trouble.

In the event that the script should be approved, he went on to say, all film shot in Israel would have to be reviewed by the military authorities before being shipped out of the country. Since the picture was being shot in color, and since there was not a single color processing laboratory in the—until that moment—Holy Land, I decided not to worry about it. Why get excited about a picture that was not going to be shot just because the film wasn't going to be developed? The fact that, when it was developed, almost nobody went to see it, merely emphasizes my point.

General Rabin, a sturdy, intelligent, tanned, and hardy soldier, then relaxed, *his* battle having been won. Was there anything else he could do for us?

I mentioned, almost apologetically, that we would like to borrow his army for the picture.

General Rabin, in reply, reminisced for a while about his days as a young officer fighting at Mickey's heroic side, and admitted the Israeli Army indeed owed the indomitable Colonel Marcus a tremendous debt. The trouble was, however, that the Knesset didn't.

The Knesset is the Israeli parliament. At last count, it was made up of twenty-six different political parties, none of whom would be caught dead in the same room with each other. This made a quorum a national event. The IDF—Israel Defense Force, there no longer being armies or secretaries of war in the world, now that we have the capacity to defend ourselves into total oblivion—was dependent upon the Knesset for the funds for its existence. Israel was fighting for its life, as usual. How could General Rabin go to the Knesset and ask for more money so the army could help poor little Hollywood make a movie, when the Knesset was thinking of asking *Hollywood* for more funds?

It was at this point that Gershon broke in with the suggestion that the IDF provide everything we needed, with the production paying the actual cost *above* normal budget requirements directly to the army. Thus the Knesset need not even be approached.

General Rabin nodded his approval of this end-around play. If we waited for the Knesset, we wouldn't get an answer until two or three wars later.

The war council broke up on a happy note, nothing having been accomplished. Everybody saluted Nate again, and we left.

CHAPTER VII

Back in Hollywood, I finished writing the screenplay. How simple that sounds. And on the seventh day I rested. After all, the Patriarchs only gave Jehovah two paragraphs for the Creation.

But within that first sentence lies an acre of soul-searching. Word had filtered down from the United Artists hierarchy in New York that they were worried. Who wants to see a movie about a Jewish general?

So, after twisting my own arm, I wrote in a considerable romance. I issued propaganda describing what we were doing as "a Middle-Eastern Western." I searched for Spectacle, to give the picture Scope. I did everything but have my head examined. That came after the premiere.

Once the script was finished and approved by the Mirisches and New York, the search for a star intensified. Kirk Douglas was making a picture in Norway, somewhere near the Arctic Circle. He was sent a script that arrived in the midst of a blizzard and had to be read by the light of a blubber lamp. Weeks went by. Months.

Then John Wayne reached Douglas by telephone, in an igloo somewhere. Duke wasn't certain what Douglas had told him because Kirk seemed to be shivering, but he thought he had heard a qualified "y-y-yes."

A short time later, Kirk's agent confirmed this by asking for more money than United Artists was willing to pay. Everyone was jubilant, for now we could negotiate!

It was like negotiating with North Vietnam. The Arctic winter had apparently frozen Kirk's price so solidly it could not be thawed out. His agent showed up for conferences wearing a parka and carrying a harpoon. I felt I was on the end of it. Finally, I called in Herman Citron and told him I was being paid too much and wanted him to tell the Mirisches I would give part of my fee back so we could afford to pay Kirk.

A "banshee" is described in my dictionary as "a spirit (Irish) in the form of a wailing woman who appears to or is heard by members of a family as a sign that one of them is about to die." Herman Citron could give any Irish banshee cards and spades in wailing and come out ten points ahead. Some brave men don't know the word fear. Herman doesn't know the words *to give back*.

But he did it. After much thought, he concluded it was better for me to get a picture made and *not* get paid a fortune than *not* to get a picture made and *also* not get paid a fortune.

The Mirisches recovered from their initial shock in time to accept quickly, and a St. Bernard was dispatched to Norway with a fat contract nailed to its brandy cask. We had our Star.

Somewhere in here I have skipped over Duke Wayne's battle with The Big C, partly because none of us really believed it could be happening. That the indestructible symbol of vitality could be faced with extinction at the hands of a tiny cigarette seemed too incongruous to merit consideration.

When the reports from the hospital could no longer be denied, it seemed relatively unimportant that the picture would now, in all probability, be shelved. The important thing was whether the Sheriff would survive this shot in the back, whether the Good Guy on the white horse could outsmart the black-hatted Outlaws from the Circle-C Ranch, even though he was surrounded.

There is a famous scene in the picture *True Grit* in which Wayne, in the role of a one-eyed, drunken, fat old Marshal named Rooster Cogburn, faces four armed and mounted killers in a meadow and magnanimously offers them the opportunity to surrender. When they sneeringly refuse, he puts the reins between his teeth, twirls two guns large enough to give any other Western star a hernia, and charges happily into their midst firing all barrels at once. Of course, he emerges victorious and unscathed, his enemies, those still alive, fleeing in dismay. Many critics applauded this scene, calling it "high camp," a tongue-in-cheek exaggeration of all the invincible Wayne roles of the past. Nonsense. This was as factual a rendition of Duke's attitude toward life and death as a government report on the national deficit. Maybe *more* factual.

Cancer will never be the same after its encounter with Wayne. He shattered its legend of invincibility, climbed out of a hospital bed while his doctor was still adding up the bill, and, with only one good lung, started shooting a Western in mountains so high the cameraman had a chronic nosebleed. Duke reported in Rome for his scenes in *Cast a Giant Shadow*—yes, *Rome,* and we'll get to that later—and hit every nightspot in the Eternal City before reporting to the set, where he shook my hand so cordially I directed the remaining scenes as a southpaw.

With Wayne on his feet, with Kirk Douglas' signature in frozen ink on a contract, my project had become a listing in *Daily Variety.* Immediately, all of Hollywood's doubts disappeared and my phone rang incessantly with requests from friends to give their nephews, nieces, girlfriends, and proctologists jobs on the picture. The fact that they had no particular talent for picture-making didn't seem to matter; wasn't it enough that they wanted a free trip to Israel?

Of course, I turned down all such requests, because I was trying to get *my* son a free trip to Israel. He had recently informed me he was leaving law school after one whole month of earnest endeavor, because a professor had told his class that, no matter how brilliant they became in the practice of law, a judge could always decide a case any way he really wanted to. My son immediately made up his mind to start studying to be a judge instead of a lawyer—a not illogical choice—but was brought up short because the university did not offer a single course in judging.

I had made the terrible mistake, when he was in high school, of introducing him to show business by getting him a part in a picture

I was directing. *The Five Pennies,* with Danny Kaye. I wanted him to spend one day as an extra—salary, $17.50—so he could watch me and find out how hard his father worked to finance his Volkswagen. However, I discovered he could not work unless he was a member of the Screen Extras Guild, a difficult matter. But, if he had a *line* to deliver in the picture, that would make him a bit player, and he didn't have to join *that* union until he was offered a second job. Being fairly certain that my son the actor would never face that danger, I gave him one line to say and get it over with.

Then I discovered that, as a bit player, his minimum employment had to be for a full week and his minimum check $250. My son was delighted, blew his one line four times in front of the camera, then sat around on the set for the remainder of the week complaining he was underpaid. Thereafter, he became, not stage-struck, but check-struck. He decided it might be worthwhile becoming a star until he had banked enough money to devote the rest of his life to his chosen vocation, goofing off. As you can see, he had developed the star temperament, all right.

After his run-in with the judiciary, he naturally looked with interest for another windfall in his old man's racket. It was then I discovered that any job he was capable—or incapable—of handling was so highly unionized there was no possibility of admitting new members for approximately eighty-five years. Even as the son of a member of the Directors' Guild, he was not allowed to work as an assistant, indicating they had either seen his father's pictures or my son's record in law school. He could, however, become a member of the Writers' Guild, merely by *writing* something. You can imagine how far the Writers' Guild got with my son with that gambit. As a matter of fact, the Writers' Guild will allow anyone to write for motion pictures who has the talent for it. This, obviously, is unfair, and might destroy the whole concept of the Hollywood Union, which is designed to keep new members out so old members can keep working until they collect on their life insurance. The average age of the motion picture audience is, I believe, eighteen. The average age of a motion picture cameraman, according to Union records, is sixty.

Finally, it was decided that *I* would finance my son's trip, while he was between universities, and when he got to Israel, we would figure out some way to keep him amused. After all, even King Solomon had to find a hobby there.

Meanwhile, military negotiations with the Israel Defense Forces had proceeded by mail.

Much to my surprise, the screenplay had been approved, with enthusiastic and detailed instructions on how to change the entire story line and restructure 31 different scenes.

I quote briefly from an official communication from General Staff Headquarters of the Israeli Army, following a meeting of military minds:

> *It seemed that the love affair between Colonel Marcus and Magda is being exaggerated. Admittedly the man is not a saint, he is only human, yet the image of the hero, the man fighting for ideals, the man the spectators are ready to worship, is being weakened by a sex-starved woman longing to be loved and have an affair with the great general.*

I could visualize the debate, between strikes across the Syrian border: the Commander of the Tank Corps insisting the sex-starved woman should not have attacked Mickey at that point and exposed her flank, the Air Corps arguing it was up to Colonel Marcus to send up flares for assistance, and several generals cutting them off with the remark that if the spectators are ready to worship this general, and if this woman is longing to be loved and have an affair with him, why is this bad for the Jews?

The Alice-in-Holy-Land quality of this correspondence prompts me to include photostatic proof that it all *did* take place. Here is a letter from General Staff Headquarters that reads as if it had been composed by the mail order department of Sears, Roebuck and Co., Promised Land division:

Tel Aviv, February 3rd, 1965
MN / 4 / 217

r. Melville Shavelson
041 No. Formosa Avenue
os Angeles 48, California
. S ; A .

aer Mr. Shavelson,

Thank you for your letter dated 14th January 1965, to which I would like
o make reference.

As you may recall the list of items the I.D.F. will be requested to loan
ou was not a carefully prepared one, but rather a vague list worked out by yourself
nd Col. Rivlin, therefore it is impossible at this stage, basing ourselves on that
ist to ascertain the loan of those items, unless we get a detailed one.

Taking in account the vagueness of the present list we can already inform
ou that some of the items requested are not in our possession at all, whereas others
re limited in their quantities. *

As regarding the number of troops requested, we would be able to put at your
isposal the following:-

An army officer fro full time employment as both technical adviser and L.O.
for the services of which you will be requested to reimburse the army;

Lt. Col. Gershon Rivlin as part time historical adviser; **

Up to 800 soldiers for a limited period of three days namely the 6ht, 7th
and 8th of June 1965. ***

Ammunition and explosives will not be supplied by the army. I suggest you
contact the Military Industries in the Ministry of Defence for the production
of the quantities and types of the ammunition and explosives required. ****

As for other items on the list, enclosed please find a detailed list of
prices. *****

I would like again, to stress the importance of a quick reply regarding the
the detailed list of items and quantities as requested.

Sincerely Yours,

SHEMUEL GAT   —   Sgan Aluf .
for/DIRECTOR OF PUBLIC RELATIONS.

Translating this coded secret message into its true meaning, we get the following military information:

* You have ordered several well-advertised bargains, which of course we do not have in stock. Does Macy's?

** Thus, you will have *two* technical advisers, Rivlin and another army officer, who will then be entitled to disagree on everything, giving your picture the true Israeli flavor. *One* technical adviser wouldn't have slowed you up at all.

*** At the time, I didn't realize that these dates for the employment of eight hundred soldiers were more rigid than my wife's appointments at the beauty parlor. Since this is a citizens' army, and each precious unit must be in a precise place at a precise time, you cannot vary its schedule by as much as one day without disrupting the taxi service in Tel Aviv or the hotel service in Jerusalem. Each soldier must be replaced in his civilian job for the exact period of his army duty, and this requires incredible logistics. It also required us to start shooting, before we were ready, with the largest and most difficult scene in the picture.

**** This caused all sorts of difficulties, because many of the guns we secured for the picture were Italian, and the Israeli ammunition would not fit. Consequently, we shipped our ammunition and explosives from Europe. They were promptly confiscated by Israeli Customs, since there is a strict law against their importation. The fact that they were being imported at the request of the Army didn't impress Customs. We finally got the Knesset to pass a special law to permit us to bring in our subversive supplies.

***** Since neither I nor anyone of my acquaintance had ever seen a Sears Roebuck Catalogue issued by a national army while it was in a state of alert, I include for posterity a photostatic copy of the list referred to above. "IL" is the designation for the Israeli pound, then officially worth about one third of a dollar, but don't count on it.

You will note that this army is on the alert and not to be outmaneuvered. For instance, while there are fixed prices for machine guns, mortars, flame throwers, hand grenades, and tanks, they were not going to be lured into supplying batteries for the walkie-talkies before they knew how much we talked.

The last item was obviously meant to be intercepted by enemy intelligence. It indicated that the last three Israel bond drives had been so successful the Israeli Army now had tanks to burn.

PRICE LIST

A. Prices of items based on list prepared bt Lt. Col. Rivlin (on monthly basis)

1. Rifle 7.62 m"m   IL   5.30
2. Rifle British   IL   7.50
3. Pistol   IL   3.30
4. Stengun   IL   1.00
5. M.G. Machingun   IL   34.00
6. Brengun   IL   25.00
7. Beza Machingun   IL 175.00
8. A.A. 20 m"mGun   IL 825.00
9. 81 m"m mortar   IL   12.00
10. Flamethrowers   IL 150.00
11. Hand Granade   IL   7.00
12. 15 Tents   IL 250.00

B. Prices on a daily basis

1. Soldiers   IL   6.50

C. Prices for limited given periods

1. Four half trucks for six days   IL 2400 excluding fuel and drivers
2. Four weapon carriers for six days IL 1440   "   "   "*   "
3. Six Walikie Talkie radio sets for IL 250 excluding prices of batteries
   one month
4. Tanks with crews. Allotment of approx
   150-200 Engine hours   IL 200 per hour excluding fuel
5. Tank Transporters   IL 200 (each)
6. Transportation for 800 Troops
   total 95 Transportation days   IL 5225
7. Three Tanks for burning purposes   IL 1000

The bandwagon was now rolling. Equipment was being shipped from Hollywood to Israel, technicians were being recruited in Los Angeles, Rome, and Tel Aviv, and two of my agents were hurrying to Palm Springs.

Yul Brynner invited me to meet him at the Hillcrest Country Club. The Moslems have their Mecca, the Catholics have Rome, and Beverly Hills has the Hillcrest Country Club. The real Wailing Wall is not in Jerusalem. It surrounds the golf course, where those denied membership beat their breasts and moan as they watch the oil wells that were discovered on the fairways pumping black gold into the club's coffers, making greens fees unnecessary. The back nine on this course has the world's most expensive oil slick. It is the richest oil deposit anywhere in the world, that doesn't allow Arabs into the parking lot.

Several years ago, Hillcrest was worried about its exclusively Jewish membership policies being anti-Semitism in reverse, so it was decided to admit some representative Gentiles. The first name proposed was that of Danny Thomas. He was promptly blackballed, on the grounds that if they were admitting Gentiles, they wanted them to *look* Gentile.

Whether Mr. Brynner is Jewish or not, I don't know. That he is a devout gypsy is true. Or as true as anything about Mr. Brynner can ever be. He has, on various occasions, admitted to being born in Bulgaria, Yugoslavia, China, Russia, The Bronx, Japan, and Outer Mongolia. He speaks the mysterious gypsy language, Romany, which has never been written down and forms an international bond. Yul Brynner can walk into any gypsy caravan in the world and have his palm read free. He can sing strange melodies all night long in strange languages no one can understand. In fact, no one can understand why he is singing them. The only thing known for certain about this mystic individual is that he directed the first telecasts of the Brooklyn Dodgers baseball games. He also claims to have devised the split-screen technique of showing both batter and runner at the same time, but this is disputed by several other gypsies who worked for the Columbia Broadcasting System.

At any rate, when I met him, he had just finished a round of golf on the Hillcrest course and we sat in the lobby, talking, as he removed the crude oil from his hands. Walter Mirisch had given him a copy of my screenplay the day before. He had read it at one sitting, until three in the morning, and wanted me to know he would play any part in it I wanted him to. With a preamble like that, I would have let him play the role of Mrs. Marcus if he had asked for it. He could always wear a *sheitel.*

I suppose the mystique of Israel is greater than that of the gypsies; all of us, myself included, read into that screenplay all the things we hoped were there. We were moved, not by what was on the page, but what was inside us. I could understand it happening to *me;* I was startled it had happened to John Wayne, pleased it had happened to Yul Brynner, and, later, absolutely astounded when it happened to Frank Sinatra, the cynic's cynic.

The only ones it didn't happen to were the Israeli General Staff.

They can't afford to lose even *one* battle.

A slight correction: there was one other who cast a somewhat jaundiced eye on my creation, at least some portions of it. Kirk Douglas had schussed down the last frozen slope in Norway, chiseled the frost out of the cleft in his chin, and departed for London to shoot the interiors of his picture in a British studio so damp, drafty, and cold, they could have shot the exteriors there as well.

En route back to Tel Aviv, I stopped off to confer with him. We had never met. It didn't take me long to discover what my main problem was going to be: Kirk Douglas was *intelligent.* When discussing a script with actors, I have always found it necessary to remember that they never read the other actors' lines, so their concept of the story is somewhat hazy. Kirk had not only read the lines of everyone in the picture, he had also read the stage directions. This is considered indecent. A writer, resigned to having every line of dialogue examined, twisted, and changed by every actor billed above the title, can at least be certain that nobody cares enough about the stage directions to change them. So this is where he does his *real* writing, the little nuances, the flights of genius, that he knows will remain there for him to read and reread after he has seen the finished picture and failed to recognize a word he can call his own.

Kirk, I was to discover, always read every word, always discussed every word, always argued every scene, until he was convinced of its correctness. Furthermore, he would listen to *logic*. He could not be dismissed as a star who must have everything his own way, making it a waste of time to fight. He listened, so it was necessary to fight every minute. This can be exhausting and damaging to the ego, but in the end, even if it doesn't produce a good picture, it does produce some very good arguments.

His basic complaint was that in the script as written, Mickey was an observer, not a participant. Kirk is not a man to mince words. I had my unblushing tape recorder along, and I quote:

> *Kirk:* Somewhere I want to see Mickey in *action*. He should take out a patrol of ten guys and they should kick the shit out of the other guys and then come home. That's how Wingate did it. [NOTE: General Orde Wingate, the British officer who secretly organized and trained the Haganah.] Then maybe one guy wants to hang around and take another shot at the Arabs and Mickey grabs him and says, "One brave guy can fuck up an army. Don't be too brave."

> *Me:* The problem is, he'd have to say it in Hebrew.

> *Kirk:* I'm sure they've got a word for it. The main thing is, this story must be geared toward one guy, the protagonist. Everything must revolve around him.

> *Me:* John Wayne and Yul Brynner might disagree.

> *Kirk:* Listen, I made a picture once, we had every fuckin' star in the business in it. We got Frank Sinatra, Robert Mitchum, and Tony Curtis, and Burt Lancaster, all to play different parts. It was this picture where everybody wears masks all the way through, then at the end everybody takes the mask off his face and we see who they are. We felt we were going to have the biggest picture in the world. All we forgot was we fell so in love with the gimmick, we were so impressed we had all the stars—we didn't have a movie.

> *Me:* Don't worry. I've written a line for Mickey: "Life isn't a spectator sport. There are too many people who stand

by and wait for somebody else to do the job. I've got to stick my neck out."

Kirk: That's a great line—give it to Yul Brynner. I'd rather see Mickey *do* it.

CHAPTER VIII

On March 14, 1965, the first wave of American, British, and Italian technicians for *Cast a Giant Shadow* arrived in Tel Aviv and demanded their expense checks. I arrived with them, script in one hand, pencil and eraser in the other, and holed up at the Dan Hotel until a house could be secured for my wife and family to join me.

Why we had to bring so many of our crew with us requires a bit of explaining. In America, every Jewish mother wants her son to be a doctor or a lawyer. In Israel, there are so many doctors and lawyers that if the lawyers didn't get sick and the doctors didn't get in trouble, they would both starve.

Consequently, in Israel every Jewish mother wants her son to grow up to be a carpenter. In a country that was building housing, at that time, for close to a hundred thousand refugees a year, a carpenter was assured of year-round employment at a salary no doctor could approach. No self-respecting carpenter wanted to give up that kind of security to work on a motion picture that was going to *tear down* everything after they built it.

When the Histadrut, the national labor union, heard we were hiring *Italian* carpenters, they immediately protested. We offered to hire any Israeli carpenter who was willing to work for us. No such person ever showed up. So we hired our Italian carpenters, flew them from Rome, bought thirty houses for them to live in, and paid their living expenses. And it cost less than if they had been natives of Tel Aviv.

Sometimes it hardly pays to be Jewish.

About those thirty houses: by the time the Mirisches were certain the picture would be made, all the available housing in Israel was gone for the tourist season. Only at the insistence of the government were we enabled to take over three floors of the Avia Hotel, near the airport, and *buy* thirty cottages the hotel had just completed on the hotel grounds, with the understanding that we would sell them back when we left.

Thus was born Little Italy of Tel Aviv. The Caesar, nay, the Nero, of this colony was the most talented, inch-for-inch, cameraman in the world. His name is Aldo Tonti and he is five feet tall when measured to the tip of his uptilted cigar. Aldo has photographed so many motion pictures in Italy and around the world for so many years, no one knows his true age.

For a while, Aldo was Mussolini's official photographer, but he quit, it is rumored, because Mussolini was too much of a liberal for him. Aldo rules his camera crew—made up almost exclusively of his sons —with an iron hand and a walking stick carved out of the bones of his last director. He shouts at them, punches at them, insults them, curses them, and promises to fire them as soon as he catches his breath. No one minds, because Aldo is a pussycat and they don't want him to realize he's been found out. His crew loves and protects him with a fierce loyalty their wives will never know.

When the uprooted Italians of the camera and carpentry crews were placed in their spare little bungalows, they immediately went out and bought up all the spaghetti in Tel Aviv, which took about five minutes.

The chambermaids at the Avia Hotel, who took care of the houses, complained there was something mysterious going on. Every day they had to clean spaghetti off the ceilings. They couldn't figure out why. One day I was invited to have lunch with the crew, and the mystery was solved. I was ushered into a little house that had no furniture in it but a huge dining room table and chairs. Since, to an Italian, the stomach is the second noblest part of a man's anatomy, they had wisely enshrined it by doubling up on their sleeping quarters and devoting one of the houses exclusively to eating. All the chores were rotated, with everyone serving as cook or waiter or dishwasher on a regular schedule.

Except Aldo. He was enthroned regally at the head of the table like a Queen Bee ruling over a hive of tomato sauce. On a gesture from Aldo, I was presented with an array of *antipasti* that would have done honor to Alfredo Alla Scroffa in Rome, followed by *insalata, scallopini parmigiana,* and a delicate *pasta* cooked *al dente.*

The cook apologized that the *pasta* was not quite perfect. The cottages had no stoves, so they were cooking on tiny hot plates, and the only way to be certain the spaghetti was the correct consistency was to throw it against something. If it stuck, it was *al dente*.

Ecco! Spaghetti on the ceiling.

Most of the rest of the company, our offices, and our projection equipment were housed at the aforementioned Avia Hotel. Unlike most airport caravanseries, it is located several miles from the terminal it is purported to serve. It is not convenient to anything, except a watermelon field which also doubles as its front yard and which, during watermelon season, contains an armed Arab who sleeps in a tent and shoots anybody who steals watermelons. This is a service Conrad Hilton never dreamed of, and, if extended to the hotel proper, could result in a remarkable saving in towels.

Being inconvenient, the Avia is inhabited mainly by group tours, who are getting what they deserve: a bargain. However, all of the air crews of the planes serving Lydda Airport bed down at the Avia, to use the term loosely. The hotel contains the most nerve-shattering, eye-filling array of luscious Swedish, British, French, Italian, Japanese, and American stewardesses this side of a nervous breakdown. These girls have a twenty-four to forty-eight hour layover, you should excuse the expression, and had we known in advance, we would never have been foolish enough to install our staff, our offices, our crew, some of our actors, and my son right in the middle of Never-Never Land.

The aforesaid son, imported to Israel as a projectionist for the production and suffering from a shattered love affair in the States, immediately began to take a renewed interest in life. One of our actors established a liaison with a young lady from Alitalia which enabled him to secure hot pizza direct from Rome, among other travel benefits. My son, disdaining such favoritism, once asked me which I would prefer that week—*smørrebrød* from Copenhagen, Napoleon brandy from Paris, or a jar of caviar from Iran? It seems he was juggling representatives from three airlines at once, a procedure he described as The Only Way to Fly. The huge swimming pool at the Avia was always surrounded by a blanket of bikini-clad young ladies from colder climates, basking in the Biblical sunshine and baking out their fear of various Commandments. At least that was the impression an older and somewhat more jealous generation received. Probably there was no more impropriety among the stewardesses here than at any other resting place, but where else could they be invited to spend Saturday night in Sodom and Gomorrah?

Richard—My Son, The Projectionist—was the first to inform me that the Avia was far from Paradise Regained. At that point, he was no longer a projectionist but an assistant director. I had nothing to do with that, but *somebody* must have gotten that caviar. The problem at the Avia was the food, never the best, but a matter of utmost concern when the Bad Rabbi was on duty. Every hotel in Israel has its resident rabbi in the kitchen, checking to see, first, that everything is dead; second, that it has been salted, so it can't come back to life. They've had a lot of trouble with that last. The personality of the rabbi can influence an entire meal, because strict interpretation of the kosher laws can make anything inedible, including Strawberries Romanoff. The Avia kitchen, being a nerve-wracking operation, maintained a staff of *two* rabbis, who spelled each other when the strain became too much. These were, obviously, the Bad Rabbi and the Good Rabbi. The Bad Rabbi gave not an inch on anything. The Good Rabbi permitted ketchup. Without ketchup, nothing was edible.

A system of espionage was set up, reaching into the heart of the kitchen itself. Word would circulate like wildfire, in heated whispers— "The Good Rabbi is on! The Good Rabbi is on!"—and the dining room and the ketchup bottles would fill up like magic. When the Bad Rabbi was on, the only way to escape starvation was to steal a watermelon.

Nate Edwards in Israel, watching the budget. (*Melville Shavelson*)

Aldo Tonti, cameraman and spaghetti king of Israel. (*Melville Shavelson*)

CHAPTER IX

Underfed and ill-housed, everyone set to work to prepare for the start of the picture, which had been rescheduled—by the Israeli Army—for May 18. Now was the final opportunity to correct whatever flaws I could find in my flawless screenplay; but other duties kept interfering. I have often said I am a writer by choice, a producer by necessity, and a director in self-defense. In Israel, the enormity of overseeing all the details of a production of this size while simultaneously casting, rehearsing, preparing to direct, rewriting and re-rewriting the script, with home base nine thousand miles away, finally dawned on me. I was, obviously, out of my mind to attempt all this single-handedly. It didn't cheer me at all to reflect that the Mirisches were out of theirs to allow me to try.

All this misery had its origin back in the days when Doris Day looked like The Girl Next Door and I was one of The Writers Next Door who wrote her dialogue and let some hardier soul stage it. In those simpler times, the way a motion picture got made at Warner Brothers was that Jack Warner would look in the catalogue of Warner Brothers Music Corporation and pick a song he would like to hear again. Then he would assign it as the title of a Warner Brothers musical to one of his producers, who would then assign it to his writers and leave for Las Vegas. Doris Day was always in it. Thus, even if the picture was a flop, her recording of the title tune would revive the sale of the sheet music and Warner Brothers Music Corporation would make half a million dollars. While this was fine for Jack Warner, Albert Warner, Harry Warner, and even Doris Day, the poor writer who had to figure out the story to go with the song title had his work cut out for him.

The song J. L. Warner selected with a toothpick one day from the music catalogue was a little opus titled "On Moonlight Bay." The writers to whom this choice assignment filtered down were Jack Rose and myself. After an initial attack of heartburn, I remembered that somewhere in the Warner Brothers Story Department files I had seen a reference to the fact that the studio owned the rights to Booth Tarkington's *Penrod* and *Penrod and Sam,* two warm and humorous studies of boyhood in Indiana after the turn of the century. What these stories had to do with the song "On Moonlight Bay" was exactly nothing, which is what intrigued me. And Penrod's sister, Marjorie, had been playing Doris Day long before Doris was born.

Jack and I wrote a screenplay based on Tarkington's classics, and somewhere near page 59 we inserted an amusement park which we named, in a fit of inspiration, "Moonlight Bay."

When the script reached Mr. Warner's desk, there was an explosion. Didn't we know that in 1919 Warner Brothers had made a series of shorts based on the *Penrod* stories which had been such a disaster several exhibitors were still fumigating their theaters? Since this was now 1951, we had assumed the odor had somewhat diminished, but J. L. was adamant. Change all the names. Change all the names so no exhibitor will know!

Change the names of Penrod and Sam? Change Romeo and Juliet? Tom Sawyer and Huckleberry Finn? Peleas and Melisande? Hero and Leander? Charlie Brown and Snoopy?

If J. L. says so. *Change.*

In Booth Tarkington's stories, Penrod has a dog who is named "Duke." When our script returned to Mr. Warner's desk, the names of Penrod, Sam, and Duke had been changed to Harry, Jack, and Albert.

Another explosion!

Rather than change jobs, we changed the names again.

Finally, our script reached the sound stages, with Doris Day and Gordon MacRae in the starring roles and a talented young boy named Billy Gray in the role of Penrod—er, Jack—that is, Wesley. One day I wandered onto the stage and found our wholesome Doris in front of the cameras, writing a letter and singing. Since, in those days, Doris never did anything, including brushing her teeth, in front of a camera without singing, this didn't surprise me. But there was something odd about that song. I wandered over to the director, a white-haired, distinguished, and filthy rich gentleman who shall remain nameless, and inquired to whom Doris was singing.

The director, who had once informed me he never spoke to actors outside of business hours, and normally never spoke to writers *during* business hours, condescended to let me in on my own story. Doris, of course, was singing to Gordon MacRae, who was outside her window, and would soon join her in a duet. I then inquired to whom Doris was writing that letter.

This puzzled him. It had never occurred to him to turn to the next page of the script and find out. As gently as possible, I explained to him that Doris was writing the letter to Gordon, who was supposedly at college, 250 miles away, and if he were going to hear Doris singing to him through her window at that distance, she would really have to belt out the tune.

It was at that precise moment that I decided to become a director myself. Especially since my distinguished, filthy rich mentor always kept the screenplay on the floor in front of his chair and turned the pages with his foot.

It was some years later, after I had directed many of our own screen-plays, that Mr. Rose and I came to a parting of the collaborators and I found myself assuming the mantle of producer as well. Now it had all caught up with me, here in the land of my fathers, far, far from home. And instead of Penrod, Sam, and Duke, or Harry, Jack, and Albert, I was involved in a story about living and fighting and dying.

Eventually there would be 125 members of our production crew, 800 soldiers of the Israeli army, one thousand extras, thirty-four featured players from Hollywood, Broadway, Greece, Scotland, and Israel, and Kirk Douglas, John Wayne, Frank Sinatra, Yul Brynner, Angie Dickinson, and Senta Berger waiting for me to tell them what to do and what to say and which side of their face to turn to the camera when they said it. And if I waited too long to make up my mind, they would tell *me.* That screenplay had better be foolproof and actor-proof, which is not always the same thing.

So, while attending to the million-and-one problems of preparing the production, I had to squeeze in a little time to revise the script I had completed in Hollywood, remembering the admonitions of

Colonel Rivlin and the various generals, the fears of United Artists in New York who were putting up the money, and my own desire to produce the kind of masterpiece Shakespeare might have come up with if he had had the good fortune to be born Jewish.

The story that finally evolved began with this foreword:

> THE MAJOR EVENTS DEPICTED IN THIS FILM ACTUALLY HAPPENED. SOME OF THEM ARE STILL HAPPENING. THE MAJOR CHARACTERS ACTUALLY LIVED. FORTUNATELY FOR THE WORLD, MANY OF THEM ARE STILL LIVING, ALTHOUGH IT WAS NOT EASY.

The first scene was set at Macy's Department Store in New York City, Christmas, 1947. We had already "stolen" a long shot of the exterior of Macy's in New York the preceding November, but the interior of the store and a portion of its exterior were to be built at Cinecitta Studios in Rome after we left Israel. Of course, this scene of Mickey Marcus—Kirk Douglas—being approached by a secret representative of the underground Jewish government in Palestine could also have been played in Mickey's kitchen, where it actually happened, but what would the Mirisches have done with all the money they saved? Probably squandered it foolishly on pictures like *West Side Story*. So, eventually, we built Macy's in Rome. We also built Coney Island there. And cut it out of the picture.

In 1947, Mickey had returned from his incredible military career in World War II and was making an attempt to be a lawyer and a husband. But he was tempted by the siren call of the representative of the Haganah, who approached him—in my version, in Macy's toy department—with this:

> I represent the world's youngest, worst-trained, least-equipped, and most outnumbered army. On May 15th, the British will withdraw and we will announce our independence. Six nations have promised to drive us into the sea. Have you heard their exact words? King Ibn Saud: "There are fifty million Arabs. What does it matter if we lose ten

million to kill all the Jews? The price is worth it." The
Grand Mufti of Jerusalem: "I declare a Holy war. Murder
them. Murder them all." We are going to fight. There is no
other place for us to go. We won't fight to the last man.
We are prepared to fight to the last child. Our children
don't believe in Santa Claus. Not any more. We need,
immediately, an experienced military adviser. We've come to
you because, frankly, no one else wants the job.

MICKEY—*Kirk*—Major, I've just been through a war and a
half. I promised the next war to my wife. If I leave home
once more, I have an idea I'm going to find my pajamas on
the front porch. Would you give up everything you love to
fight some insane war for a country that's going to get its
brains blown out in a couple of weeks?

MAJOR SAFIR—If it were *my* country. You're a Jew, aren't
you?

MICKEY—I'm an American, Major. That's my religion. The
last time I was in Temple I was thirteen years old; I made a
speech and got forty-two fountain pens. I don't have to go
again. I've got enough fountain pens.

Of course, by the end of the scene Mickey had made up his mind
to go. Then he had to go home and tell his wife Emma about it, which
he did, in bed, while making love to her, a procedure somewhat complicated by the fact that I decided to flash back during the lovemaking
to his career in World War II, and a scene with John Wayne as "General Randolph," and to Mickey parachuting into Normandy on D-Day,
and then back to the bedroom with Emma—Angie Dickinson—who
somehow had managed to preserve her sexual enthusiasm throughout
the entire flashback. With her arms around Mickey-Kirk, she whispered in his ear:

EMMA—I've got to send you off to your flea-bitten war. . . .
It gets you more excited than I do, doesn't it? . . . Hey, did
you ever notice we don't have any children? I want yours—
ours—*now*. There's a chance, isn't there, that I might never
have *you* again?

Then they turned off the light—we *always* turned off the light in movies at that point, in those archaic days—and in the darkness we heard Emma say:

> Oh, Mickey . . . you're a wonderful lover . . . and such a lousy husband.

A line, incidentally, which Emma Marcus herself had quoted to me.

So the situation was set up for Mickey-Kirk to meet both a new country—Israel—and a new woman—Senta Berger, playing an Israeli —making not a triangle but sort of a Star of David out of the whole affair. Since the British were still in control of Palestine, Mickey entered on a false passport under the name of Michael Stone, a name he used throughout his adventures there, and Senta played the part of a member of the underground who provided his cover. The dialogue, when they met at Lydda Airport near Tel Aviv, ran like this:

> MAGDA—*Senta*—You are to live at my apartment. It is better than a hotel if the British ask questions. From now on, I am your sister.
>
> MICKEY—What's the attitude on incest in this country?
>
> MAGDA—Very Biblical. Especially since I am also married. But you can try, if you wish. It makes life interesting.

Get the picture? Boy meets Girl, Girl has Husband, Boy has Wife, but you can bet your bottom dollar even though it's not kosher, Boy will get Girl.

Somewhat incidentally, there was a war going on around them. Mickey was taken to underground headquarters where he met a commander of the Haganah who looked suspiciously like Yul Brynner. Yul took an instant dislike to this American interloper—possibly because he had a full head of hair—which prompted a scene in which Mickey offered to leave Israel if Yul were not willing to accept his military counsel.

Yul was saved from having to make a decision by the sudden word that British troops had spotted a refugee ship filled with illegal immigrants from Europe, and were heading for the beach to prevent a landing. Taking Mickey and Senta with him, Yul reached the beach with some armed men and helped the refugees land, until the British arrived. The British troops leaped out of their trucks and ordered the refugees to surrender. At that point, the people of Tel Aviv, summoned by hundreds of telephone calls—this, like most of the picture, is based on true incidents—poured onto the beach and changed clothes with the refugees so the British soldiers could not tell them apart. This gave me an opportunity to be both historically accurate and have Senta Berger remove her clothing. What filmmaker could resist?

Colonel Marcus, by that time, was developing a growing awareness of the spirit of the people themselves, a factor the British and the Arabs never really took into consideration. But the Jewish military was still suspicious of Mickey as an interloper, an officer from a huge army who could never understand their limitations and needs. He met the youthful leader of their Commandos, the Palmach, played by the young Greek actor Stathis Giallelis—in real life, their commander was Yigael Allon, at present Deputy Premier of Israel, from whom I learned this part of the story—and together they visited an old Berber chieftain who was thinking of defecting from the Arab side but still had his doubts. Haym Topol, the wonderful Israeli performer who plays Tevye in the motion picture version of *Fiddler on the Roof*—also for the Mirisches—portrayed the seventy-year-old Arab chief so realistically you could almost smell the camel dung. The scene ran something like this:

ARAB—*Topol*—From Damascus, from Amman, from Cairo, they send messengers to tell me the Jews will destroy our land and ravish our women, so I should send my men to the Grand Mufti's army. What answer have you?

MICKEY—*Kirk*—Your own eyes. The Jews aren't destroying your land. They are not ravishing your women. They don't even *like* your women.

ARAB—That is not much of an answer. They don't even like *their* women.

MICKEY—For fifty years you have lived beside them without hate—why, now, a holy war? Because the Grand

Mufti and King Abdullah and the rest see a chance to win
money and power and land. They won't leave one camel for
you and your people. You will fight their war for them, and
when it is finished, your people will be worse off than
before, or you will be dead. When was the last time they
sent help to *you?*

The chief demanded proof from the Jews that they had the strength
they claimed. To convince him, the Palmach attempted to blow up an
ammunition dump inside Syria, but ran into serious trouble. Mickey,
along on the raid as an "observer," injected himself into the proceed-
ings as a participant. While this incident *may* have occurred, its actual
genesis was in that meeting I had with Kirk Douglas in London:
"Somewhere I want to see Mickey in *action.*"

In the raid on the ammunition dump, Senta's husband was conveniently killed, which shows what can happen when authors are put
in charge of the casualty lists.

Out of this came the scene of the first meeting between Mickey
Marcus and David Ben Gurion, called Jacob Zion in the script because
I didn't want to get involved with Ben Gurion. A very talented actor,
Luther Adler, played the part, but since Luther refused to wear a wig
to simulate Ben Gurion's famous shock of white hair, the make-up
man had to blow powder and shellac on Adler's own hair, which
made him look like a Jewish O'Cedar mop.

Colonel Marcus demanded unification of all the diverse forces—the
Haganah, the Palmach, and the private armies of the Irgun and the
Stern Gang—under one command, his own. Ben Gurion-Adler, after
detailing the intense rivalries and jealousies among the various Jewish
forces, informed him gently, "Believe me, we could have a very nice
war *without* the Arabs. And you want me to give you absolute authority? Please, Colonel Marcus, if you find out how to get it, let me know.
Because then, if anything went wrong, it would be nice to have an
American to blame it on."

Next came the attempt of an armored convoy from Tel Aviv to
break through the "Arab Volunteer Army" lying in ambush in the
Bab El Wad, the deep gorge through which ran the only route to besieged Jerusalem. Mickey-Kirk and Asher-Yul Brynner made the

journey in an armored car; Magda-Senta was driving a truckload of chickens as a volunteer. Again, a chilling incident I had heard became the basis of the scene: during the War of Liberation, a similar convoy had been ambushed and partly destroyed; one truck and driver were separated from the rest, the motor stalled. Some of the others shouted to the driver to come on; then, from the hills, the Arabs echoed the "Come on! Come on! Come on!" derisively, waiting, guns at the ready, for the last truck to pull into the open where it could be blown apart. The catcalls went on and on. Finally, in desperation, the driver got his truck to move and gunned his way through the shattering fire; but his hair turned white overnight and he went out of his mind.

In the screenplay, I placed Magda-Senta in the same predicament, and had her freeze at the wheel in terror until Mickey-Kirk could get to her side and slap her into awareness. They made it to safety, Senta's hair didn't turn white, and no one went out of his mind until the day we tried to shoot the scene and not one, but twenty, trucks stalled and refused to move.

It was at this point in the story that Mickey decided to leave Palestine and return home. Emma had written that she had had a miscarriage and was in the hospital. That, plus Mickey's disillusionment with the role Ben Gurion was limiting him to, helped him make up his mind to pack and get out.

Of course, this was also the moment that Magda-Senta, in a virtual state of shock since the incident with the convoy, chose to call him a coward, burst into hysterics, and then attempted to seduce him—before suddenly succumbing to the sedative the nurse, the censor, and I had carefully placed in her medicine at the beginning of the scene to avoid embarrassment to the real-life Emma Marcus.

Mickey's return proved short-lived; Emma-Angie Dickinson was not in the hospital. She had been out for some time and hadn't told him because she wanted him back. Mickey was outraged. Then he was called to Washington to receive a World War II medal and got into an argument with John Wayne-General Randolph, who was conveniently receiving a medal of his own. Mickey asked Wayne-Randolph if he thought the United States would recognize the government of Israel if and when the new state were declared.

GENERAL RANDOLPH—*Wayne*—What the hell for? What's in it for us but trouble? Your friends may have the Bible in their favor . . . but the Arabs have all the oil. You think our State Department's going to hesitate choosing up sides? They're already putting the screw on your pals to postpone independence. What's a few more years . . . or a few more centuries . . . to those people? Thank God you got some sense and pulled out of there before it was too late.

MICKEY—*Kirk*—(grabbing him) Listen, you brass-buttoned, bigoted, ignorant—have you any idea what the stakes are over there? A people fighting with their bare hands because this is the last place on this whole earth they can go and be—

GENERAL RANDOLPH—*Wayne*—(without turning) Then how come you came home so soon? Wouldn't they let you be captain?

MICKEY—*Kirk*—(releasing him) You know me too damn well.

GENERAL RANDOLPH—*Wayne*—And you don't know me at all. Don't you give the rest of us any credit for being human beings, too? Who gave you those trucks and blankets when you liberated Dachau? You've got friends, Mickey, although maybe it upsets you to find out. I'll ring every damn doorbell in Washington for you, from the White House on down, if it'll help. But what about you? Are you too big to go back and help your own people unless they bow down and kiss your West Point ring? What happened to that insubordinate son-of-a-bitch who jumped out of one of my planes over Normandy? Are you proud of your Distinguished Service Medal and ashamed you might win the Star of David? Stand up and be counted, Mickey, and a lot of us will stand up with you. (he raises his glass) *L'chaim.*

When Duke Wayne, fresh from his victory over cancer of the lung, poured himself into that last speech the day we shot it at Cinecitta in Rome, and wound up belting out the Hebrew toast to life, I wouldn't have changed places with any writer or director in the world. Maybe I should have, but you would have had a hard time convincing me. Duke was standing up to be counted; that was why this picture got to be made.

Mickey-Kirk, of course, was convinced. He returned to Israel to find that his training program and table of organization had been put into effect by Ben Gurion's order. Asher-Yul met him at the plane when it arrived at night at a secret airstrip, and laughed at Mickey's surprise that this acceptance could happen after all his military proposals had been sneered at.

> ASHER—*Yul*—Didn't you realize you were dealing with *Sabras?* We have to pretend to know everything, because we know so little. We'll still criticize everything you suggest. But that doesn't mean we won't do it.
>
> MICKEY—*Kirk*—I'll bet if Moses came down from Mount Sinai, the Palmach would turn down five of the Commandments just so God wouldn't get a swelled head.

Mickey was followed out of the transport plane by a pilot from Texas, recruited into the Haganah's air force, like many Americans, because of the Jewish underground's lack of trained airmen. This part had not been cast yet—but we'll get to that later.

Mickey had returned just in time to hear David Ben Gurion declare the creation of the Jewish State in a historic speech in the Dizengoff Museum in Tel Aviv, which we recreated on Israel's only so-called sound stage. And Mickey joined in the singing of the national anthem, "Hatikvah," interrupted—in my screenplay, at least—by the arrival of a cablegram announcing that the United States had become the first nation to recognize the new State of Israel.

In the next sequence, Tel Aviv went wild celebrating its first Independence Day, and Mickey and the Texas pilot drove a jeep through the cheering throngs to a rendezvous Mickey had arranged with Magda-Senta, climaxed by their first kiss and the city's first air raid, both with devastating results.

By this point, the story had reached its frenetic stage. Egyptian tanks rolled across the Sinai. Mickey counseled attack—attack with anything at the little Israeli Army's command, even if only a column of jeeps. Ben Gurion agreed but also insisted that Jerusalem must be defended to the last man.

> ASHER—*Yul*—It will cost ten times as much to hold the city as it's worth.
>
> BEN GURION—*Adler*—How much is Jerusalem worth? What did it close at on Wall Street today? What's the price of a hundred foot frontage on Solomon's Temple?
>
> MICKEY—*Kirk*—It won't be worth a plugged nickel when the desert is full of Arab tanks and you've wasted your arms trying to defend the impossible.
>
> BEN GURION—*Adler*—There will be arms for the desert and arms for Jerusalem.
>
> MICKEY—*Kirk*—Do you believe in miracles?
>
> BEN GURION—*Adler*—You came back, didn't you?

The jeep force that Mickey had assembled raced into the desert by night, secretly armed with recoilless rifles and grenade throwers. Mickey went with it, and a battle ensued in the Negev desert in which Tex, the pilot, was killed in an attack on the tanks with a Piper Cub. But the jeeps managed to divert and stall the tank force, and continuing hit-and-run raids by night kept the tanks confused. They never reached the coast, which would have cut the country in two, or Tel Aviv, which would have decapitated it.

The real problem was Jerusalem, which was being strangled by the Arab siege. In a scene with Ben Gurion, Mickey argued that it had no strategic value, that half of it was already in Arab hands, and that it didn't make sense to risk everything to save the rest of it.

> BEN GURION—*Adler*—Did it make sense for a fellow with a nice, steady job building pyramids to march his friends into the Red Sea? Mickey, Jerusalem is starving. It was destroyed once by Nebuchadnezzar, a second time by Titus of Rome. Not again, not again! Without Jerusalem there is no Israel.

MICKEY—*Kirk*—I'd be interested in knowing how you intend saving it.

BEN GURION—*Adler*—In the Bible, there is a Hebrew word I've never seen anywhere else. "Aluf." It means "Commander." More than that, it means "Leader." I am placing the unified command of all forces on the central Jerusalem front in the hands of Aluf David Marcus.
(he extends an order to Mickey)
Well . . . don't you want to be the first General of the Army of Israel in two thousand years?

Mickey-Kirk, like Colonel David "Mickey" Marcus in real life, finally had what he wanted. He accepted the command and traveled to Kibbutz Hulda, headquarters of the little army trying to capture the fortress of Latrun, which was manned by the crack Arab Legion and had used massed artillery time and again to decimate the attacking Israeli forces. Mickey-Kirk, of course, was taken to the kibbutz in a jeep driven by Magda-Senta. The real Colonel Marcus probably had had no such coincidental good fortune.

Taking over command from Asher-Yul and Allon-Giallelis, Mickey called all the officers together and laid out a plan that demanded split-second timing.

MICKEY—*Kirk*—(looking at his wristwatch) We'll synchronize to mine. When I say "Hack," it will be exactly 4:05 P.M. Ready? Three . . . two . . . one . . . Hack!

AN OFFICER—Aluf—(Mickey looks at him; the officer indicates the other officers) You'll excuse us, but we don't have a watch.

Thus Mickey came face to face with the Israeli Army's supply problem. But at dawn of May 31, 1948, the attack against the fortress of Latrun was launched under his command. First came the busses, carrying the new recruits from Tel Aviv—recent immigrants from the concentration camps of Belsen, Auschwitz, and Buchenwald, who had arrived by way of Cyprus. Most of them spoke no Hebrew. But on hand signals they rose out of the wheatfields facing Latrun in the blistering midsummer heat and attacked the fortress that was strangling Jerusalem. A makeshift force of Jerry-built armored cars actually breached the walls of the fort, using homemade flamethrowers, and blasted their way into the interior. But the diversionary force sent around to the rear to cut off reinforcement failed to reach its objective. The Arab Legion massacred the infant Israeli Army with artillery fire and forced another bloody retreat.

Mickey had been beaten, and beaten badly. In a makeshift hospital set up outside the kindergarten at Kibbutz Hulda, he and Asher looked over the casualties. Orders had been given during the battle in seven languages, yet many of the immigrant soldiers still hadn't understood. But the men and boys had never faltered in their advance. Their bodies were found in the wheat, the safety catches still on their guns. They hadn't even known how to release them. And yet had advanced.

There was no choice, as Mickey saw it. They would have to attack again. At least he *thought* there was no choice. But then, *deus ex* screenplay, arrived Topol, the old Berber sheik, to tell them of a secret way through the mountains out of sight of the Arab guns that could get them through to Jerusalem—if they could build a road. And it would have to be built in a week.

The use of the Berber chief in this connection was my invention, but the basic facts were true. The old route was found. The people of Tel Aviv and Jerusalem, the *people,* working from both ends of the route by night with their hands and a few bulldozers, almost within earshot of the Arabs, secretly built an entire military road, bypassing the fortress of Latrun and lifting the siege of Jerusalem, in one week. It traveled, incredibly, across mountains and up cliffs and through gorges. It is still there. You can see it if you turn off the highway that now passes through the Bab El Wad at the historical marker that now announces "The Burma Road;" Mickey's name for it. But the people who worked on it still call it "The Marcus Road." And in the Bab El Wad, the Israeli government has left as a national monument the burned-out hulks of the armored cars that were destroyed in convoys attempting to break through to Jerusalem before Mickey's secret road was completed.

The road had to be finished before the United Nations truce in the war went into effect, for if Jerusalem had still been isolated at the time of the truce, it would have legally passed entirely into Arab hands.

The road was completed on the night before the truce. The Israeli forces under Mickey's command encamped at the Monastery of Notre Dame at the Arab town of Abu Gosh, in sight of the hills of Jerusalem. In the screenplay, Mickey left his quarters, passed a sentry, and wandered into a vine-covered ruin for a prearranged meeting with Magda-Senta. There he told her their romance was over; that he was going home to his wife, because he had been in love with Emma all his life and had just found it out. Magda-Senta kissed him and also, figuratively, the United Artists front office, and said, "Shalom, Mickey. You bastard." And left.

Mickey started back for his quarters and was challenged by a new sentry in Hebrew, a language he had never bothered to learn. Mickey thought it was a joke and started to run and was shot through the head.

The final scene of the picture depicted the panorama of convoys and soldiers moving up the Marcus Road toward Jerusalem as a single jeep made its way down in the opposite direction, carrying the coffin of Colonel David "Mickey" Marcus, U.S.A., "A soldier for all humanity," as his headstone at West Point was to read.

I have included this rather detailed sketch of the screenplay for two reasons: so that the progress of shooting the picture can be more easily followed, and so that those readers who fancy themselves motion picture critics—and their name is legion—can see how and where the screenwriter erred.

One final note, for those unfamiliar with the ways of our industry. A motion picture is not usually photographed in the sequence in which it is written; it is photographed in whatever manner makes it least expensive to shoot. Most of our settings for interiors were to be built in Rome, where stage space was plentiful. Consequently, all the scenes with John Wayne and Angie Dickinson were photographed in Italy, after we had left Israel behind. In Israel itself, the sequence of photography was determined by many things, primarily the Army. Thus our shooting started with the main portions of the battle for Latrun, which required the use of Israeli soldiers, then shifted from there to the scenes in the Negev desert, utilizing the Israeli tank corps. A director is forced to carry a road map in his head of the twistings and turnings of plot and character and mood, and to turn it around and around, depending upon the vagaries of the schedule, so that when it is all put together it will have unity and flow. It is a little like doing a jigsaw puzzle upside down and backward, and sometimes just about as successful.

Macy's Rome branch. The exterior of the set we built at Cinecitta instead of playing the opening scene in Mickey's kitchen. Everything's cheaper at Macy's, isn't it?

Kirk Douglas and Angie Dickinson in their working clothes. "Mickey, you're a wonderful lover . . . and such a lousy husband."

Kirk and Senta Berger exchanging clothes with the immigrants in our mass Jewish striptease. Everyone wanted to exchange clothes with Senta.

Kirk playing Mickey Marcus and Luther Adler playing David Ben Gurion and an O'Cedar mop. "Well . . . don't you want to be the first General of the Army of Israel in two thousand years?"

Senta and Kirk in the chicken truck, running the gauntlet of Arab fire in the Bab El Wad en route to Jerusalem. It was the director's hair which turned white in this sequence, when two-thirds of our convoy developed vapor lock.

Senta and Kirk in her bedroom in Tel Aviv, just before the sedative placed in her medicine by her nurse, the censor, and me took effect. Obviously, in the nick of time.

Tel Aviv made up to look like Jerusalem for the arrival of the convoy after the incident in the Bab El Wad. Originally, we had attempted to shoot this scene in Jerusalem itself, with our "soldiers" throwing food to the actual residents of the city who, being both bewildered and prosperous, immediately threw it back, with considerable accuracy. So we reshot, in Tel Aviv, with our own extras.

Colonel Marcus and General Randolph (John Wayne) after receiving medals at the British Embassy in Washington, built at Cinecitta. Duke is trying to remember the pronunciation of "L'chaim."

The real Colonel Marcus.

CHAPTER X

Nehemia Graf owned orange groves. Several of them. This made him a rich man, for Israel. It also made him an Israeli and, therefore, curious.

What kind of idiots make moving pictures?

To answer this question, he got himself a job on "the production." By this time, you see, in and about Tel Aviv, we were simply "the production." Every year, some American company decided to support the entire Israeli economy by shooting a picture about Israel *in* Israel. The year before it had been Paramount's *Judith,* starring Sophia Loren as an Israeli. This year it was our turn.

Nehemia signed on as a driver. It was early Spring, there would be no orange crop for several months, and besides, he liked to drive. This, in Tel Aviv, is akin to a passion for Russian roulette.

The Israeli government has seen fit to impose a duty of 300 percent on imported motor cars. This makes the average American Ford or Chevrolet retail for around $12,000. Any Israeli paying out this kind of money for a Ford or Chevrolet figures he has bought the road as well, and as the proud owner of the road, he tries to remove any other car trespassing on his property. One of the truly inspiring sights in this country is an Israeli who owns his own car making a left turn. First, he waits until the light turns red against him, thus reducing the competition somewhat. Then he swings from the right to the left lane several times, to brush aside tourist-driven automobiles and chickens, and dashes forward, foot on the throttle, through the intersection. Every horn within a quarter of a mile starts to blow from drivers who have *also* purchased the road, but our hero ignores them and turns right. As the enemy, deceived, charges forward to force him into the ditch, he swings left, tires screeching, eliminating several of the attackers, and hurls his machine in the proper direction, but the wrong lane, where he comes to an abrupt stop, either because he has run out of gas or because he has not run out of gas. Israeli gasoline, except for that reserved for the Army, has an octane rating of about 13, and needs to sit down occasionally.

As a consequence of the high proportion of Jewish Kamikaze drivers, the accident rate in little Israel is the highest in the world. The death rate from accidents is the highest in the world. Automobile insurance starts out at $9,000 deductible. On our production, at the end of each day the transportation manager would chalk up our losses on a blackboard. It was like an RAF briefing room after a raid on Cologne. Every returning driver stood stiffly at attention, head erect, induced by whiplash during the day's combat. Crumpled fenders were carried in for repair, bits of pedestrian clinging to them. A three-tone auto horn played "Taps." After seeing the damage caused by a Volkswagen during rush hour on Dizengoff Street, I am not surprised the Egyptian Army abandoned five hundred armored vehicles at the Mitla Pass when faced by these same drivers inside eighteen-ton tanks.

Although Volkswagens in Israel may sound a little strange, there is a reason for it—of sorts. The West German government, as part of its war reparations, has given a complete Volkswagen factory to Israel. Some Israelis think it is a continuation of Hitler's search for the Ultimate Solution.

During the production of the picture, West Germany established diplomatic relations with Israel for the first time, and thousands of Israelis carrying anti-Nazi signs demonstrated against the arrival of the new German Ambassador's plane at Lydda Airport. And then, according to Tel Aviv's newspaper, *Ma'ariv,* "The demonstrators got back into their Volkswagens and drove home."

Nehemia, fortunately, was a conservative driver. He only drove on the wrong side of the road when there was no *other* side of the road, as frequently happened. And he didn't consider a traffic light an attempt by the Establishment to limit his freedom. With his orange groves, Nehemia *was* the Establishment. It was with considerable pride that he drove my wife and me to see the house the production had rented for us in Savyon, which, he informed us with quiet pride, was the Beverly Hills of Tel Aviv.

I had been living in my hotel room for several weeks, and my wife had just arrived that afternoon from Rome, excited and impatient to begin housekeeping in a new land. With a flourish, Nehemia threw open the door of our new home. It came off the hinge.

The walls were bare of any decoration except for a few Picasso-styled cracks. The furniture resembled the props in the second act of *Fiddler on the Roof*. The stove didn't work. The cupboards were empty of the pots and dishes my wife had ordered by mail. But that was all right, since there was nothing in the refrigerator to put in the pots and dishes anyway.

I had been subsisting on soybeans for so long I had looked forward to my first home-cooked meal with the anticipation of a sailor with a three-day pass to the Playboy Club. Lucille—my wife—had promised me a feast.

She looked around the house, sat down quietly, and burst into tears. The effect on Nehemia was astounding. He ran out of the house, jumped into the car, and drove away.

Unable to puzzle this out, I was doing whatever I could to brighten the situation—knowing all the time it was partly my fault for not having checked the house earlier—when Nehemia returned, with Menehama.

Menehama is supposedly Nehemia's wife, but she hasn't fooled me. She is the Angel of Mercy, with a degree from the *Cordon Bleu*. She came bearing potato *kugel* and a brisket. Also a few dishes and pots and pans. In five minutes the stove was working. In six minutes, Lucille was talking to me again. In an hour, we were having dinner.

Nehemia had acted, not as a driver, not as an employee, not even as a friend, but as a patriot. In my wife's tears he saw an indictment of all of the shortcomings of today's Israel. Seeing Savyon through her eyes, it was no longer Beverly Hills, but Coney Island. And there is a deeper truth: Israel is one family, and he wanted to show us we were a part of it. So he included us in his.

Menehama agreed with Lucille that it was terrible to thrust her into a place like this. But don't worry, awful as the house was, it would be a palace in no time—this while lighting the candles, because the lights didn't work either. Menehama and Lucille had already become old friends, communicating in English, Yiddish, and Hebrew—no mean achievement, considering my wife didn't know any Yiddish, had never before heard Hebrew, and Menehama's English was shaky, to say the least. But no matter. Women must communicate continuously or they can't exist, so a little thing like language is no obstacle.

How, Lucille wanted to know, were all these miracles Menehama promised to be accomplished? Menehama's answer was simple: Yaakov the Electrician.

Yaakov the Electrician showed up the next morning, a big, burly, cheerful man, who rode up on a bicycle that seemed to be bending under his bulk, and greeted us with, "Good morning."

Having exhausted his knowledge of English, he and my wife conducted the rest of the conversation, about the repairs necessary and the prices to be paid, in Hebrew, a language Lucille had acquired the previous night, apparently while I was sleeping.

Yaakov the Electrician helped buy the dishes and the pots and pans, fixed the door and the cracks in the wall, rearranged the furniture, and took care of the garden. He introduced Lucille to a butcher, recommended a beauty parlor, secured a discount on a pair of bicycles we wanted, fixed the flat on the Peugot the production had given me to drive, and notified us we were entitled to a membership in the local tennis club, as residents of Savyon.

The only thing he was a little vague about was the electricity. But he got the refrigerator working by kicking it.

He also adopted us. We didn't discover this until the next day when we wandered over to the tennis club to hit a few balls and discovered we weren't members. There were a few technicalities to be worked out, since we were only renting in Savyon. But don't worry. Come back tomorow.

I have no doubt that, some day, those technicalities will be worked out. Some day, also, we may be allowed to swim in the club pool. I'm looking forward to it.

Returning from the courts, I suggested we work off our frustrated energy by taking a bicycle ride. Lucille agreed, and we went to get our bicycles from the garage.

Yaakov, not trusting the bicycle locks we had bought, had thoughtfully chained his bicycle to both of ours, so they would be safe. They couldn't have been safer. We had the key to our locks, but Yaakov had the key to his.

So we went for a ride in the Peugot instead. This proved to be a mistake. The street we lived on was named Olive Grove Lane. That, we were told, was the translation of the Hebrew *Simtat Cherem Hazeitim.* Simple enough, except for one thing: all the street signs were in Hebrew.

If I hadn't gone out of the window in Hebrew class, I might have been able to decipher them. I could hear my rabbi snickering somewhere in Valhalla, "Schnook! I *told* you, pay attention! Some day the sacred language of Abraham and Moses would lead you to heaven, and also to Simtat Cherem Hazeitim!"

We turned a corner, and I was absolutely lost. Every street sign looked the same to me—indecipherable. I had encouraged Lucille in the pleasant delusion that, of course, I had a knowledge of everything pertaining to my heritage that no Pennsylvania semi-shiksa could ever acquire. This didn't seem the time to mention that I appeared to have forgotten the alphabet.

So I kept driving and turning corners, hoping to find some recognizable landmark, without success. After half an hour we were getting low on gas. The last thing I wanted to do was drive into a gas station and allow my wife to realize I didn't know how to say, "Fill her up." *She* probably knew.

It started to grow dark, and Lucille was getting a little restive. It had been a very nice ride, eighteen times around Savyon, but now could we go home? It was time to prepare dinner. Hunger finally overcame my pride, and I confessed my difficulty. My wife promptly pointed to a street sign we had passed seven times in the last half hour.

"*That,*" she said, "says Olive Grove Lane."

I stared at the Hebrew hieroglyphics.

"How do *you* know?" I shouted, as reasonably as possible.

"Because that word is 'Simtat,' " she replied. "It's very simple. I noticed it when we left the house. It's an *O* with a tail on it, an upside-down *L,* and a backward *C.*"

I didn't have the heart to tell her that she was reading the sign from left to right, which, of course, was backward. She never really accepted the fact that the Hebrew language ran in the other direction. Also, the word she was deciphering was "Cherem," but that, too, was beside the point: *she* could read Hebrew, and I couldn't.

I tried to pretend, after that, that I had suffered only a temporary lapse of memory, but I was soon exposed. We were invited to the apartment of General Shlomo Shamir, the man who had originally recruited Mickey in his kitchen—or Macy's Toy Department. He was now the director of a chemical plant near the Dead Sea, but, fortunately, his apartment was in Tel Aviv, and he had written down the directions in Hebrew, which I merely handed to a taxi driver—I was too wise, by this time, to drive the Peugot to any destination I had not already scouted.

Arriving at an apartment house that looked as if a general would live in it, I paid the driver and, puffed up with my success, led my wife into the lobby.

But the general had failed to tell me the number of his apartment. Quickly, I crossed to the wall beside the elevator where the directory was located.

It was in Hebrew.

With my wife eyeing me, I attempted to pick out the name "Shamir," reading from right to left. A Hebrew S—*shin?*—that should be simple.

I found it quickly, and we took the elevator to the eighth floor, the numbers being easily decipherable. Strange how well I could read Arabic numerals.

Nobody on the eighth floor spoke English or looked like a general.

We came down again. I found another letter that looked as if it could be pronounced as a sibilant opposite the number "4."

We went up in the elevator. Nobody on the fourth floor looked like even a lieutenant.

Back to the lobby again, where help arrived in the shape of the janitor. I addressed him in sign language, but he didn't speak it.

My wife introduced herself to him in his native tongue, Kurdish, which she had never heard of until that moment, and he directed us to General Shamir's apartment on the ninth floor.

We spent a pleasant evening with Shamir, talking about Mickey Marcus. When we left the general's apartment, we hailed another taxi, I told him our address on Simtat Cherem Hazeitim. Apparently he was a foreigner, for he could not understand my impeccable Hebrew pronunciation.

My wife told him we wanted the street that had a backward *C,* an upside-down *L,* and an *O* with a tail on it.

He took us home.

My final humiliation came on a drive into the countryside, when I couldn't find Jerusalem. You must admit, in a country that has only four or five cities large enough to have more than one highway leading to them, losing a town that has been in the same place for over five thousand years takes a certain amount of talent.

But I did it. We came to a crossroad that had signs pointing in opposite directions, with the names of the cities clearly visible—in Hebrew. Any red-blooded Jewish boy who can't decipher the word "Yerushalaem," which occurs some 14,000 times in the Old Testament, should be subjected to a saliva test. Any Jewish boy who can't remember what the first letter looks like is, obviously, a simpleton.

I found it, of course, turned to the left, and drove us proudly to the Mediterranean.

All of this came to a climax in a meeting we had in Tel Aviv with Yigael Allon—*General* Yigael Allon, naturally, who was then Minister of Public Works, in charge of the nation's highways.

Lucille listened to his stories of his war experiences dutifully enough, then got down to the *real* business of our meeting. As Minister of Public Works, how could he expect Western tourists to visit this country if they couldn't even find Jerusalem?

Nonsense, the Minister of Public Works insisted. What tourist could be stupid enough to lose *Jerusalem* in this tiny country?

My wife indicated her husband.

"The Jewish Daniel Boone," she replied.

Not too long after that, every road sign in the State of Israel blossomed forth with an English translation under the Hebrew.

Several police officers were given the license number of my car, with instructions to *point.*

By that time, it wasn't necessary. I always carried with me a card which had on it a backward *C,* an upside-down *L,* and an *O* with a tail on it.

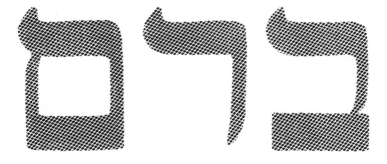

CHAPTER XI

We were rapidly approaching the day set by the Israeli Army for the start of our picture, and things were growing more and more hectic. Outside of Tel Aviv, we were assembling machine guns and ammunition, building bombs and grenades, and constructing armored cars. The ammunition consisted of blanks, the bombs of smoke powder, and the armored cars were made of plywood; but the prices were real.

At this point, one of the young Israelis working as an assistant director asked to see me in private. He had run across the price list the Israel Defense Forces had sent to me. What had I done to make the Army angry?

I couldn't think of anything offhand. I hadn't attacked any border *kibbutzim* or blown up any busses that I could remember. I had bought Gershon Rivlin a bad lunch the week before, but I couldn't believe a punitive raid would be launched in retaliation for some spoiled gefulte fish. However, the Israeli Army is very touchy. I wasn't certain.

The assistant shook his head. I didn't understand. He had been an assistant director on Paramount's production of *Judith.* He had seen the price list the Army had given *them.* We were being charged double.

I thanked him for the information and began to worry. After all, you can't go to the Better Business Bureau to complain about the Army. Also, you can't go to the Army and make an accusation that may not be true; after all, *their* guns had real ammunition. Furthermore, I had been disturbed about our deteriorating relations with Israel's armed forces for some time. The promised jeeps and tanks had never materialized, and I was on the verge of employing Pinhok, the world's champion smuggler, to perform his specialty.

My dilemma was solved by the arrival in Israel of Mrs. Mickey Marcus. The lovely Emma had been invited for the ceremonies attendant to the launching of the picture, and to receive the honors the Israeli government wished to bestow posthumously upon her heroic husband. When she stepped off the plane at Lydda Airport, the country was at her feet. A red carpet had been spread. A band was playing. A contingent of troops paraded. Emma smiled fondly at the soldiers as she descended the ramp, but they continued to parade right past her. The Foreign Minister of Ethiopia had just landed in another plane, and that's what all the fanfare was about.

Not that Israel didn't love Emma Marcus. But she was family, she was Jewish, *she* didn't have to be impressed, while the Ethiopian Foreign Minister had come from Cairo, and Israel mustn't look like a poor relation in his eyes.

Emma understood and laughed about it, and was whirled off by people I didn't know into a series of parties and testimonials that could only in part reflect the depth of the feeling for her and Mickey. The climax was to be a meeting with the Prime Minister, Levi Eshkol, which I was to attend with her.

Is an Israeli Prime Minister also Commander-in-Chief of the Army? I intended to find out.

Levi Eshkol, the one-time Ukrainian farmer who had succeeded Ben Gurion as Prime Minister, was a kindly appearing, baldish man who wore glasses but no tie. Early in the chit-chat with Emma, it appeared he had a considerable sense of humor, at least for a former Finance Minister. Most Finance Ministers are understandably short-tempered, and the former Finance Minister of *Israel* had even more right to be somewhat liverish. However, Eshkol's easy attitude and ready smile encouraged me. When he paused in his reminiscences with Emma and asked me if all were going well with the production, I said, "No."

He seemed a little surprised. It was like asking a friend, "How are you?" and having him tell you; but I wasn't going to let the opportunity get away.

What was my problem?

Nothing much. Only the Army.

He smiled an understanding smile. I wondered what kind of price list the Army had given *him*.

I told him that almost everything we had asked for, the Army had been unable to let us have in the quantities we needed. Oh, it had all been explained logically enough: they could not supply us with the tanks they had promised because that would mean taking them out of the forward areas facing the Arabs, and they had no replacements. The same for jeeps. The same for guns. This little Army was spread so thin, they couldn't loan us a fountain pen unless they had a pencil with which to replace it.

Eshkol nodded. True enough. Wasn't it?

"Mr. Prime Minister," I said, "the other day I attended Israel's Independence Day celebration. You were there, too. I saw fifty or sixty tanks, a hundred jeeps, uncounted guns, jet airplanes, and fountain pens. Now, everyone knew you were holding this parade. TWA and Air France ran excursions to it. You advertised it in *The New York Times,* which several Arabs read at breakfast. So if you don't have enough jeeps and tanks to go round, who was watching the store?"

Eshkol's eyes twinkled.

"The Lord watches over Israel," he said. And then he added, "but we don't depend on it."

Having made a point, I continued. The only purpose of the Independence Day Parade, as far as I could see, was propaganda, to impress the country, the Arab nations, and the Hadassah tours. But one international motion picture would be seen by more people than a *hundred* Independence Day Parades. Here was propaganda going begging!

Now I pressed my advantage: Why should the Israeli Army charge twice as much to allow their soldiers to play Jewish soldiers as they did for them to play *Egyptian* soldiers?

The Prime Minister looked a little startled. What was I talking about?

In *Judith,* I explained, the Israeli Army had had to play the part of the Egyptian Army attacking a *kibbutz,* since no one wanted to issue a casting call to the real Egyptian army. In our picture, Israeli soldiers would be playing Israeli soldiers—but the army had doubled the ante.

Eshkol smiled again. He asked me a simple question: when the Army had submitted its price list to the producers of *Judith,* had they bargained? Of course not, I replied, who bargains with an Army?

Paramount paid every penny demanded in the first Army price list? Every penny, I insisted.

And now the Army was asking double?

That's right.

"So what did you expect," asked the Prime Minister, "discounts?" Then he looked at Emma, and he said, "For Mrs. Marcus's sake, I think I should talk to the Army—if they're still talking to me."

He telephoned Army headquarters and asked for the price lists on both *Judith* and *Cast a Giant Shadow*. When they arrived on his desk the next day, every price on the *Giant Shadow* price list had been cut in half.

The jeeps and the tanks showed up, too.

CHAPTER XII

Kirk Douglas arrived in Tel Aviv and took over the King David suite at the Dan Hotel. Normally, when a movie star invades a hotel, there is a lot of bowing from the manager and the assistant manager, and the chambermaids are too awestruck to clean the apartment for a few days. But this was Israel. The chambermaids didn't clean the apartment, but they weren't awestruck. In fact, a couple of them had sons who were nuclear scientists, and they were leaving it to The Bomb to dust the place off some day. And I never saw anybody bow in Tel Aviv unless a lot of other people were applauding.

Kirk didn't mind. While he will match his ego with any man's, he was Jewish before he was an actor, and he understands. In Israel, pride is as important as gun powder. And sometimes as effective. An actor who has made it in *Hebrew* is an Actor. An actor who has made it in English is a rich man and deserving of no great attention unless he is making a donation. Haym Topol was the toast of Tel Aviv at the time because of his successes on the Hebrew stage and in local Israel movies that sometimes cost $20,000 and a case of chocolate matzos. Children followed him, crowds gathered in the lobby of the Dan when he appeared, autograph books were shoved at him—from right to left—when he walked down the street with Kirk Douglas. People were always asking Haym for his autograph while they were usually trying to sell something to Kirk. Incidentally, Topol, who was thirty at the time, had spent most of those thirty years playing old men similar to our Berber chief, and is perpetuating that image in *Fiddler.* His main worry is that by the time he is as old as the roles he plays, he will be too old to play them.

I had secured Topol's participation in the picture by sitting down and reading him the part, aloud. Since I am notoriously one of the world's worst actors, I can only assume that either the role was superbly written or Topol needed the money. Kirk, I discovered, was not convinced that his part was superbly written, as yet. We paced up and down the King David suite, discussing it line for line and syllable for syllable. And, more importantly, motivation for motivation. This kind of dissection may help an actor come to grips with a characterization, but there are many times in a play or a novel or a screenplay where an author cannot tell you *why* his way is correct; it is a matter of instinct and inspiration that cannot survive argument. Kirk wouldn't stand for that kind of evasion. So we went round and round, and continued in that direction during the shooting of the picture. Sometimes he went round clockwise and I went counterclockwise, producing the inevitable collison. I couldn't say now if the picture would have been better if he had listened more closely to me, or if I had paid more attention to him. I only know that I lost sixteen pounds during photography on the picture, and it wasn't *that* hot in the Negev.

On a softer note, by this time, the beautiful Senta Berger had been hired for the role of Magda, the Romantic Interest, and all the males on the production, including my son, were considerably disturbed to learn that she already had a romantic interest of her own. He lived in Vienna, which should have eliminated him for a while, but love and the Boeing 707 conquer all. Senta went home for weekends.

I was prepared for this, having been matured on the legend of William Faulkner, who came to Hollywood to work for Warner Brothers. Faulkner dropped by Jack Warner's office one day and inquired if it were all right if he worked at home. Warner magnanimously agreed, and it was several months before he discovered that home, to Faulkner, was Mississippi.

Home, to Senta, was Vienna. The problem was that she and her romantic interest were happy together. Instead of quarreling, worrying, and losing weight, like sensible lovers, they wandered from the whipped cream delights of Vienna's famed Demel's confectionery to the Hotel Sacher's restaurant and its Sacher Torte, holding hands and eating. When Senta returned to Tel Aviv, she had always added ten pounds—she plumps rapidly—and her Monday closeups could not be cut in with her Friday closeups, which had been shot on a spartan

Israeli menu of soybeans and dietetic chicken fat. However, since she always brought me one of the Sacher Tortes, I found ways to shoot around her until she had become her ravishing soybean self again.

We rounded out most of our casting in Tel Aviv by hiring a group of fine Israeli performers, including Michael Shillo, Rina Ganor, Shlomo Hermon, Hillel Rave, and others.

One of the Israeli actors who shall be nameless proved to be a considerable problem. The salary he was demanding was beyond our budget for the part and I held many meetings with his agent, a former waiter, trying to reach an accommodation. Someone—I prefer to be understandably vague on this point—finally suggested that, the Israeli income tax being what it is (according to some bitter informants, it is 105 percent of earnings; however, since most of this goes to the Army, and everyone is in the Army, nobody starves), if two-thirds of the salary were paid in America in American dollars, the actor would triple his take-home pay, as long as he didn't take it home.

The waiter-agent agreed that this made sense, but obviously it all had to be hush-hush. There followed a series of secret maneuvers that would have given James Bond a nervous breakdown. The money was to be paid in cash, in small, unmarked bills, in New York. A friend of the waiter-agent just happened to be leaving for New York that week on El Al, and would collect the money from the bank in person. Then he would rush to a telephone, put in a call for Tel Aviv to the waiter-agent to tell him the ransom had been paid, and, if the call got through, the waiter-agent would call the actor. If *that* call got through, the actor, who would already have his make-up on, would immediately begin to act—for by that time the picture would be in production. All my suggestions that the actor should begin acting *before* the telephone call, in case it took the usual forty-eight hours to complete, fell on deaf ears.

But, I protested, how will the vice-president of the bank—the waiter-agent insisted it must be at least a vice-president—know that he is faced by a bonafide secret representative, to whom it is safe to entrust all that cash?

No problem, the waiter-agent informed me. The friend would whisper to the vice-president a secret code word, which would identify him. The code word? The nickname of the waiter-agent, "Lover Boy."

Never having been involved in international intrigue before, I was fascinated by the clever details of the scheme. I promised to cable these instructions immediately to the vice-president of the bank in New York, and was stopped by the horrified expression of my co-conspirator's face. *Cable?* Was I out of my mind?

I understood the problem immediately. Cables were sent on the Telex machine from the Avia Hotel. The telephone operator at the hotel was the only one who could operate the machine. She was, to say the least, a friendly, chatty soul. Many times when I entered the lobby, she would discuss with me the casting of the picture or the state of a shipment of camera equipment from Rome, displaying a fund of knowledge which could only have been acquired by reading cables I hadn't received yet. In fact, it was she who informed us Frank Sinatra had signed for his role twenty-four hours before we received the official confirmation. She had saved the Telex to show to her girl friends before bothering to deliver it.

When faced with the impropriety of her actions, she immediately became indignant. She *had* to read all the cables. She was, in fact, not only a telephone operator, but a member of the Israeli Army's Secret Service. *Everybody* knew that!

To entrust a password like "Lover Boy" to her eyes would obviously be suicidal. Our cover would be blown, we would all be taken into custody, and the delicate diplomatic balance between Israel and the United States would be utterly destroyed. The U.S. would undoubtedly send Egypt a dozen F-104's in retaliation.

Consequently, I sat down and wrote a long and detailed letter about the entire secret plot to the vice-president of the bank in New York, with instructions to burn the letter as soon as he read it; or, if surprised while reading, to swallow it. Then, with a sigh of relief, I sealed it carefully, put double the required amount of airmail stamps on it, and mailed it at the airport.

On *Shabbat.* The mailman, of course, disdained to take it out of the box until the following week. Besides, the stock market wasn't doing very well and he was working part-time as a butcher, so he didn't get around to the mail as often as he used to. The secret emissary arrived in New York before my letter had left the mail box. He marched into the bank and demanded to see the vice-president. He was thrown out.

However, he, like everyone else, had been in the Israeli Army and didn't know the meaning of defeat. He marched back in and insisted again, so loudly that finally it was decided to admit him to the *sanctum sanctorum.*

The vice-president eyed him warily.

"I came for the money," said the secret emissary conspiratorially.

"Get out," said the vice-president.

The secret emissary leaned across the desk.

"Lover Boy," he whispered confidently.

The vice-president called the police.

Still shouting the secret code word, our emissary was led to police headquarters and interrogated by a suspicious lieutenant of detectives, who finally decided his story was so preposterous no one could have invented it. He was released.

Moments later, he telephoned the waiter in Tel Aviv to tell him they had been hoodwinked. No one would give him the money, I was probably a double agent, and he should keep the actor from acting until an investigation had been made of my connections with Al Fatah. The waiter immediately telephoned the actor not to act and phoned me on our location to tell me that, unless I straightened the bank out immediately, none of his clients would ever work for me. Since he only had one client, this wasn't too much of a threat, except for the fact that I *needed* that one.

Sometime in the next twenty-four hours I managed to get through on the telephone to the bank in New York. On the overseas phone from Tel Aviv, it is safe to pass a secret code word, because the connections are so bad no one can understand what you're saying anyway. However, by shouting, the essentials of Operation Lover Boy were more or less communicated. The secret representative was informed, and he once more entered the bank in New York, a little diffidently this time. The vice-president was waiting for him.

"Lover Boy?" inquired the vice-president.

The secret representative nodded glumly, the magic having gone out of the situation somehow. The money was counted out in small bills, the two men shook hands and took a vow of silence, and the secret representative raced out of the offices to the nearest telephone booth. In six short hours, he had gotten through to the waiter again. The waiter put in a call, and the actor, who had been crouching in full make-up for two days, sprinted to our location and raced in front of our camera in time to make his first shot.

It wasn't very good.

The real David Ben Gurion and the very real Emma Marcus, shortly after her arrival in Israel for the start of the motion picture.

Kirk Douglas and the author engaged in one of the many script conferences that went on before and during the shooting of the movie.

CHAPTER XIII

I have a confession to make. I have a secret vice, which I share
with a mere 300,000 denizens of the planet Earth. It is not an
uncontrollable urge to indulge in continual sexual excesses—mine,
alas, is only too controllable—or a need to smoke pot, hashish, cocaine,
or other interesting flora. I trip out if I inhale English lavender. No,
my vice is something deeper and more insidious: I am a Radio Amateur. In the vernacular, a "ham." I have spent untold hours soldering
wires together and building equipment so I could speak to mysterious
parts of the world; many times I have turned on the power in my
transmitter and, immediately, carried on interesting conversations with
my next-door neighbors who threatened to come over and smash the
damn thing if I didn't get off Channel 2.

I had had several reasons for wanting to go to Israel; one was to
make the picture; another, and possibly a more important one, was
that Israel at that time had no television. If I could find some way to
operate from that Promised Land, not only would I be free of neighborhood complaints, but any station I could hear would be *foreign!*

Furthermore, the overriding, urgent, earth-shattering purpose behind
what was about to befall me was that, somewhere in Brentwood,
California, which is the Beverly Hills of Beverly Hills, an even more
enthusiastic enthusiast than myself was waiting for me to call him
via the ether. There is something about the thrill of amateur radio
that makes it increasingly enjoyable to talk to your friends the further
they are away from you. There may be a deeper meaning here, but let's
not go into *that.* At any rate, I knew he was waiting for me to establish
radio communication because he cabled me every day he was waiting.
I cabled back every day that I was hurrying, but my equipment hadn't
arrived. Then he cabled back that he was glad I was hurrying, but
he was still waiting.

105

My alter enthusiast was Ernest Lehman, the distinguished screen-writer and producer of such films as *Who's Afraid of Virginia Woolf?* and *Hello Dolly!* but this is merely a cover for his real occupation, which is being enthusiastic. He works so hard at enjoying his hobby, he sometimes doesn't realize he's enjoying it. I once drove up to his house in Brentwood and found him riding up and down the street on a bicycle, speaking into a tiny walkie-talkie.

"What are you doing, Ernie?" I inquired.

"I'm talking to Australia from my bicycle," he said enthusiastically. "What are *you* doing?"

I was only talking to Hawaii from the transmitter in my car; I realized he had one-upped me by several thousand miles and 280 horsepower, so I didn't mention it. It turned out he was remote-controlling the powerful transmitter in his home via the walkie-talkie, thus his seemingly miraculous ability to communicate with the other side of the world while riding no-hands. The only thing left for him to do was communicate with Antarctica from a unicycle, which he has probably managed by now. He has also spoken to Japan while floating in his swimming pool. On December 7th.

From the time of my very first trip to Israel, I had instituted, through Gershon, negotiations with the Israel Post Office Department and the Army. After some delay, I was granted permission to bring in radio receiving and transmitting equipment and an antenna.

Note that last: *an antenna.* A modern directional rotary beam antenna is some thirty feet in length and contains three or more "elements" over twenty-six feet long. Even knocked down, it makes a considerable package to ship nine thousand miles; but that is nothing compared to the problem of putting it together and raising it thirty or more feet into the air.

Yaakov, the Electrician!

There was the answer to everything, electrical and constructional. I spoke to him about it. He smiled enthusiastically and asked my wife what I was saying. She explained as best she could in basic Hebrew, a language not constructed to distinguish between linear power amplifiers and beat frequency oscillators—but then, neither is my wife—and he assured her it was no problem. Whatever she was talking about.

Thus encouraged, I waited for the equipment to arrive from the United States.

The Israeli government had given the production a blanket clearance for all equipment and supplies to pass duty-free through customs. Unfortunately, the blanket had a few holes in it. First came the problem of the ammunition, which required an act of the Knesset, and the customs agents still weren't certain what kind of plot we were hatching. Then a crate of secret-looking and complicated radio transmitting apparatus arrived at the port of Haifa, together with an antenna that looked as if it were meant to communicate with Mars. While Israel had never had trouble with Mars before, from sad experience the Israelis felt the odds were pretty good that whoever lived there was anti-Semitic. Customs refused to clear my radio equipment.

I finally reported my problem to the government, in the form of Asher Hirschberg. Asher was then the one-man ruler of the Israeli film industry. To his credit, he has done more than anyone else to bring foreign productions—and money—into the country, and make it simple and easy for them to operate. As simple and easy as anything can be in the Land of Job. Asher is also the leading race car driver in the country, no mean feat since Israel contains no race tracks. Asher hasn't noticed this yet. He drives between his offices in Jerusalem and Tel Aviv as if he were on the Indianapolis Speedway, and sometimes gets as far as halfway. It's a little like the story of the drunk who phoned his wife and said, "Get the kids off the streetsh. I'm drivin' home!" When word leaks out that Asher is driving someplace, mothers grab their children, truck drivers pull into the ditch, and the Asher Hirschberg Rescue Tow Truck warms up its engine, waiting for the sound of breaking glass.

Colliding with Asher in the course of the performance of his duties is a little like trying to pass him on the right. Five minutes after I had called him, he was on the phone to the commander of the Port of Haifa. I don't know what he said to him, but it must have included a hint of a firing squad.

A few short hours later, an old Plymouth, laboring mightily under a load of aluminum tubing, coils, condensers, transformers, receivers, and assorted subversive equipment, turned into Simtat Cherem Hazeitim and coughed to a stop at our door. Two boys climbed out of the windows—there was no possibility of getting the doors open with all that aluminum plumbing lashed to the outside—and introduced themselves as the sons of the president of the Eilat Shipping Company. Apparently there was some sort of national emergency and they had been ordered by their father to deliver this *immediately,* even though today was *Shabbat.* They would unload the car as quickly as possible if I would show them the command post, then they would have to return to Haifa, where no doubt they would be called up by their units.

A little embarrassed, I explained as well as I could that this was a toy. In somewhat of a daze, they carried the equipment inside, circling carefully around me as they did so. My wife felt obliged to cheer things up a bit by asking if they would like a gin and tonic.

"Yes, of course," said the older instantly. And then he added, "What's a gin and tonic?"

After learning several times, both young men were in a more understanding mood. We all shook hands and they returned to Haifa to report that, thank God, the enemy had seen all that sophisticated equipment being installed in Savyon and had called off the attack.

Yaakov the Electrician, arriving the next morning, looked over the array of wires and tubes and dials and knobs and couldn't understand why I wanted to use this to talk to America. Didn't I know Israel had telephones? When I asked him if he had ever tried to make a long-distance call on that system as I had during the "Lover Boy" incident, his eyes lit up with understanding. You mean with this you could *hear* the person on the other end? What would they think of next!

The aluminum elements of the beam antenna were set out in our front yard, the ends hanging over into the street. We carefully assembled it according to the instruction book, a process that took only three days. Meanwhile, any visitors to the house had to use the back entrance. Somewhere, Yaakov located thirty feet of pipe—I thought I saw a legend on one length that read, "ARAMCO–British Arabian Oil Company," but I can't be certain. Eventually the antenna was to be raised on top of this pipe, if we could locate a flying carpet.

Finally everything was in readiness, except the motor. If you are not acquainted with the insanity of amateur radio, it would never occur to you that anyone would attempt to install a large motor at the *top* of thirty feet of pipe, remotely controlled so it will turn one hundred pounds of antenna from the ground. The purpose of turning the antenna is to point it at various parts of the world in the hope of hearing them better. It is also handy for shaking off pigeons.

The motor didn't work. Fortunately, I discovered this *before* placing it atop the thirty feet of pipe, which, for me, approached genius. Having done my part, I handed the motor to Yaakov the Electrician to fix.

Yaakov inspected it carefully and told me he knew just what to do with it. He had a friend at the hospital. I assured him the motor was not critically ill, just lazy, and hospitalization would not help much, unless his friend was a psychiatrist. Yaakov explained patiently that this acquaintance of his was *chief electrician* at the hospital. A motor would be child's play for him. I hesitated to mention that I had hoped it would be child's play for Yaakov, for fear of hurting his feelings. But Yaakov the Electrician, I was beginning to understand, was frightened of electricity. He didn't really believe in it.

After much telephoning, we were informed that the chief electrician would receive us that evening, at his home. Yaakov suggested I bring the motor, and some honey cake, since the chief electrician was a gourmet.

That night, after destroying the honey cake and a bottle of Mt. Carmel wine I had thoughtfully brought along, the chief electrician took the motor completely apart, explained to me exactly what had gone wrong, and in fifteen minutes had reassembled it. We congratulated him, finished another bottle of the wine, and plugged in the motor.

It whined pitifully and suffered a mild coronary.

The chief electrician of the hospital took it apart again, with the rueful smile of a surgeon who had sewn his tobacco pouch inside a patient's kidney, and in only two hours discovered the wire he had connected incorrectly. This, he explained, could happen to anyone, and he reassembled the motor. When he finished, we had some more wine, some more honey cake, congratulated him again, and then my wife noticed several parts of the motor sitting on the floor that should have been inside it.

With the rueful smile of a surgeon who had forgotten to sew his tobacco pouch inside a patient's kidney, the chief electrician disassembled the motor, installed the parts, reassembled the motor, and asked for some more wine. This time the motor worked and, as I recall—my memory of everything that occurred after we finished the third bottle is strangely incomplete—we carried him around the apartment on our shoulders and promised to come down to the hospital and applaud the next lobotomy.

Yaakov took personal credit for repairing the motor and, for all I know, for the lobotomy.

Now the moment of truth had arrived. The next day it was time to get a hundred and more pounds of antenna and motor raised above the roof of our house on thirty feet of shaky pipe from the British-Arabian Oil Company. Yaakov had come up with some guy wire that had once been used as a hawser for the *Queen Mary,* and insisted we needed a winch for the job. However, I knew better, having done this many times before; all we needed was a lot of manpower, to place one end of the pipe in a hole in the ground as several men *walked* the pipe up into place, with several others to hang on to the guy wires in case it wavered and threatened to topple onto the house.

There was, as usual, a problem: it was Passover, and none of the Israeli crew of the production was available for work. So we called the Italians away from their pastime of throwing spaghetti on the ceiling and asked them to help. Led by all five feet of Aldo Tonti, they came over en masse to help *il regista* (me, the director) get his curious arrangement of aluminum crosspieces high into the air. I had informed them that once it was raised, I would be enabled to speak directly with Rome, and from the approving looks they gave me I am convinced they thought it was some sort of huge crucifix to show my Savyon neighbors I had finally been converted.

Not daring to disillusion them, I masterminded the operation which saw ten Italians straining at the guy wires while ten others walked the pipe with its motorized Gentile symbol at the top into an upright position against the roof. Several Americans from the production had come over to assist in what, as it happened, turned out to be a house lowering.

Our unit manager had climbed to the roof on a ladder and decided to direct traffic. The Italians pulled the guy wires like assembled pup-peteers manipulating a mammoth aluminum-and-steel Pinocchio; other Italians thrust mightily against the pipe. Unfortunately, their enthusiasm got the better of their judgment. The pipe rose rapidly, to a storm of Italian *bravos,* the huge antenna swaying at the top, and kept right on going toward the house.

The unit manager stepped back on the tile roof, and that is the last we saw of him for fifteen minutes.

In Israel, a tile roof is made of tile. That's all. Tile. Underneath there is no supporting wooden structure. Who would see it, anyway? One piece of tile, resting on another piece of tile, resting on another piece of tile will cover a nice area, if you hold your breath. The pieces are fitted together carefully, possibly by angels lowered by cable from helicopters. When the unit manager took his step onto the roof, the whole angelic mess disintegrated into a mass of brick dust and pottery shards that resembled the archaeological digs I had seen at Masada and Caesarea. Now I understood why so many ancient civilizations in the Holy Land collapsed: their roofs were constructed by Jewish masons who were saving a little money on the job.

Meanwhile, the antenna and its supporting pipe wavered, hesitated, then, like a huge redwood under the axe, fell in slow motion to the ground under a stream of Italian curses, damaging, in the process, several of the aluminum elements and the morals of any neighbor within earshot who understood Italian.

The Italians refused to be frustrated. They attacked again, hauling, lifting, sweating; the antenna again rose to heaven and came to rest in a somewhat vertical position, its bottom end securely in the hole Yaakov had somewhat wonderingly dug for it, its middle leaning against a piece of jagged tile that remained on the roof.

There were cheers and shouts. I was congratulating the workers on the first unified Italian effort since the last time their government surrendered, when I realized one of the shouts was coming from *inside* the roof. The unit manager! I ran into the house, climbed to the attic, opened the trap door, and lo and behold, there he was, flat on his back amid the wreckage. He was helped out and, after several trips back into the shambles to locate his wallet, his wristwatch, and one of his shoes, persuaded to join in the victory celebration in the back yard, consisting of a case of Passover wine, a sickly sacred liquid made of one part alcohol, two parts grape, and three hundred parts sugar. In ancient times Jews were accused of using not wine for Passover but the blood of Gentiles; however, this myth was exploded when everybody realized you couldn't get diabetes from the blood of Gentiles.

After everyone left, congratulating each other because we were more than two weeks away from the rainy season, and surely the roof would be repaired in two weeks—I think my raincoat is still there, covering a hole in the roof shaped like a unit manager—I feverishly turned on the radio equipment to find out what God had wrought. The pipe was some ten degrees off the vertical; two of the elements were twisted; when I turned the control for the motor to the north, the antenna rotated to the west; and it was necessary to reach one hand into the high voltage section of the transmitter to turn a balky switch, within inches of four thousand volts; but to a real enthusiast, being electrocuted by four thousand volts is an admirable way to go, proving our hobby *does* have some practical value.

I have neglected to mention that the cables from Ernie had been accumulating daily, and by now made a neat pile the size of a small child, which we both undoubtedly were. Our last exchange of $2.40-per-word communication between Israel and California had set a target date of 6:30 A.M., Tel Aviv time, the next morning, which would be 8:30 P.M. in Brentwood, for us to have our first momentous meeting on the air, talking *free.*

By the time the antenna had been erected and the house cleaned of debris, it was already evening. In twelve short hours, I knew, Ernie would be crouched at his receiver, heroically ignoring the pain from writer's cramp in the hand that wrote the cables, waiting for the miracle of hearing my voice. Moses, one hand cupped to his ear on Mt. Sinai, could not have been more attentive. I had to be certain everything was in operating order so I would not disappoint Ernie the next morning. With bated breath I threw the switch to put the transmitter on the air and see if I could actually talk to someone. I did at once— my wife, who wanted to know where all the smoke was coming from.

It was 2:00 A.M. by the time I had repaired the damage and located the faulty switch that had caused the short circuit. Then, as I mentioned, it was necessary to hold my hand in close proximity to the high voltage to get the switch closed, but I was *on the air!*

The first gentleman I spoke to was named UA3KBD. We *aficionados,* of course, address each other by our radio call letters. UA3KBD's given name was Victor, but that didn't sound half as romantic. I myself had *two* names. I had been christened W6VLH by the Federal Communications Commission, but my Hebrew name was now 4X4UT. In the phonetic code, that became Four X-ray Four Uncle Tom, which has a lovely anachronistic sound to it.

Victor was in Moscow. I never asked him what he was doing up at two in the morning, but I thought, possibly, he was worrying about who to vote for in the next election. Anyway, it was only *1:00* A.M. in Moscow. But he could *hear* me, which was the most important thing, and I could hear *him!* We spent half an hour assuring each other of this miracle—Victor's English and the atmospherics made it a real challenge—and then I spoke to two gentlemen in Germany who had had too much *Hasenpfeffer* for dinner and couldn't sleep. Finally, I retired to snatch a few hours rest before my momentous appointment with Ernie.

I awoke, somewhat refreshed, at about 6:00 A.M. and dashed to the transmitter and threw all the switches. Everything was fine, except that I couldn't hear anybody. Instead of its usual delightful cacophony of atmospherics, automobile ignition noises, and the voices of my brother hams pleading with each other to get off the frequency, the receiver gave forth only a gentle, contented hiss. I tried another frequency band. Utter silence. It was as if a huge, godlike hand had been clamped over the mouth of every radio amateur in existence, perhaps to prepare for the return of the Messiah. I hastily looked out of the window, in the direction of the Mount of Olives, but there was no undue glow in the sky.

What there was seemed to be a loose wire.

I went outside and stared up at the antenna, erected the day before at such expense of time, wine, Italian perspiration, and unit manager's rear end; it was still leaning ten degrees off the vertical and the elements had been somewhat twisted by their hectic adventures, but those, I knew, were not the problem. What was the problem was that the lead-in wire that connected the transmitter and receiver to the antenna was hanging loose, thirty feet above the ground, and I immediately knew why. I had soldered it to the antenna with an Israeli soldering iron. An Israeli soldering iron is designed, basically, to save money. It gets just warm enough to melt the solder, then turns off the electricity automatically so God forbid you shouldn't run up a bill.

I was standing there, horrified at the thought of having to lower the entire affair to the ground to fix the wire, and more horrified at the thought of attempting to raise it again. One more unit manager through that roof and we might as well live in a tent, like the Arabs.

It was at that moment that Yaakov the Electrician arrived, took in the situation at a glance, and announced he could fix it.

Well, *he* couldn't exactly fix it, but he had a friend in the Petah Tikvah fire department. A hasty call to the fire department elicited the news that they could come, but their ladder wasn't working. Yaakov suggested they take their ladder to his friend at the hospital, which they promised to do. I wondered vaguely what they would do if there were a fire, since obviously they wouldn't have a ladder for several days unless they had a lot of honey cake, but Yaakov shrugged that off. You could reach the roof of most buildings in Petah Tikvah by standing on a chair, and the chairs at the Petah Tikvah fire department worked fine.

I stared again at that loose wire, thirty long feet above the soil of the Holy Land, and prayed for a miracle. Yaakov answered my prayer. In Israel, today, when they need a miracle, they no longer rely on long-haired Saviors running around in sandals; they call on the Army. Didn't I, Yaakov inquired, have some kind of drag with the Israel Defense Forces?

Five minutes later, I was explaining my situation to Sgan Aluf Gershon Rivlin, unsung hero of the War of Liberation. Rivlin was sympathetic, and announced he had a friend who had worked with him in the underground for twenty years. I explained patiently that we had a problem here for the *over*ground, and twenty years would be too long. Ernie Lehman's nervous system would never make it.

Rivlin explained just as patiently that his friend had survived numerous attempts by the occupying British forces to blow his head off, and was now chief of the fire department at Ramat Gan, where they had the tallest fire ladder this side of the Sahara. Gershon would phone him immediately and explain this was a matter of life and death— Ernie's.

In half an hour an olive-drab jeep came roaring through Savyon, towing behind it a trailer containing the Tallest Fire Ladder This Side of the Sahara. It screeched to a halt in front of the house in a cloud of dust, and three Jewish firemen leaped out, clutching axes and sniffing for smoke.

Where was the goddam fire? they inquired in Hebrew, according to Yaakov, who was translating into Yaakovese to my wife, who translated into English for me. I sent back, through the chain of command, the information that there was no fire. What there was was a loose wire.

Yaakov refused to translate their reply, except to remark that for a dead language Hebrew certainly had a lot of life in it. The firemen were in no mood to stay, feeling somewhat naked without a holocaust; I was prepared to light one for them if that were the only way open. But, gradually, I managed to get through to them the information that this was a vital radio installation that had the secret blessing of the Army, and they would do well not to question me further. They looked somewhat dubious, so I played my trump card. I had imported, in my luggage, one of the first Polaroid color cameras to be found east of Suez, and while they were arguing, I snapped their picture. Sixty seconds later I handed it to them, in full color, and I thought for a moment they were going to kneel at my feet. However, they probably recalled all the trouble they had got into with the Romans the last time they did that, so instead they agreed to do what they could to repair the antenna at the fixed fee for fighting fires—sixty Israeli pounds per hour. It seemed only logical that a country that had a set price for burning tanks would also have one for burning houses, so I was not too surprised. I agreed, and they seemed somewhat disappointed. I gathered that, usually, there was a bit of haggling over the charge, depending upon how close the flames were getting to the owner of the house, and they rather missed it.

However, the lure of more Polaroid pictures overcame their disappointment, and the jeep hauled the trailer into the backyard, knocking down two hedges and a rose bush so they could feel they were accomplishing something, and in no time the Tallest Ladder This Side of the Sahara had been cranked up into position, placing a spacious work platform right at the antenna.

But there was nothing to work with. The only soldering iron I had was the frugal Israeli model, and the firemen had never had any necessity to solder a burning building together, so they carried no iron of their own. Lucille and Yaakov were dispatched in the Peugot to buy a new and more spendthrift type. An hour went by. Two. They had not returned. I was running out of Polaroid film and realized I soon would be running out of firemen, when Yaakov and my wife finally appeared, 120 Israeli pounds' worth of fire department time later.

It seemed that, since this was Passover, all the stores were closed. They had finally located an Arab establishment in Jaffa that had surreptitiously opened the back door and allowed them to make a purchase, if they promised to keep their mouths shut.

But at last I had a soldering iron that *worked* (it had the Arab Good Housekeeping Seal), and in a short time the firemen, clambering up and down the ladder like Hebrew Tarzans, had straightened out the bent elements, forced the water pipe into a truly vertical position, and soldered the loose wire firmly to its connectors. They descended, and cranked down the ladder. I paid them their fee and offered a bonus, which they indignantly refused. They were civil employees, fire money was the property of the community—do you tip the President of the United States for doing his job? I admitted nobody had wanted to lately, we shook hands all around, I promised to send enlargements of the Polaroid pictures to be hung in the Ramat Gan firehouse, and they got back in their jeep and drove it through the shrubbery again, waving a fond goodby as their trailer ripped a small olive tree out by the roots.

By this time, my original schedule time with Ernest Lehman had long passed. I had cabled him suggesting he leave his receiver long enough to eat something and possibly say hello to his wife, who hadn't seen him recently except when she accidentally passed the Western Union office. He had cabled back that his confidence in my abilities had been severely shaken, but he would be listening again the next morning, also at the same ungodly 6:30 A.M., Tel Aviv time.

I dragged myself out of bed, turned on the receiver, and was rewarded with the sound of a hundred signals pounding through the loudspeaker with exciting volume. I called Ernie for twenty-five minutes, or until I was hoarse, whichever came first—I don't remember. I had quite a nice conversation with YU3LB in Lubljana, Yugoslavia, and UB5BX in Odessa, though. They didn't know Ernie.

In the next few days, I received three angry cables from Ernie. Every morning I got up at 6:00 A.M. and turned on the transmitter. I talked to Finland, Italy, England, Crete, and the U.S.S. *Saratoga.* I was beginning not to miss Ernie at all. Then I spoke to Boston, Chicago, Montgomery, Alabama, and my brother-in-law in Spring Valley, New York. I had ensnared him in the hobby several years ago in an effort to cut down telephone tolls between New York and California; by now he had $4,800 invested in equipment and had cut his telephone bill by $3.25 a month. We figured out if we both lived to be 420 years old, we would break even. If we were still talking to each other.

Several weeks went by. Ernie was calling me by radio every day. I was calling him. No contact. The cables were piling even higher. My wife was using them to light the barbecue. Now I was talking to stations in San Francisco, San Diego, and Santa Barbara. I had every one of them phone Ernie. He was never in. Naturally. He was down at the telegraph office, sending me cables.

According to my log book—by international regulation, we are required to keep a record of all this misery—it was April 17th at 15:39 Greenwich Mean Time that I finally heard, very weakly, a voice calling me on 14.246 kilohertz.

"4X4UT . . . 4X4UT," I heard Ernie's voice, "this is K6DXK. Do you read me? Over."

Excitedly, I grabbed the microphone.

"K6DXK!" I shouted, "this is 4X4UT! Ernie! Do you hear me?"

"Yes," Ernie shouted back, "I hear you! I hear you!"

Then we kind of lost interest.

CHAPTER XIV

I have mentioned one crisis that occurred during Passover, but not the most crucial to our existence. At the insistence of the Religious Party, no bread is sold in Israel during this sacred holiday, only the unleavened bread—matzos—the Children of Israel baked on their heads during the trek through the Wilderness. I had always looked on this story in the same light as that of Jonah and the whale, a harmless fiction, a striving for literary effect. However, having spent a week in the merciless sun of the Negev, I am now convinced you could not only bake matzos on your head, but also pizza, bagels, chocolate soufflé, and a complete casserole dinner. My apologies to Moses.

This strange stomach fetish the Hebrew patriarchs had, this dietary religiosity which made them proscribe the tastiest foods, was rather difficult to explain to the *goyim* in our cast, who believed we were making it all up to save money on the box lunches. However, I felt I could make it clear to them, including Senta Berger (Protestant), James Donald (Scotch Methodist), and Stathis Giallelis (Greek Orthodox), all of whom were playing Jews, by explaining, first, that all the kosher laws were based on logic. In Biblical times, with neither ice cubes nor electric refrigerators readily available, food spoiled easily. Meat spoiled, and milk spoiled. Therefore, they had to be eaten separately, never together.

Why not?

"Shut up," I could hear my mother explaining while salting the brisket to make it tough, and therefore legal. Meat and chicken had to be salted in the raw state to be kosher. Fish didn't have to be, because salted fish tastes good. The dietary laws are a kind of gastronomic masochism.

So there is a prohibition against pork. And certain species of fish. Not only shellfish, but sturgeon. The problem with sturgeon is that no matter what you do to it, it still tastes wonderful, so the patriarchs got rid of it before it could corrupt the young. There are also some game animals a good Jew is not allowed to eat, although there is no prohibition against them eating him. And, in case you should think you have the system beaten by subsisting only on beef, certain parts of the cow have also been declared off limits; you need a road map to locate which parts.

It is almost impossible to remember all the things you are not allowed to eat, and in addition, just about everything you *are* allowed to eat must have been killed by a rabbi. This doesn't make the chicken or meat any tastier, but it certainly helps the rabbi, who needs every penny he can get to buy sacramental wine to help him forget what he's eating.

For those who are willing to fight it out, constant vigilance is required. My wife and I were ensconced at the Dan Hotel one weekend while our Savyon mansion was being repainted, and I was nursing the flu. I decided to call room service for a solitary dinner as Lucille was to dine with friends. An hour or so after I called, our waiter stormed in, a short but imperious man with a gimlet eye. Obviously I wasn't sick at all, I was a *shtarker* who should be down in the dining room, not bothering him with this nonsense.

He shoved the menu into my faltering hand and waited impatiently. Not wishing to offend him, I ordered the first two dishes that struck my fancy—the cheese blintzes with sour cream and the pot roast with potato pancakes.

You would think I had struck him in the face. He informed me coldly that I was in Israel, the Dan Hotel was strictly kosher, and I could not order a meat dish and a milk dish at the same time.

"All right," I said, thinking quickly, "*I* will have the pot roast and my *wife* will have the cheese blintzes."

He grabbed the menu from my hand and drew himself up to his full height—five foot three.

"Not on *my* floor!" he announced, seeing through me immediately, and marched out of the door.

This patriotic hysteria over the subversive mixing of meat and milk is one thing; but when a sovereign state prohibits the staff of life itself—bagels—revolution may well result. The official edict against all forms of bread during Passover was a hardship to the Americans in our cast and crew, but it was a tragedy to the Italians. Without something to sop up the marinara sauce, half of their cooking was wasted. Their faces became gaunt, their bellies hollow, and the only thing that prevented them from begging for bread on street corners was their pride and the fact that everyone else in Tel Aviv on Passover was also starving for bread.

It was Lucille who discovered the bread-easy in Jaffa. Jaffa is the Arab-populated neighbor of Tel Aviv. On Friday nights, when the Religious Party closes down all the Tel Aviv theaters and nightclubs, you can find the Jewish younger set jamming the streets of Jaffa until the wee hours, for here it is legal to swing on *Shabbat*. Nightclub life begins about midnight, and goes on until the *muezzin* sounds the morning prayers from the tower of the Jaffa mosque—incidentally, by tape recording, for the *muezzin,* too, has been celebrating at the Omar Khayam Club and doesn't trust himself to climb all those stairs.

We all felt, of course, that this attitude of *laissez-faire* would certainly extend to the Jaffa bakers during Passover; but we were quickly disillusioned. The Religious Party, possibily at the urging of the matzo manufacturers, clamped down a net of Bread Agents who effectively closed every oven in Jaffa. It was as if Prohibition had suddenly worked. Men and women tramped the streets, bread deficiency showing in their trembling hands, hunting for some little Arab cooking up a home-brew batch of *pitta* (the delicious Arab bread) on a hidden fire. They didn't have much success.

Somehow my wife located the bread-easy. We had to drive there in the dead of night, through dark and twisted Arabic alleys haunted by the ghost of Pepe le Moko. Then we descended a series of steps, hewn out of the rock, to the doorway of a hut. A panel opened in the door, revealing a pair of eyes. If you uttered the correct password— something like "Shlomo sent me"—you were silently admitted to a small, warm room where other bread addicts were jammed about a counter, averting their eyes from each other in the depths of their degradation, as the loaves of hot, corrupting, delicious-smelling Arab bread were taken from the glowing ovens and placed before them. Mammy's little baby loves short'nin' *pitta.*

Our purchases were placed in plain brown wrappers and we ascended once more to the car, driving cautiously past the Israeli police, who sniffed suspiciously—and hungrily—as we went by.

We had a secret feast at our home on Simtat Cherem Hazeitim, the Americans and Italians wolfing loaf after loaf, happily mopping up butter and marinara sauce as we kept the blinds drawn and a lookout stationed in the front yard.

We felt rather smug about our success until Lucille and I were invited to attend the *seder* at the home of Menehama and Nehamia. It was a warm and happy family group, representing four generations, who clustered about that table and ate the bitter herbs and heard again the story of the first Passover: how the Lord passed over the homes of the captive Israelites on the way to slay the first-born of their oppressors, of the Exodus and the wandering in the desert.

When the children began to sing the incomprehensible Hebrew songs I could dimly remember being forced to learn in my recalcitrant childhood, it suddenly occurred to me that they understood every word, for they were singing in the same language they spoke every day, the language they used in school and to argue with their friends. These were not strange liturgical chants but the songs of other children of another day whose language had vanished from daily life for thousands of years, and has suddenly returned to these children of the twentieth century, who used it casually, as a mother tongue should be used. No one had to teach them a dead language. This language was alive, and it was learned as naturally as walking and running and kicking a ball and swinging on a swing. And one of the things that had kept it alive was evenings such as this, even though it had once meant risking your life to read to your family the story of the escape from bondage.

The escape had taken place, not in some mythical land with an impossible alphabet no one could ever learn, but only a few miles from here, across the desert where tanks had recently rumbled out of that same land of Egypt, only to be turned back in defeat by the descendants of those who had written the very songs the children were singing.

Menehama's food was wonderful, as wonderful as the children's voices, and when the matzos arrived, they tasted every bit as good as the illicit *pitta*.

And the wine was sweet, but not too sweet.

CHAPTER XV

LATRUN FORTRESS
(Special effects)
Silhouetted against the night sky.
OVER THIS we SUPERIMPOSE:

LATRUN
MAY 31, 1948

As the LEGEND DISSOLVES OUT,
the sky begins to lighten. It is dawn.
We realize we are looking at the
fortress through binoculars.

MICKEY—*FULL SHOT*
He is standing, in battle dress, beside
an acacia tree on a slight rise,
binoculars to his eyes. Slowly he lowers
the glasses and turns away, CAMERA
PANNING as he moves down the
slope, revealing:

FIELD—MED. SHOT
A command car and two radio jeeps
are drawn up beneath some trees. A
group of mortars has been set up.
Magda (Senta Berger) is seated beside
the Radio Operator, serving as inter-
preter. A row of Tel Aviv busses is
rolling into position, filled with the
immigrant infantry. Behind them we
see the first trucks of the convoy
which is waiting for the fortress to be
silenced so they can break through to

On May 18, 1965, *Cast a Giant Shadow* began principal photography at the fortress of Iraq Suidan in central Israel, reenacting the climactic engagement of the Battle of Latrun. We weren't ready, but the Israeli Army was. As always. So we shot.

Kirk Douglas, Yul Brynner, Senta Berger, and Stathis Giallelis were unlucky enough to be in those scenes. It was 115 degrees in the wheat fields in front of the fortress. Senta's make-up ran off in streaks. Kirk had picked out an Australian Army forage cap that he decided to wear throughout the picture. It kept the sun off his face, but since he was the only one who wore such a hat in our entire army, he looked as if he were fighting World War I with the Aussies at Ypres all by himself. I never could talk him out of it. Yul was the only

*the relief of Jerusalem. Asher Gonen
(Yul Brynner) is hurrying toward
Mickey.*

ASHER—*The busses were held up by
mechanical trouble, but they're
ready now.*

MICKEY—*So is the Legion. It'll be
light enough in half an hour to read
your obituary.*

*Gonen signals the units to move up
as Mickey crosses to the radio jeep.*

MICKEY—*Any word from Aleph
Battalion?*

MAGDA—*They have almost reached
Imwas, in the rear of the
Arab positions.*

*Ram (Stathis Giallelis) and a group
of other officers are pinning colored
ribbon to their shoulders.*

MICKEY—*What's this?*

ASHER—*Ram had an argument with
some soldiers on the road who didn't
believe he was old enough to be an
officer—so we sent to Tel Aviv for
some ribbon to identify all of us.*

MICKEY—*(indicating himself) How
about the commander?*

RAM—*We're out of ribbon.*

MICKEY—*The story of my life.*

*ROAD—MED. SHOT
A bus is moving along near the
mortar emplacement, filled with
immigrant soldiers. They are leaning
out of the open windows, their*

one who seemed comfortable.
It was probably his hair-do.

Iraq Suidan was our
second choice as a location;
we had made a bold attempt
to secure permission to use
the still-standing Latrun
fortress itself, across the
Jordanian border. I had
dispatched a cable to King
Hussein, although the telephone operator at the Avia
Hotel debated with me for an
hour before consenting to put
it on the wires. It had to be
sent to Cypress, since there
is no direct communication
between Israel and Jordan.
It was then transmitted to
Amman, thus presumably
cleansing it of deadly Hebrew
bacteria and hidden micro-
phones. In the cable, I told
the king that, although I did
not know him, I felt he was
a fair man. (Incidentally,
I still do. Even before the
Civil War, his poor little
country had been all but
swallowed up by his friends,
the Syrians and the Egyptians,
and the Palestinians who
keep attacking Israel from
his territory and provoking
her to keep striking back
at *Jordan.* It's the old story
of the fight manager whose

weapons clutched in their hands,
chanting something in
Hebrew.

MICKEY—*Where are they from?*

ASHER—*Belsen ... Auschwitz ...*
Buchenwald ... by way of Cypress.

MICKEY—*And the song?*

ASHER—*A prayer that was sung on*
the way to the gas chambers. Like
many of the prayers it begins,
"Next year in Jerusalem."

DISSOLVE TO:
A STALK OF WHEAT—CLOSE
SHOT
Brilliant and golden in the blistering
sunshine. CAMERA STARTS TO
ZOOM BACK to reveal a peaceful,
pastoral scene: acre upon acre of
ripening yellow wheat against a blue
Mediterranean sky; suddenly, directly
in front of CAMERA a group of
immigrant soldiers rises out of the
wheat and charges forward, falling
out of sight into the grain upon a
signal as the entire field becomes
alive with similar ranks of soldiers,
charging and dropping into the wheat
field for protection as CAMERA
CONTINUES BACK to reveal, on
the hill, the ominous outline of the
Latrun fortress. The first mortar
shell bursts against the fortress. The
artillery fires back. A shell explodes
in the wheat directly in front of
CAMERA. The battle is on.

AT RADIO JEEP—MED. CLOSE
Mickey and Gonen listen anxiously.

client is being cut to ribbons,
shoving his battered boy
back in the ring with the
encouraging words, "Hit him
again! He can't hoit us!")

The cable asked for
permission to film the battle
scene in its actual location;
since this was an outstanding
Arab victory, the king
certainly would not object.
Of course, if Hussein ever
received the cable, he knew
as well as I that this was an
obvious publicity ploy. Any
Arab king who helped a
Jewish director make a
movie about the war in
which Israel won its independence, and invited the
Israeli Army over to act it
out, had little chance of
surviving to read the notices
in *Variety*. (Had *I* read those
notices in advance, I wouldn't
have been too happy about
surviving myself.)

At any rate, the reply
from Jordan was a loud
Arabic silence: either the
cable had been received and
ignored, or the telephone
operator at the Avia, in her
official capacity as Sgan Aluf
of Intelligence, had ordered
it seized and destroyed.
Fortunately, the British, dur-

GIRL'S VOICE—(*on loudspeaker*)
Gafna Blue . . . this is Petach Red . . .

MAGDA—(*into microphone*) *We read you.*

GIRL'S VOICE—*Shalom, Magda. I am in the lead armored car. We are approaching the gate under heavy fire. Our flamethrowers are a surprise—*

FORTRESS GATE—MED. SHOT
The armored cars move through an opening blown in the barbed wire. One of them is hit and blazes furiously. The others crash through the gate and attack the inner gate of the fortress with flamethrowers.

THE WHEAT FIELD—MOVING CAMERA
Ram is in the lead. The line has grown ragged but is still advancing. CAMERA PANS DOWN to their feet in the wheat. A soldier's foot hits a trip-wire concealed in the grain. There is a tremendous explosion as CAMERA PANS swiftly down the line of soldiers. Mine after mine explodes under them.

FORTRESS COURTYARD— MED. SHOT
Four armored cars have broken into the interior which has been set ablaze by the flamethrowers. Silhouetted against the flames is an Arab antitank gun which is whirled into position by its crew and starts to fire at the armor.

ing their years of mandate over Palestine, had built a string of identical fortresses throughout the country. The one at Iraq Suidan looked exactly like Latrun. One of the major battles of the war had taken place here. Iraq Suidan had been attacked six times by Israeli forces, and when it finally succumbed after a fierce engagement, the Israelis allowed its surviving defenders the signal honor of marching out with their arms, led by their commander, a Captain Gamel Abdel Nasser. Knowing what they know now, I suppose, the Israeli Army would have attacked a seventh time.

Latrun was an entirely different matter. The full story had been told me by General Chaim Laskov in our earlier meeting, after which I had obtained the *other* full stories from General Vivyan Herzog and General Yigael Yadin. As Laskov told it to me, at first they did not know that it was not Abdul Humpty Dumpty behind those huge walls directing the fire of the artillery, but the crack British-trained Arab Legion under the command

INSIDE THE ARMORED CAR—
THE GIRL
Tensely now, into the microphone:

THE GIRL—*You will excuse please*
the expression, where the damn hell
is the Palmach, they're supposed to
be attacking the rear, do they want
us to be fried like chickens?

THE RADIO JEEP—FULL SHOT
Mickey grabs Magda by the shoulders.

MICKEY—*What about Aleph*
Battalion? They should be coming
up from the rear right now!

Magda speaks in Hebrew to the Radio
Operator, who replies in
Hebrew.

MAGDA—*(to Mickey) They have*
decided to withdraw.

MICKEY—*Withdraw! Who the hell—*
how many casualties?

MAGDA—*Two. Two dead.*

MICKEY—Two?

MAGDA—*Try to understand. Aleph*
Battalion is all from the same
neighborhood. Eighteen families lost
sons in the last attack. Now two
more. They are withdrawing.

GIRL'S VOICE—*(on loudspeaker)*
Magda, Magda, do you read me? This
is Rona . . . we are on fire . . .
we are . . .

The radio goes dead. Mickey turns
abruptly and heads for a command
car.

of the famed Glubb Pasha,
a seasoned British officer.
Israeli Intelligence, at least in
this instance, was terrible.

The Israeli Army had no
artillery, only mortars. The
raw recruits advancing into
the wheat fields surrounding
the fortress in the scorching
mid-summer heat were
mowed down in wholesale
lots by the accurate fire from
Latrun. Their first attacks
failed miserably. Then Mickey
was given command of the
Jerusalem front and arrived
on the scene. He attempted
to bring some precision and
coordination into the effort,
by planning several
simultaneous military moves,
as sketched in the scenes
from the screenplay included
here.

Laskov's brigade with its
home-brew armored cars
actually breached the outer
walls of the fortress and
reached the central area before being decimated and
driven back. Israeli girls participated in the attack as jeep
drivers and radio operators;
many of them never returned.
It was only later that the
Israeli command withdrew

MICKEY—(*to the others*) *Let's go.*
They don't need generals now.

THE WHEAT FIELD—FULL SHOT
Back through the wheat comes the
retreat, the men dazed, battered, most
of them carrying weapons of others
picked up on the battlefield, more
precious than life. CAMERA PANS
to reveal a group of command cars,
led by Mickey's, plowing through the
wheat, picking up the more seriously
wounded.

THROUGH JEEP WINDSHIELD—
(*Hand-held camera*)
SHOOTING OVER MICKEY, we
see Ram, carrying an assortment of
weapons, bleeding from a head
wound. The jeep halts. Ram leans
against it.

RAM—*I'm sorry.*

women soldiers from the actual fighting, after a series of Arab atrocities against them.

General Laskov, in detailing the battle over a lemon splash that quiet day in the vegetarian dining room of a a Tel Aviv beachfront hotel, had startled me considerably. The idea of a Jewish soldier had always seemed an anomaly to me, an uncomfortable role assumed only because there was no way out. But as he talked, I could hear echoes of Bar Kochba and Joshua and other Hebrew warriors of the past. These men, all of them, enjoyed what they were doing. Laskov

praised the bravery of his own men, of course, but a light came into his eye when he described the clever strategy of Glubb Pasha, the careful disposition of the Arab forces, the swift reaction of their British officers to every stratagem he countered with.

It doesn't matter whether you win or lose, it's how you play the game that counts.

What? What *game?* Didn't he know there is only one criterion to apply to anything in the universe, be it war, peace, catastrophe, or the side effects of The Pill—is it good or bad for the Jews?

Israel was dying, and Laskov was concerned with tactics! He was right, of course, and I was wrong. Passion is fine in the bedroom but a handicap on the battlefield. Had I Laskov's detachment and professionalism, I might have brought a little more reality to my recreation of his story.

In my futile search for authenticity, I had asked Laskov to suggest an officer who had taken part in the attack to serve as technical advisor on the sequence. One after another, he suggested four men who, he felt, would be excellent. And then, to his own astonishment, realized that all four had fallen in that battle, sixteen years earlier. So near are our yesterdays.

And then he told me the story that made me understand a little more about him and the little army he loved. Before the battle, troops were encamped across the highway leading toward Latrun. Laskov ordered them off to make room for the hoped-for busses with reinforcements. At that time, the commander of the Israeli armored forces was a very young man indeed, for all his importance, and most of the soldiers hadn't seen him before. So they ignored him, or, worse, laughed at him when he shouted his commands.

It was then that he unilaterally decided that if his army were going to have officers, there ought to be some way to tell who they were. Of course, it had taken much haggling and rulings by committees to determine that there should be officers in the first place. It had been the Jewish experience that making a man an officer, especially in the Russian or German armies, did not necessarily improve his disposition. Reluctantly, the army was allowed to have its officers, but the signs of rank were considered a little *goyish*. So, there was no appropriation in the military budget for bronze, gold, or silver bars, stars, maple leafs, or noodles. Laskov dug into his own pocket and scouts were sent through the enemy lines. They returned with a quantity of colored ribbon, which was cut into small pieces and pinned to the shoulder of the uniform of each officer. However, by the time they got to Laskov, they had run out of ribbon.

End of story. Beginning of legend.

General Herzog had also filled me in on the Latrun incident. In a jeep, Herzog, Rivlin, and I had visited the actual battlefield in front of Latrun which we later duplicated at Iraq Suidan. We were only a few yards from the Jordanian border, in the buffer zone maintained by the United Nations, when I climbed out of the jeep to take some photographs. Herzog gently suggested I get back in.

"You see," he said apologetically, "we were a very inexperienced army. We never bothered to keep maps of our mine fields. And you're standing in one."

I got back in the jeep.

It was then he told me of the days at Kibbutz Hulda when Mickey arrived bearing that letter from Ben Gurion appointing him to the Biblical rank of Aluf. Herzog and some of the others, before Mickey's arrival, had tried in vain to get a delay of a week before attacking the fortress, but Yigael Yadin, who was in command, had ordered an attack at all costs. Mickey blew up when he heard this, saying that any officer who issued such an order should be prepared to be responsible for the consequences.

Then had followed the subsequent attacks, and failures, against Latrun under Mickey's leadership.

After talking with Herzog, I had visited with Yadin. Over tea at the Dan Hotel, I asked him why he had ordered an attack when his men were still unprepared. He smiled at me. Didn't I know, he asked gently, that it was Ben Gurion who had insisted Latrun must be taken at once and at all costs?

Right, Wrong, and *Aha!*

Whatever the truth, it was simple enough to visualize the battle while Laskov and Herzog and Yadin were telling me about it; but recreating it in the heat at Iraq Suidan was another matter. In the first place, the Army had allowed us exactly four days to shoot it; the soldiers would be withdrawn at the end of that period whether we were finished or not. Their timetable was inflexible and their budget was fixed. Further, the Army would not order any of its men to don Jordanian uniforms and play the parts of the defenders of the fortress, but they did allow us to ask for volunteers; almost every Israeli soldier enthusiastically raised his hand, because it did not take a very practiced eye to see that you could spend a much more comfortable day as an Arab lying on the masonry of the fortress shooting blank cartridges at the Jews than fighting the heat, the wheat, and the flies down in the fields as a heroic patriot.

Each day it became hotter and hotter; by the end of two days we had shot a great deal of the battle, and now, on the third day, it was time to stage the arrival of the Tel Aviv busses, loaded with refugee soldiers from the rear. Things move slowly in a motion picture, more slowly than in a war, and some of the soldiers had to sit in those busses, in the heat, for hours, waiting for the cameras to roll.

When the cue was given for them to start, nothing happened. An assistant came running up to me to announce that our Army was on strike; it had gotten out of the busses and refused to get back in. You must understand that this group consisted not of actual members of the Israeli Army but of youths we had hired to augment the eight hundred soldiers supplied by the IDF. They would not be required to fire weapons, and thus could be civilians. Furthermore, I felt that their very unfamiliarity with military discipline and guns would add to the authenticity of the scene, since the refugees who fought and fell at Latrun had probably been as unmilitary as our extras.

Something had to be done immediately. In two days all our soldiers would be rotated back to civilian life—me along with them, unless we finished on time.

So I walked down to the wheat field and, through several interpreters, some official and some merely kibitzers, attempted to reason with the exhausted kids sprawled in the wheat. I tried the Rockne approach, exhorting them to win one for good old Ben Gurion, explaining the historical significance of the battle. I tried shaming them, reminding them that I was older and just as hot as they were; they saw the justice of that, and offered to get back into the busses if they were paid my salary.

I hastily changed the subject back to patriotism. Through the interpreters, I was startled to discover that these Jewish boys had never heard of the battle of Latrun, and had certainly never heard of Mickey Marcus; but what was most shattering was that most of them looked upon the War of Liberation as some distant historical event. Many of them had been born after Israel was already a nation.

My initial resentment suddenly changed. It dawned on me that this tiny Jewish state had existed long enough to raise an entire generation within its borders, when the world would have given odds and points it would never exist in the first place. The reason it was able to survive was this very recalcitrance, this ingrained stubbornness that refused to give an inch in a traffic jam, shoved its way to the front of every queue, argued even the most obvious points, and scorned ties, cosmetics, and authority. The Israelis disagreed among themselves at every possible opportunity. Now these Sabras were exercising their independence to refuse to make a picture about Independence itself.

One of my Israeli assistants watched wisely as I continued to exhort them without success, perspiration streaming down my face.

"You know," he said finally, as it became obvious I was not succeeding, "the only thing that's held this country together for so long has been the Arabs. Now, thank God, we have the Arabs and you!"

At the time I didn't think it was very funny. Now I'm beginning to admit it might have had a little humor in it. I turned away hopelessly; several precious shooting hours were now completely wasted.

The kids got up from the wheat and climbed back into the busses, shouting and laughing and starting to sing.

I turned around. They waved at me. They had made their point. They were getting back into the busses not because they had been ordered to, not because I had persuaded them, but because *they* had decided to.

Also, by that time it had gotten cooler.

We made one shot, but it was too late to finish the scene.

When I returned to the Avia Hotel late that night, the telephone operator stopped me cheerily.

"You're going to get a cable," she called loudly, "from your bosses." And she added reassuringly, "If I were you, I wouldn't be in a hurry I should open it. First have a drink, you'll feel better."

I took the Telex from my box and read it:

> SHAVELSON FROM MIRISCH RE FIRST DAYS WORK
> WE VERY DISAPPOINTED IN RESULTS. CERTAINLY
> HOPE THIS NO INDICATION OF FUTURE PROGRESS.
> WOULD APPRECIATE YOUR ASSURANCES.

I had a drink. I felt better.

Let me add a postscript to the battle of Latrun that did not come to light until recently when I delivered a lecture on my experiences in Israel before some group in Los Angeles who didn't realize *I* was the one who should have received a lecture. I was approached by a forthright, middle-aged man who introduced himself as a former officer who had been with the Israeli forces at Kibbutz Hulda during the assaults on Latrun.

War—at least, a war in which the Jews had weapons, too—was a new experience for all of them. After the first awful defeat, the little army was in danger of falling apart. It was made up of diverse nationalities and temperaments, a tentative alliance run through with fear and doubt. Morale was at its lowest ebb. Nothing the officers said or did seemed to be able to unify the confused little force which had faced the grim facts of mass slaughter and concentrated artillery fire for the first time, and knew it would have to face them again.

At this point, the officer was visited by a young Yemenite soldier. Now, the Yemenites are a group of Jews apart. The women have a dark, oriental beauty that would make them stand out on the streets of Stockholm or Paris. In Tel Aviv, they are absolute lighthouses. The men have a fiery temperament which is more Italian than Hebrew. The Yemenite soldier had a simple request: he wanted to go home.

The officer explained, patiently, that Kibbutz Hulda was the front line; going home meant desertion. The Yemenite shook his head. He would be back. All he needed was twenty-four hours.

The officer told him, carefully, that no passes were issued during a battle, no matter how extenuating the circumstances. The Yemenite said *his* circumstances were so extenuating, it wouldn't be a bad idea to stop the war until he returned.

And then he told his story. It seems he had been in love with the most beautiful Yemenite girl in all creation. His love was returned, but among the Yemenites, the bride must be *bought* from her father, and this girl's father knew the value of his merchandise, especially in Israel, where female beauty is in short supply and even your closest relative can't get it for you wholesale. The price for the girl was put sky high.

The poor Yemenite boy then worked for five years in a cement plant, covered with dust and sweat, denying himself everything, saving every penny, until finally he had raised the required sum. On the day he paid the money to the girl's father, he was notified of his call-up into the Army. He was to report within a week.

Another thing you must understand about the Yemenites: the reason the prices for their daughters have remained firm is because so have the daughters. Virginity is prized above life itself, and there is a religiously sanctioned examination before and after the honeymoon, after which the groom may demand his money back. Under this system, most weddings in America wouldn't earn the father of the bride a nickel.

After five long, arduous, but healthy years in a cement plant, the Yemenite boy was understandably frantic. An immediate marriage ceremony was arranged and performed.

Following the ceremony, the bride revealed to him she had just gone through her menstrual period. While this may sound like gratuitous information at a romantic moment, it was far from it. Under Yemenite law, the husband cannot have intercourse with his wife in this circumstance until *one week after*. In the race to the finish line, the Israeli Army won by twenty-four hours.

And now, after the first disaster at Latrun, it had dawned on the boy that he might get killed before cashing in on five years of hard labor. All he asked was one chance to find out if he had been overcharged, one chance for at least a down payment in return for 1,826 days of shoveling cement. Could any army in the world be so unfeeling as to deny him?

The war had been put in its proper perspective at last. The officer ordered the young man to write down every detail of his heart-rending story in a letter to the commanding officer, which he guaranteed to deliver. It arrived, ten pages of agony and frustration, written in the centuries-old Yemenite lettering similar to the beautiful Hebrew script in the scrolls from the Dead Sea.

The officer carried this missive into the tent where the recently arrived Aluf Mickey Marcus was holding his first tense strategy meetings with Yadin and Herzog and Rabin. At first they refused to listen, intent on their own earthshaking problems in which the survival of a race and a nation lay in the balance. When the officer insisted *this* problem was greater than theirs, Mickey finally condescended, somewhat irritably, to read the letter.

In half an hour the Yemenite soldier was on his way to Tel Aviv, the proud holder of the only one-day pass ever issued a private in the middle of battle.

Twenty-four hours later, as he had promised, he returned to Kibbutz Hulda. The road was lined on both sides by every available soldier in the Hulda Brigade of the infant Israeli Army. As the Yemenite stepped out of the jeep that had returned him, a mighty cheer went up. On every side he was interrogated—had he been successful? How was it? Was it worth five years in a cement plant?

To every question, the Yemenite gave an enthusiastic affirmative. The cheers increased.

My informant smiled at me as he told me about it. At last, the weary, dirty, undisciplined soldiers had something in common, so basic it proved all men are brothers. And all women aren't sisters. The beautiful Yemenite girl had done her bit. She had unified the little Army of Israel.

The officer didn't know if the boy came through the battles at Latrun alive. But the nation did.

Iraq Suidan. While the honeymoon was still on. The director, Kirk, Senta, and Mrs. Mickey Marcus, on the first day of shooting.

The Israeli Army. As worried as usual.

Three cameras, 110 degrees in the shade. No shade.

The mutineers listening to the director coax them to return to the busses. That is *not* Yul Brynner in the foreground.

Stathis Giallelis in the wheat field taking direction. The extra on the left holding a gun on the director is negotiating his salary.

Kibbutz Hulda. How you put romance on a silver screen. Aldo Tonti, the director, Kirk, and Senta in one of our almost rehabilitated jeeps.

Senta and Kirk inspecting a convoy while the Israeli Army inspects Senta.

CHAPTER XVI

I would never have survived the ordeal by heat prostration at Iraq Suidan, or the one that was to follow shortly in the Negev desert, if it hadn't been for Moishe. I don't know what size or shape guardian angels are supposed to assume when they appear on earth, but mine was short, tough, and chubby. He was assigned to me as my driver at the beginning of May, when Nehamia was needed for more important things, and immediately assumed responsibility for my health, good humor, weight, diet, temperature, transportation, perspiration, sleep, thirst, and ice cream.

Moishe was a young Sabra who would gladly have fought his weight in tigers if I had requested it. This was no mean feat, since Moishe at the time was some thirty pounds overweight, all of it solid muscle. When our car had a flat tire, he would haul one side of the rear end off the ground with one hand while searching for a place to put the jack. He had the proverbial heart of gold, but when some member of the cast or crew was giving me trouble, he would ask me quietly if I would like him taken care of. I was often tempted, but since I wasn't certain our cast insurance covered mayhem, I never put him to the test.

Moishe was desperately in love—with automobiles. He had a knowledge and respect for them that seemed entirely out of place in a country where cars were more a means of attack than transportation; and where an automobile stood a better chance of emerging alive from a ten-car smash-up than from a week in the repair shop. In a land where the average mechanic repaired a balky carburetor by the Yaakov method—hitting it over the head with a monkey wrench—Moishe could do wonders with a tiny screwdriver, a piece of wire, and infinite patience.

For some reason he had given me his allegiance. Like everything he did, it was with his whole heart. Standing in that pizza oven which was the Iraq Suidan wheat field, attempting to direct members of the Israeli Army and the Screen Actors Guild of America at the same time, listening to Aldo Tonti explain that the film in three of the cameras had buckled because of the heat, and ducking the premature explosion of dynamite charges simulating artillery fire, I would feel a firm hand on my shoulder. When I turned, there would be a glass of ice cold Jaffa orange juice, or a thermos filled with ice cream, with Moishe at the other end, urging me to drink or eat, and applying a cold cloth to my forehead. He made the average Jewish mother seem like Medea.

Only once did he fail. By dint of much scrounging, argument, and threats of bodily harm, he had secured for me one of the few cars in the production which had air conditioning. He would drive me, proud and shivering, to our locations, then open the door and support me when I staggered back from the impact of the inferno outside. By this time, Kirk Douglas's sons, Joel and Michael—Michael, of course, is now a movie star in his own right—and Kirk's beautiful wife Anne had arrived in Israel. Anne visited us on the location one day and drove back to Tel Aviv in Kirk's production car—also air-conditioned. We finished the shots in which Kirk was needed and Kirk looked around for some means of returning to his hotel without getting charcoal broiled. Our transportation manager, a large and extremely vociferous gentleman, told Moishe to take Kirk home in my air-cooled chariot.

"Listen," Moishe explained to him, "I can't do it—is The Boss's car." Only to Moishe, I assure you, was I "The Boss."

"Goddammit," said the transportation manager, who had a colorful though limited vocabulary, "do as I goddam say, goddammit!"

"No," said Moishe, "is The Boss's car."

"Goddammit! You wanna be goddam fired this goddam minute you goddam idiot?"

I was not a witness to this scene, but I was informed that Moishe glared at the transportation manager, who was a large, beefy, and muscular 250-pounder, with a look that implied that he was debating whether to disembowel him before or after strangulation. He told me later he was afraid any trouble he caused would reflect on the production, and therefore on me, so he decided to bow to unjust authority and take Kirk home. But he would do it so rapidly, he would be back in time to pick me up at the end of the day's shooting.

It is an hour-and-a-half drive from Iraq Suidan to Tel Aviv, under the best of conditions. A bewildered Kirk Douglas arrived at his hotel half an hour before his stomach. Moishe had made the run in something under forty-five minutes, a feat which would have given Mario Andretti heart failure. It didn't do Kirk much good, either. Then Moishe turned the car around and raced back.

But for some reason we had wound up shooting early, and I was already on the way home to Savyon, jammed into a packed, parboiled, un-air-conditioned station wagon with the grips and assorted ordinary mortals. Moishe never forgave himself. He should have murdered the transportation manager, or ditched Kirk behind a sand dune and turned back. It did no good for me to assure him that one small, perspiring journey with the hoi polloi was not going to injure my health permanently. What Moishe was worried about was that I would lose face because the star had more power than the director. And he had a feeling I was going to need all the power I could muster before long, not only with the actors but with a production office that was shot through with jealousies, with costs that were beginning to snowball beyond reason, and with the various liaisons—heterosexual, homosexual, and *tsimmis*-sexual—that always materialize in a group of high-strung individualists under continuous pressure far from the restraints of home.

He was right. We were on a collision course with at least eight of the Ten Commandments.

While we are being Biblical, this might be the moment to bring up Moishe's father. The only reason Moishe worked for us was because we had some of the best automobiles in the country. He could always have made a far superior living by working for Moishe *père,* who owns the largest pig ranch in Israel, and a highly successful chain of pork sausage stores. In the land of Moses.

My wife, who was rapidly extending her knowledge of the finer points of the Hebrew language, was having difficulty remembering one phrase until Moishe came along; the phrase was, *"Hag Sameach,"* meaning, "Happy Holiday." After his arrival, she had merely to look at Moishe to be reminded of ham hocks, which, as any fool knows, leads you directly to *"Hag Sameach,"* and her problem was solved.

If you think I am inventing any of this, including my wife, you are mistaken. The Israeli appetite for pork products is a demonstration of that same stubbornness and intransigence mentioned earlier. While Rome is full of cathedrals, and Mecca is full of mosques, there are very few synagogues in Tel Aviv. The few there are do not cause visiting Catholics to consider adding more gold leaf to the interior of St. Peter's to give it a little more class. Among many Israelis there is a slight feeling of bitterness toward Israel's Religious Party. I have mentioned the party before; it controls less than 17 percent of the vote in the country, but since Israel is fragmented by so many political factions, no government can survive without including it. In return, the Religious Party exacts a certain tribute: the continuance of laws requiring the observance of the kosher rules in all hotels and restaurants, since these are visited by Jewish tourists from America who expect the Holy Land to be Holy. When they return home, cleansed spiritually by a week or two of not drinking milkshakes with their hamburgers, these pilgrims like to reminisce about their religious rebirth over the morning bacon and eggs, far from the clutches of the waiters at the Dan Hotel.

But the average Israeli will go out of his way to show the government that while *it* may compromise with the Religious Party in order to exist, *he* certainly won't. In a land where eating pork is considered daringly anti-Establishment, Moishe's father was doing very well, especially with the young. It was as if smoking ham had become the equivalent of smoking pot. Moishe could have had a lucrative job with his father, far more lucrative than driving a car for the production, but, as he explained, "I can't stand the salami business." Fortunately for me.

Moishe was almost patheticallly eager to have me meet his parents and get a conducted tour of the pig ranch, but I never found the time to oblige him. However, returning from one location with my wife, he persuaded her to make the trip with him to Nahariya, a small town within shouting distance of the Golan Heights and the borders of Lebanon and Syria. There he proudly showed her his parents and their television set.

I mentioned before that Israel, at the time, had no television stations. It did, however, have an import duty of 200 percent on television sets. While a number of my erudite friends in America would happily pay $600 for a television receiver if the government would promise there would be no television stations for it to receive, I was startled to learn that there were twenty thousand expensive sets already operating in Israel, where there were no programs.

But the *Arabs* had television stations. There was one in Cairo and one in Beirut. There were stations in Lebanon and Syria and Jordan that could be received, with suitable receiving antennas; I was told they usually ran old Arab movies. Now, the Arab people may seem backward in some respects, but they are years ahead of us in their motion picture tastes. In a society where family life often begins in a harem, their entertainments make *Oh, Calcutta!* look like an overdressed *Sound of Music.* An officer who was in charge of Israeli intelligence during the first Sinai campaign told me there was an extra incentive for Israeli tanks to overrun Egyptian desert outposts, because they were always equipped with motion picture projectors and a collection of the wildest stag films this side of Andy Warhol. Apparently, the Egyptians built their forts in the desert first, then brought in the stag movies, and after that started looking around for water.

When television arrived in the Middle East and news spread that this kind of entertainment was electronically crossing the borders of the Holy Land, twenty thousand patriotic Israelis bought television sets to keep an eye on Arab propaganda. The antennas they erected to receive the distant signals grew larger and taller; in fact, my wife and I got the reputation of being the most avid pornographers in Savyon because of that tremendous monster of an antenna towering above our house. Nothing would convince our neighbors we didn't have a television set on the other end that was capable of receiving programs directly from Saudi Arabia, where it was rumored the instant replays of the activity among Ibn Saud's three hundred wives and concubines were outrating the reruns of *Father Knows Best.*

Naturally, there were a number of Arab programs that were not in this category. Immigrants to Israel were allowed to bring in their television sets duty-free; and since most of them spoke no Hebrew when they arrived, they found it comfortable to watch the programs from Lebanon—many of them in French—or Jordan, which were sometimes in English—and, of course, many of the immigrants understood Arabic.

Moishe was proud of his family's television set because they were *not* immigrants; thus they had paid the full price and therefore the set was an important status symbol. He showed it to my wife—there were no Arab movies on at the time, otherwise she might still be seated there, watching—and then took her to see the pig ranch.

It was a revelation. The Israelis have studied the Danes, who raise their pigs scientifically and hygienically. The pens were spotless; the pigs were immaculate, cheerful, friendly, and looked Jewish. My wife spotted one which, to her, resembled a certain member of our production staff, and she couldn't resist snapping several pictures with her camera. Returning to Tel Aviv, she regaled me with stories of the ranch and the photos she had taken until I was impatient to see for myself.

But, alas, she had given the film to an Orthodox developer. The roll came back with prints of all the photographs of Moishe's parents, one of Moishe, one of the television set—and none of the pigs. The developer had refused to print them.

Not on *my* floor.

The photographs the Orthodox developer refused to print. (*Lucille Shavelson*)

CHAPTER XVII

THE CLIFFS OF BEERSHEBA—
FULL SHOT
A group of BEDOUIN with their
camels are framed against the
morning sky. They look down as
CAMERA PANS to reveal an
Egyptian tank column roaring
directly past Camera.

EYN AVDAT CANYON—(dawn)
A line of Israeli jeeps, Mickey and
Safir (James Donald) in the lead
jeep, roars down the desolate desert
canyon and turns into a protected
area behind some boulders. Soldiers
leap off and start taking their sleeping
bags off the hoods to bed down
for the day.

RADIO JEEP—MED. CLOSE
It has pulled alongside the lead
jeep.

SAFIR—*(to Mickey) They've picked*
up the radios in the Egyptian tanks.
They're heading north to knock out
the Har Safit Kibbutz.

MICKEY—*How long will it take us*
to reach them?

SAFIR—*Too long. It will be broad*
daylight. The orders were for night
assaults only.

Beersheba stands on the edge
of the vast and terrible Negev
desert, where it has stood since
time immemorial. Sheer cliffs
drop off to the desert itself,
which extends to a horizon beyond which lie Suez and Port
Said and Cairo. It is the gate-
way to the Sinai peninsula,
battleground of three separate
wars since 1947. Out of this
desert Egyptian tank columns
came roaring during the War
of Liberation, to be met by
suicidal squads of Israeli jeeps,
those same jeep units which
Mickey Marcus helped train
and equip for just such an
eventuality. These jeeps had
antiaircraft guns mounted on
them on special pivots so they
could fire straight forward;
they were designed to strike at
night, moving across the sand
with a speed and agility that
kept the Egyptians off balance.
The Israeli Army had no
tanks to speak of; they relied
on the jeeps, and on courage

MICKEY—*You've got no choice. Hit those tanks with everything.*

SAFIR—*Risk this entire force?*

MICKEY—*They don't know this is the whole Armored Corps. Go for broke. This has to be the biggest bluff since the invention of falsies.*

SAFIR—*But you're just an adviser! You can't countermand an order of—*

MICKEY—(*interrupting*) *David, there's a mountain over that way called Masada. The last stronghold of the Hebrew army in the revolt against the Romans. They had an adviser, too. After they held out under siege for three whole years, he advised them they didn't have a chance . . . so nine hundred and sixty of them committed suicide on top of that mountain and some of you people are* proud *of it. What do you want? Another eloquent philosopher to give you a nice speech and then we'll all cut our throats? David—attack. There have been enough Masadas for your people.*

HAR SAFIT KIBBUTZ—FULL SHOT
A group of BOYS and GIRLS are leading some goats through the barbed wire when an ALARM SOUNDS. CAMERA ZOOMS to the desert far below where a line of Egyptian tanks emerges from the shimmering mirage.

THE ISRAELI JEEPS—FULL SHOT
They separate into two columns,

and ingenuity, and a sense of humor. Some of the jeeps carried loudspeakers, over which they broadcast recordings of artillery barrages in the darkness. On one occasion, I am told, the Israelis even used thunder sheets, an old theatrical device that hasn't been used to simulate gunfire since boys stopped playing girls onstage. (Or have they?)

The Israeli Armored Corps of today, which maintains a training base near Beersheba for somewhat obvious reasons, had promised us enough tanks to recreate this battle. The jeeps, of World War II vintage, we had purchased and optimistically overhauled ourselves. They formed the spearhead of our attack, which rolled out of our armored-car-and-explosives factory on the outskirts of Tel Aviv and headed south. They were followed by Kirk Douglas and his air conditioning, James Donald, the fine British—and Protestant—actor, who found it a little disconcerting to be playing a Jewish officer, and our army of assistants, makeup men, wardrobe women, script girl, camera crew, special effects experts, grips, la-

*moving off at right angles to each
other in flanking maneuvers against
the tanks.*

*THE TANKS—FULL SHOT
As they wheel into position and
start to fire at the kibbutz. The two
jeep columns come in from opposite
directions, opening fire with machine
guns at the Egyptian infantry which
has been using the armor as a shield.
Simultaneously, a tiny Piper Cub
appears, alone and lonely in the desert
sky, bearing the Israeli colors.
It dives for the tanks.*

borers, carpenters, supporting actors and actresses, and accountants with the expense money who were supporting all of us.

Since I hadn't had a full night's sleep since the start of shooting, my wife suggested we put our recently arrived Volkswagen camper to double duty and make up a bed in it so I could rest royally en route to Beersheba, as King Solomon might have done if he could have been persuaded to ride in a German car. The Volkswagen had barely made it across the Israeli border; our friendly customs officials had held it up at the port of Haifa. They confiscated it as evidence that I was planning to open a grocery store.

That takes a bit of explaining. Knowing the rigors of location shooting and being acquainted with the quality of location food throughout the world—in most countries, it is a cardboard box containing the mortal remains of a weary, though muscular, chicken—we had cleverly bought the camper months before in Europe. It had been delivered in Rome unbelievably resplendent in yellow curtains, yellow and white checked upholstery, table, stove, icebox, closets, and the ability to convert itself into a double bed when frightened.

This portable Hilton had been waiting in Italy for a ship to carry it to Israel. While it waited, friends of ours decided to stock it with emergency supplies. To Italians, rations for survival in a strange and hostile Hebrew land consisted of a hundred pounds of spaghetti, a complete wine cellar, loaf upon loaf of Italian bread, a mountain of salami, cans of tomatoes, anchovies, eggplant, peppers, octopus, several huge cheeses including parmesan, peccorino, Romano, and gorgonzola, and a box of toothpicks. There were also spices, herbs, an espresso maker, coffee beans, and five gallons of olive oil.

Any customs inspector checking out this supply of edibles, which filled the trucklike Volkswagen to the bursting point, could only conclude that the intended recipients were expecting to be besieged, possibly for the duration of the next Thirty Year War, or else were planning on turning a nice profit in a land where the height of the culinary art is a waterproof noodle.

In Israel at that time, a chef was usually a cousin of the owner who was marking time in the kitchen until an opening showed up in his real vocation, brain surgery. Waiters were nephews who spent more time figuring out how they were going to take over the business than in keeping their thumbs out of the soup. No one, in short, had any interest in the service trades except as a stepping-stone to greater things, after which they could afford to hire their own servants, who would be marking time until *they* could practice brain surgery.

If food supported life, that was all that was required of it, except that it should taste like chicken fat. Besides, only the tourists ate at restaurants or hotels; the Israelis ate at home, where their mothers cooked, and if the food tasted like chicken fat, they were lucky.

However, there was a growing underground movement which maintained if you paid attention while you were cooking, food could be made to taste like food. El Al pilots, returning from Rome, reported rumors that chicken could be cooked in wine, and that wine could be made from grapes, not just from prune pits, as in Slivovitz. I suppose the great danger the customs officials could foresee was that the illicit sale of our flavorsome Italian groceries, which required so long to prepare, would cut down on the time available for Israeli mothers to study brain surgery.

At any rate, our blanket customs clearance had developed another hole, and it was not until after strenuous efforts by Asher Hirschberg and others that the suspicious Volkswagen was allowed entry, stuffed with delicacies obviously calculated to undermine spartan Israeli stomachs, toughened by centuries of *kreplach* soup. The food in Israel has improved immeasurably since then, but at that time our bus contained manna from heaven, a dish no one has yet explained to me, even in the country where it originated.

The most welcome sight after we started shooting was the awkward, ugly-duckling green Volkswagen. With Lucille first at the wheel and then at the stove, it bumped and rattled its way to our locations from Iraq Suidan to Beersheba, from the Negev to The Galilee, rolling up a total of five thousand miles of lunch in a land in which, at some points, you could throw a *fellafel* from border to border. (A *fellafel* is, in part, an Arab matzo ball, made of ground chick peas. You hope.)

Simultaneously, Moishe and I discovered an ice cream mine, the only place in the country where the ice cream is not made from yoghurt. It is in the partly Arab town of Ramle, and for all I know the ice cream store is run by Al Fatah; but no matter. Moishe and I always stopped by when we were within twenty-five miles and filled the wide-mouthed gallon thermos jug we placed in the icebox of the Volkswagen. The first time we visited this shrine of chilled nectar, I asked for an ice cream soda, and got a blank stare. Then, through Moishe, I ordered a bottle of seltzer, some syrup, some ice cream, and some milk, and manufactured my own soda on the spot. It was passed around among the owners and workers and patrons and the police and a few visiting Bedouin and I became an instant hero. I believe Moishe told them I was from America, that my name was Thomas Edison, and that this was not my first invention, although it was obviously my most important. Thereafter I acquired a certain celebrity in the area and considered inventing other things for the natives, like Dr. Pepper or root beer floats, but I worried that then they might expect me to walk on water, and I wasn't sure I could manage that, even with Moishe's help.

With the ice cream and other delicacies deposited in various sections of the Volkswagen, it didn't take long before that bus became more important than the camera on our locations. The actors, hearing, or more probably scenting, its arrival, would become affable, talented, and hard-working, finishing the morning's scene with a flourish and then waiting expectantly for the invitation to lunch.

I quote from one of Lucille's letters to a friend: "We usually serve at least eight people. Yesterday we had pickled tongue, roast beef, hot rye bread, a marvelous mixed green salad with a dressing prepared by Eliot Elisofon of *Life* Magazine, fresh fruit salad, ice cream from Ramle, cheesecake, and coffee. Our guest list included Kirk Douglas (the official bread-slicer); Yul Brynner (who sliced the vegetables); Senta Berger, who broke the thermos containing the ice cream (she was penalized two Sacher Tortes); Stathis Giallelis; James Donald; Rina Ganor; and Aldo Tonti." Elisofon, a gourmet so fastidious it is rumored he drinks his wine only while lying on his side, became the *Gauleiter* of these meals. In the midst of the Negev, he insisted on the lettuce being chilled to the proper temperature in the icebox before being *crumbled* into the salad. At one point, he wangled an assignment in Holland from *Life* partly so he could fly to Amsterdam over the weekend and bring back a wooden keg of Dutch herring for our afternoon feasts. Any man who will fly four thousand miles for a herring must be considered a serious eater.

All this attention to gustatory delight had its inevitable consequence. Our Italian crew called a complete shutdown on a hot, dusty location one afternoon until we all sampled the food supplied by our so-called "caterer," which *they* had to eat every day. One taste brought us back to reality. Under the eyes of the nauseated Italians, we ate the entire lunch. It was an experience calculated to bruise the palate of a goat. I believe the main course was camelburger, well done.

I had a heart-to-heart talk with the "caterer," and we came to a parting of the stomachs. After that, although we secured better food for the crew, I never felt quite comfortable eating chilled Lettuce Elisofon in the bus.

But I forced myself.

The night we left for our location in Beersheba, the bus had been carefully stocked with all manner of edibles to support life in the for-didding desert. The last item to be put aboard was the director. I found myself stretched comfortably in the double bed in the rear, a pillow under my head, bread and a salami under the bed, ice cream in the refrigerator, and my wife at the wheel. All I had to do was sleep blissfully while she drove. However, the highway to Beersheba was not conducive to bliss; I spent most of the journey grabbing for door handles and bouncing into the air with the bread and the salami, while frantic auto horns from the other cars in our group blared an obbligato. Mirisch's Marauders bounced toward the dark, mysterious desert en masse and arrived just before dawn in the ancient, brooding, Biblical city of Abraham and Isaac, where the two sons of Samuel escaped judgment and Elijah sought refuge from the vengeance of Jezebel, and where Howard Johnson has come to pray for forgiveness.

Well, if not Howard, one of his admirers. On the outskirts of Beersheba is the Desert Inn Motel, complete with palm trees, swimming pool, nightclub, and no room service. It even has a resident camel—

the crowning insult—which guests of the motel are allowed to ride, if the camel is willing, which is not very often. This camel is indignant about the whole thing, as well he might be, and has green teeth, halitosis, and a tendency to spit at anyone who gets too close. As for the nightclub, it is called The Bedouin Tent. Cover charge is $3.00. But they serve a good Bloody Mary, if you have a spark of sacrilegion in you.

On the edge of the desert is Sde Bokar, the *kibbutz* in which Ben Gurion lives. It is filled with strange structures, with which he is experimenting to find the type best suited to desert living. There are also a variety of plants and trees being tested for growth in this unlikely environment. The midday temperature at that time of year—late spring —was well above 110 degrees. On the floor of the desert it rose above 120.

I never met Ben Gurion—he was always out planting something. It is this never-ending crop experimentation that has a great deal to do with the growth of Israel's economy. When the British gave up their mandate, it was their stated opinion that Palestine could never support an agricultural community. The Arabs had tried for thousands of years, and the desert still resisted their efforts. The Israelis, however, once the land was theirs, sent their best students abroad to acquire the most modern scientific knowledge available on the subject. Tractors did the work that thousands of camels—indignation, green teeth, and all—had never been able to accomplish. The first major crops were citrus fruits. Later it was discovered that cotton could be grown more economically, and cotton fields replaced many of the orange groves. The Jordan was dammed, and the irrigation canals extended further and further into the desert. It was learned that an even more economical use of the available land space and water could be made with a crop of cactus, and the cotton fields diminished. I saw thousands of cactus plants, imported from the Philippines, covering large portions of the desert. I couldn't imagine what anyone could do with all that cactus except shoot a Hebrew *Butch Cassidy* until I was assured that this was the source of Abaca fiber, or Manila hemp, from which, among other things, the strongest and most durable rope in the world is made.

Some weeks earlier, the Israeli Air Force had supplied me with a Piper Cub and a young pilot, to hunt a suitable desert location for the battle scenes. We flew south from Tel Aviv, the pilot holding a map on his knees to be certain we didn't inadvertently wander over the border, a rather risky business at that time, or any time in the foreseeable future. At one point, the State of Israel is only ten miles in width, and I was told the jets of the Israeli Air Force had to fly out to sea in order to execute a left turn without exceeding their country's territorial limits.

I encouraged the pilot to be, if anything, overcautious. I wasn't too happy about flying in a Piper Cub in the first place, never having flown before in a plane that didn't show movies. But I needn't have worried about the pilot reading his maps wrong; the most accurate map lay immediately below us, full scale. On the right it was green; that was Israel. To the left, it was brown; that was Jordan.

The pilot kept telling me that, any minute now, we would be over the desert. But, to his astonishment, it never appeared. He hadn't been south in a year, and in that time the waters of the Jordan had been piped even further. The desert was blooming—with cactus, but still, blooming, every inch of available soil under cultivation. It was only when we reached Beersheba and the edge of the desolate Negev that we found the beginning of the endless Biblical wilderness of sand and heat that has remained untouched through the centuries.

But there is a white-haired old man living at Sde Bokar who is figuring out how to make it produce strawberries. Considering what he has already accomplished, this should be only a minor problem. If I were the Negev, I'd start looking around for some sour cream.

Ben Gurion had not yet solved the problem by the time we were ready to shoot; the desert was still barren and empty and forbidding. We went down into it with five cameras and a crew of over a hundred men, twelve tanks manned by Israeli soldiers but painted with Arabic markings, and thirty jeeps of World War II vintage on which machine guns had been mounted. There were also trucks painted with the insignia of the Egyptian army, and several hundred soldiers in Egyptian uniforms.

The official temperature was 126 degrees. The metal of the tanks got so hot a man could blister his hand if he touched one. We imported over a thousand gallons of soft drinks; they were consumed in a few hours. Moishe had turned into Gunga Din and was forcing liquid down my throat at regular intervals. The air was so dry there was not one drop of perspiration in that entire army; amazingly, the thousand gallons of liquid were consumed by that relatively small group of men and no one urinated the entire day. The liquid moved directly through the pores in a frantic and unsuccessful effort to keep our brains from being parboiled.

On the first shot of the day, we mounted a Panavision camera close to the muzzle of one of the tank cannon, to get a spectacular closeup when it fired. We got the closeup, and shattered a $40,000 lens into a pile of ground glass. The Mirisches thought it was pretty spectacular when they got the bill.

Within one hour, half the jeeps had vapor lock. We towed them with the other half until *they* got vapor lock. By the end of shooting, we had two jeeps that would still operate. In one, we put the camera; in the other, we put Kirk Douglas and told him to look like an army. Kirk could almost do it; there is something in his combative nature that gives him an authenticity in violent situations beyond mere histrionics. The hungry, relentless battler of *Champion* is still fighting, several million dollars later, slugging his way toward some invisible championship that continues, apparently, to elude him. In the broiling sun we rehearsed his speech about Masada, and when he finally delivered it, he brought two stones together, one in each hand, a bit of business we had worked out to give the line emphasis. The stones shattered in the intensity of his gesture.

The machine guns on our jeeps were supposedly armed with blank cartridges. During the first run-through of the action, three soldiers were seriously wounded. The dummy ammunition—and I am not certain whether it was Israeli or Italian—was sealed with small wooden plugs which were to disintegrate on firing. Some of them didn't. Realism on the screen has its limitations; from then on, the guns were never pointed at anyone. Not even the director.

The heat intensified. Several of the crew and even some of the desert-hardened soldiers passed out from heat prostration. The others crawled under the tanks and trucks between shots to get out of the direct rays of the sun. There was no other shelter—not a tree, not a stone, not a blade of grass. It is rumored that this is where Moses led the Children of Israel out of the Wilderness and told them that, at last, after forty years, they were in sight of the Promised Land and could end their journey. The standing joke among the Israelis is that if he'd only kept going, they'd all be on the French Riviera.

In spite of the heat, when it came time for the tanks to swing into action, they performed with unified fury. Under the command of a Tank Corps captain at my elbow who controlled them by radio, they swept up out of the desert in unison exactly in camera range, fired salvos from their menacing cannon toward the *kibbutz,* and battled the wheezing jeeps as they swept around the sand dunes with Kirk Douglas and James Donald in the lead. By this time, incidentally, the actors were wheezing louder than their transportation. The Piper Cub joined the battle from overhead, dropping seltzer bottles on cue—a military maneuver that will require a great deal of explanation in a moment—and the tanks roared up precisely to the mark that had been given them, directly in front of the cameras, thus completing the shot.

As I turned to the captain to congratulate him, I noticed the tanks had failed to stop. They continued to roll forward, heading right for us and our cameras.

"Stop those tanks!" I shouted at him.

The captain shrugged. "I can't," he told me and saluted.

"Try 'Halt,' " I suggested frantically. "It works in lots of war pictures! If that fails, try 'Whoa!' "

The tanks were almost upon us.

"I'm very sorry," he said, indicating the field telephone in his hand. "I just received orders from my commander. We are leaving." He saluted again. "Goodby."

"Leaving!" I shouted. "How can you leave in the middle of a scene?"

"Watch us."

"Where are you going?"

"That," he answered, "is a military secret."

I stared at him, horrified. By this time we were surrounded by lumbering, clanking monsters.

"We only got the first take!" I cried. "We have a whole battle to finish!"

"What a coincidence," said the captain, shaking my hand. "Shalom," he added. "Peace." And he leaped onto one of the departing tanks and waved at me.

I never saw him again. Or the tanks. They swept up out of the desert and headed for home.

Later we learned that Syrian commandos had launched a sudden raid across the Galilee border while our scene was in progress. Our soldier-actors, full of soda pop and seltzer, were flown north immediately. They were the best tank crews in the Army; on arrival, they climbed into tanks somewhat more modern than those we had been using and crossed into Syria in reprisal.

I hoped that, at least, it was cooler in the north.

Kirk Douglas and James Donald and the crew and the young Israeli actors and actresses who had been playing soldier returned to the Desert Inn at Beersheba that evening. In spite of chapped skin and sunburned faces and nervous exhaustion, none of us felt like complaining.

We didn't feel like going down to The Bedoin Tent for a Bloody Mary, either.

A sidelight to this desert adventure: recently I received a note from my erstwhile radio operator friend in Brentwood, Ernest Lehman. I have, perhaps, overstated our loss of interest after we had managed to communicate with each other. We did maintain a tenuous sort of radio contact between Tel Aviv and California, made necessary by the fact that in Israel on *Shabbat* the overseas telephone does not operate. While this made it only slightly less difficult to use than on the days when it *did* operate, the situation was further confused by the fact that we were permited to shoot our picture on this same Sabbath. Where it says in the Bible you are allowed to make movies in Israel on the day of rest but you can't use the telephone, I don't know. But it's a tradition.

Therefore, if any problems arose during shooting on a Saturday, there was no way open to me to share my grief with the Mirisch Corporation. Except through Ernie. However, there was another complication. At that time, international regulations forbade amateur radio operators in Israel from communicating with anyone in the United States who was not also a licensed operator. This, unfortunately, eliminated Harold Mirisch. Furthermore, no business affairs may be discussed on the amateur frequencies. This eliminated everything else.

Unless the operator at the other end were Ernest Lehman. The author of *The Sweet Smell of Success* was not going to admit failure in his chosen avocation. When we made contact by radio, he would just happen to telephone Harold Mirisch and forget to hang up the phone. Then I would cry a little, and Harold would hear me.

Which brings us back to the note I received from Ernie. It read:

In cleaning out my radio position desk drawer I came across this fragment of paper. Note hastily scribbled notes. Some day it might be worth more than the Dead Sea Scrolls.

On this historic fragment, which I reproduce here for posterity, you will notice the optimistic tone of my comments to Ernie after we had blown the entire battle sequence and a Panavision lens. This was because I knew Harold Mirisch was listening and was running short of Alka-Seltzer. Not to mention money. Ernie had scribbled: "120 degrees in desert . . . yesterday army left in middle of shot. Doesn't believe too serious."

I can just see Pharaoh reading the daily report from his Minister of Information: "Angel of the Lord just knocked off first-born in every home. Don't believe too serious."

In the upper right corner you will see a scrawled sentence in Ernie's handwriting that is almost an afterthought. It reads, "Near mutiny in the crew."

I had forgotten all about that until I read Ernie's notes. It had happened so often, it hardly seemed worth mentioning.

Mel read film in desert
Film supposed to go each
midday. 'Hve seen 4 days
of rushes — looks okay

120° in desert — yesterday
army left in
middle of shot.
Doesn't believe
too serious

[Will be writing Marvin
a letter soon.
Been working in the
crew]

May have to defer
up + rout out on it.

The Ernest Lehman Scrolls.

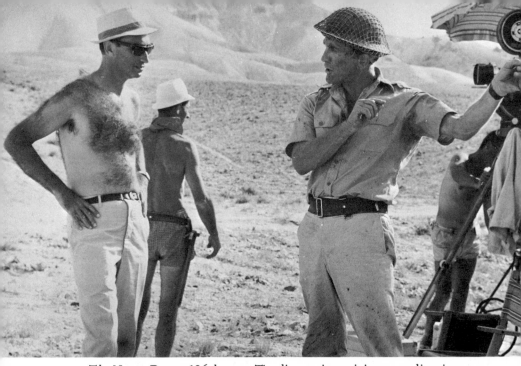

The Negev Desert. 126 degrees. The director is receiving some direction.

Kirk and James Donald receiving the director's suggestions with unbounded enthusiasm. The young lady in the rear used to be a director herself.

Kibbutz in the Negev being attacked by our special effects department.

CHAPTER XVIII

My daughter has been notably missing from this account, mainly because she was comfortably occupying herself in America with whatever it is pretty nineteen-year-old girls occupy themselves with these days without getting into the headlines. She, too, finally arrived in the Holy Land shortly after our Battle of Beersheba, but unlike my peripatetic son, she knew exactly what she wanted to do.

Mostly she wanted to stay as far away from the production as possible. And to work on a *kibbutz*. Since she had never evinced any overwhelming desire to work at anything, including the dishes, since she was six, this came as somewhat of a revelation. I could not ascribe it to her love of her people, because *her* people led peace movements and played rock guitars. Her religious training was almost nil, and her knowledge of Jewish history was gleaned from a recording by the New Christy Minstrels of "Shadrach, Mesach, and Abednego."

But the *kibbutzim* are "in" with the new generation. Boys and girls of every faith and many nationalities come to Israel to slave on them, to experience their way of life and system of communal values. Here, where everyone works for the common good, where money has little meaning, where there are no class distinctions, is the kind of Utopian society they wish they had been born into. The fact that in Utopia they speak Hebrew, or English with what sounds like a Brooklyn accent, is irrelevant. The fact that many Utopians leave Utopia after a while because they can't stand it is also understandable. There are people who would leave heaven because they didn't like the angel next door.

In the days of the British Mandate, the *kibbutzim* were the training ground for the Haganah, the underground army. The soldiers spent a certain number of hours drilling, and even more hours planting. The farm trucks became the hidden transport of an invisible military. The

Red House in Tel Aviv, home of the Union of Agricultural Workers, had in its basement the secret telegraph and radio network which controlled the *kibbutz* forces.

I remember on one occasion being taken with my wife to visit the most famous chicken coop in Tel Aviv. It is on a hill above the city, in what is now a residential area. A tough old man led us into the coop and showed us the stove used for heatiing the incubators. It was hinged at the bottom, and when pushed back revealed a round hole and an iron ladder leading into the depths below. He switched on some lights and nimbly led us down it. Thirty feet below the surface, we were in a tremendous cave used in Biblical times by shepherds to shield their flocks from the elements. It had been completely surfaced with cement and covered with racks from floor to ceiling, for the storage of weapons during the Occupation. The old man told us he had been a building contractor; every night he and a friend had personally driven his cement trucks to the site, so as not to implicate any of his workers. The two men took seven years to complete the cave—in military parlance, a "slick"—and it was thirteen years more before the weapons stored here were used in combat. In that time, it was noticed that some of the guns were showing signs of rust, so the old man and his friend, working alone and in secret, installed a complete air-circulating system to reduce the humidity. All this under the very eyes of the British. It was never discovered, and today is the site of the new Israeli War Museum.

Similar "slicks," and even factories, were built underground in the orange groves of various *kibbutzim*. Sometimes the British would surround a *kibbutz* and pour water down the iron fence posts until they discovered one that wouldn't fill up. This meant it was an air vent for a concealed work area, and a raid would immediately follow.

To this day, the *kibbutzim* are still the first line of military defense. Slit trenches lead to the bomb shelters beside the schoolrooms; they have been maintained—and used—almost constantly since 1947. In the War of Liberation, it was the defense by the Kibbutz Yad Mordechai that blunted the advance of Egyptian tanks; that's what the picture *Judith* was about, in addition to Sophia Loren's chest expansion.

But the military aspect of the *kibbutz* was the last thing that interested my daughter Lynne. Her curiosity about a selfless society was much more important. Through the good offices of Gershon Rivlin, she was taken in by Kibbutz Tsorah, where Rivlin's daughter Goni also worked. Tsorah was known as the Anglo-Saxon *kibbutz,* because it had a tennis court, and most of its members came from South Africa and could be forced to speak English. The fact that the cows used the tennis court more often than the residents didn't seem to bother anyone. There was very little time for tennis anyway.

Lynne became a *metapeleth,* which, she informed us, is a combination nurse and mother. After my first startled reaction, she clarified it. The heart of the *kibbutz* system is the group education which takes over the care of the children so the parents are freed for other work. At a very early age, children and parents are separated, and the children sleep with their "peer group" instead of at "home." The *metapeleth,* to a large extent, must substitute for mother, father, and teacher. The family group is by no means broken up, and the *metapeleth's* toughest job is convincing a Jewish mother she is taking proper care of the mother's child.

The children in my daughter's group were from eight to ten years of age. Her greatest difficulty was in explaining to them how she could be nineteen and not have been in the army, and not have to worry about ever going into the army. The United States, they concluded, has a somewhat backward culture. What do they do in America when the Arabs come?

The children were, on the surface, one large, happy family. But the lack of home life and privacy caused a certain amount of loneliness, which they tried to conceal to avoid the disapproval of the group; but, being children, the pretense didn't last very long. There is still considerable disagreement among experts on the emotional results of the system. Some believe it is harmful; others believe it substitutes other values for those it removes. One observer has noted that *kibbutz*-reared children tend to be less aggressive and more stable, but those who join the Israeli Army's shock troops are good fighters and do not break down under stress as easily as the "normal" recruits. *Kibbutz* children also show evidence of greater personality maturity and more positive attitudes toward their families.

What no one disputes is that all this puts a tremendous load on the *metapeleth,* who has to be resident psychiatrist while preparing meals and washing clothes. I am sure the children under my daughter's care gained a great deal from her, but a clinically unexplored area is what the *metapeleth* gains from her kids. In being the helper and playmate and overseer and parent of a dozen children, a nineteen-year-old girl from an overpermissive society achieves a certain stature and confidence and maturity that, otherwise, she would never reach unless she married a Catholic who couldn't afford a maid.

I guess for me the climactic moment came when my wife and I visited the *kibbutz* and saw our daughter, whose father holds the track record in the *minyan* dash, solemnly lighting the ritual candles for Friday night dinner with her flock of twelve children.

One postscript. Although my daughter didn't particularly enjoy the plum-picking season, during which everyone on the *kibbutz*, regardless of age or importance, must join, it did produce the entertaining spectacle of one of her neighbors, a tractor driver, eight months pregnant, being unable to squeeze out from behind the wheel of her tractor until help arrived. And *kibbutz* life also has its social aspect, the young people gathering at night for a *kumsitz*, a group singing around a campfire, or listening to folk rock on someone's semi-smuggled hi-fi set. Every night at eleven, my daughter told us, the girls would bring out some cake and start to divide it; three youthful sentries patrolling the fences near the Arab border would somehow manage to be in the area at exactly the right time; they would stack their submachine guns and toss their ammo belts on the ground while they munched the cake and sipped some tea and rapped with their young confrères. Then, with the sound of electric guitars twanging in their ears, they would strap on the ammunition, pick up their guns, and return to the Middle East.

CHAPTER XIX

TEL AVIV AIRSTRIP—MED. SHOT
A Piper Cub is warming up on the
strip as a catering truck races toward
it, blowing its horn. The truck is
lettered:

TEL AVIV DAIRY RESTAURANT

It screeches to a halt and two
waiters climb out, race to the rear
and open the truck's doors. They
start to haul a case of seltzer siphons
out of the truck.

AT PLANE—MED. CLOSE
Tex opens the door to the cockpit
and leans out.

TEX—*Come on, come on, boy.*
There's a war on.

One of the Waiters starts handing
him the siphons. A piece of metal
has been slipped over the neck of
each siphon.

TEX—*What's this for?*

WAITER—*A trick we learned from*
the Stukas in the other war. It's
like a whistle—it screams on the
way down.

TEX—*Great. That'll make two of us.*

If you were making a movie
in the heart of Israel,
sweltering in the heat of the
deadly *chumsin,* the wind
from the southern desert, and
you needed an actor immediately to play the minor role
of a Texas aviator, whom
would you cast?

Right the first time. Frank
Sinatra.

That is, if the *chumsin*
lasted a long time. The lore of
the Middle East declares
emphatically that during the
period of this incessant, searing
breeze, the human mind is not
responsible for its actions.
Crimes of passion, including
murder, committed during the
chumsin, are likely to be
pardoned by an understanding
judge who has kicked his
mother in the rear on the way
to the courtroom for asking
if it's hot enough for him.

I could be excused, then, in
my unhinged state, for
thinking that the Living

They get the siphons inside and close the cockpit door. Tex guns the motor.

TEX—(*calling*) *Hey—where can I get a bet down on the other side?*

The Piper Cub pulls away and starts down the runway.

Legend from Hoboken, New Jersey, would give up thousands of dollars in nightclub and concert engagements to fly halfway around the world for a two-day bit part.

I had some slight acquaintance with Mr. Sinatra, however, and I knew that what he was most likely to do was what he wasn't most likely to do. Some years back, Jack Rose and I had been included in his entourage for the inauguration of President John F. Kennedy. Our job was to help write the Inaugural Gala, a star-studded entertainment Mr. S. had whipped together for the purpose of pulling the poor Democratic Party out of a hole. The Gala raised several million dollars, although the night it was presented, Washington was hit by the worst blizzard in its history and the audience, including the President-elect and Jackie, couldn't reach the auditorium until after 11:00 P.M. It might have been better had they not showed up at all, because the show itself was not one to go down in history; by 2:00 A.M. most of the audience had turned Republican. The Kennedys graciously waited through it all, and then helped host a party given by Joseph Kennedy that lasted hours longer.

I was startled, the next morning, to roll bleary-eyed out of bed, turn on the television set, and see that Jack Kennedy had actually made it to his Inauguration. Not only that, he looked as handsome, rested, and self-assured as I didn't feel. His speech was literate and inspiring, his performance better than any he had witnessed the night before. If I had been Khrushchev, I would have retired right then.

That night Sinatra hosted a party at the Statler for all of us who had labored on the Gala. Downstairs one of the many Inaugural Balls held at various hotels that evening was already in progress. We were wading into the second or third elaborate course when Peter Lawford entered, crossed to Frank, and informed him that the new President had arrived at the Inaugural Ball and would like all of us concerned with the show to come downstairs so he could shake our hands and thank us personally.

Sinatra looked up from his soup and said, "Tell him we're eating."
Lawford blanched slightly.

"I'm only his brother-in-law," he said. "You tell him."

"Okay," declared Mr. Sinatra, getting to his feet, "I'll tell him."

And he walked casually out of the banquet room. Or as casually as
anyone could who was immediately surrounded by five brawny Secret
Service men.

They escorted him downstairs.

Fredric March, one of the diners, turned to the rest of us and remarked, "In about five minutes you're going to see one unhappy Italian
nailed to the wall."

A few moments later, Frank returned.

"Ladies and gentlemen," he announced, "the President of the United
States."

And Kennedy entered, smiling. "I'm sorry," he apologized, "I didn't
know you were eating."

There is an epilogue to the story that may prove Camelot was not
all it was cracked up to be. The new President stayed for a quarter of
an hour, enjoying himself immensely, happy to be away from the
political scene for a brief moment. My wife had made Frank promise
earlier that, if the opportunity arose, he would introduce her to Kennedy. Frank immediately called her over, and she graciously included
me in the invitation. We all chatted for a few moments; I told the
President that, as a writer, I wanted to compliment him on his Inaugural Address, if he had written it. He smiled again and admitted he
wasn't entitled to a solo credit. We returned to our table and Phil Stern,
the photographer, came over, his face a mask of gloom.

"I knew you would get me a job as an associate producer, at least,
if I got a dozen shots of you and the Prez," he moaned, "but the Secret
Service took my camera."

It seems that, all of the time we had been talking, Kennedy held a
highball glass in his hand. It is forbidden to photograph the Chief
Executive being too human. If there is a curse on that gallant clan,
perhaps it is the flaw of humanity which characterizes them all.

The entire incident went through my mind when I decided to ask
Sinatra to do something completely illogical. At the moment he, too,
was agented by the indomitable Herman Citron, who called Frank

from Hollywood—Sinatra was in New York at the time—to laugh at this crazy offer. Sinatra told him to mail him the screenplay.

Shortly afterward, I received a shocked letter from Herman, informing me that Frank had read the script, was delighted with the part, and would be ready to start shooting the morning of June 25th.

Herman's signature at the bottom of the letter looked a little shaky.

June 24th, Sinatra landed at Lydda Airport in the first private Lear Jet with a piano and cocktail bar to arrive all morning. He had brought along a few friends from New York, but he was all business.

The Piper Cub appears overhead and dives for the lead tank.

A TANK—MED. CLOSE
An Egyptian officer is in the open hatch, directing the action. We hear the shriek of a falling object and a seltzer bottle hits the tank beside him and bursts with a tremendous explosion.

INT. PIPER CUB—MED. CLOSE
Tex has the window on the pilot's side open. He reaches for another seltzer bottle as he puts the Piper into a steep bank, then hurls the bottle from the window.

TEX—(*he can't help it*) *Bombs away!*

A sudden burst of machine gun fire is heard. Tex whirls and looks over his shoulder.

SKY—POV SHOT
From Tex's point of view, we see a pair of Egyptian fighter planes diving on his tail, guns firing.

INT. COCKPIT—(Transparency)
Tex tries some desperate evasive action. Bullets stitch through the

The part he was to play was that of an American who flew with the Israeli Air Force. As I have mentioned, many American flyers, Jew and Gentile alike, were recruited for the War of Liberation, for among the Israelis there were few who had been allowed by the farsighted British, in whose army many of them had fought valiantly in World War II, to be trained as pilots. Of course, since that time, Israeli flight training has improved somewhat.

The first scene to be photographed with Sinatra concerned the unlikely incident detailed at the left, in which a pilot in a lone Piper Cub attacked Egyptian tanks with seltzer bottles. A young captain of the Israeli Air Force came to me while we were preparing the scene to protest officially what the Air Force

fuselage behind his head. He ducks
and looks ahead at:

SPITFIRE—FULL SHOT
Heading directly toward Camera,
machine guns blazing.

INT. COCKPIT—(Transparency)
The cockpit is being splintered about
him as Tex tries to pull the plane into
a climb, but the controls are useless.
He picks up a Sten gun and leans out
of the cockpit window to fire it, but
the gun jams. He throws it away. At
the last moment, he reaches for a
seltzer bottle. As bullets rattle about
him, he holds the bottle up and
squirts his last weapon at the
approaching enemy. There is an
explosion that OBSCURES THE
SCREEN.

considered a fictitious slur on
its history. He came at a
fortuitous time, for visiting
our location was an American
who had flown one of those
very Piper Cubs for Israel in
the early days of that war.

"How many bombs did
those planes carry?" I asked
him, making certain the young
captain was listening.

"Bombs?" he laughed.
"Who had bombs? Sometimes
we used hand grenades, and
when we didn't have any, we
dropped anything that would
explode and *look* like a
bomb."

"Like what?" I prompted him.

"Half-empty beer bottles," he said. "Sometimes seltzer bottles, but they were more expensive."

I turned to the captain and offered him his choice of beer or seltzer.

Now, I realize, it was a Pyrrhic victory. Frank Sinatra dropping seltzer bottles on a tank smells of Hollywood, not war. Truth in Israel is not only stranger than fiction, it is often less dramatic. Unless you happen to be on the other side.

But, at that time, no one could have talked me out of that scene.

Sinatra climbed into the cockpit of the tiny plane on the runway of Dov Airport, a military field near Tel Aviv, to make the first shot. There was to be some dialogue before he gunned the plane down the runway. He offered to take the plane into the air, since he holds a pilot's license, and I agreed.

Then we started to rehearse, and to my amazement, I couldn't understand a word the Living Legend was saying. "Y'all sho yo no thayss awurron?" he repeated.

It took me a while to realize Frank was speaking with what he firmly believed was a Texas accent. He had taken the characterization in the script literally. It took a great deal of tact for me to explain to him carefully that we had prudently changed this pilot's home town from Houston to Hoboken, New Jersey, and his name from Tex to Vince. Frank was somewhat disappointed, having worked on the accent for fully five minutes, but then figured he wouldn't have won the Academy Award with it, anyway, and switched back to himself, a character he plays to perfection.

The cameras rolled. Frank exchanged dialogue with the waiter who was loading seltzer bottles into the plane, then swung the Piper Cub onto the runway for the take-off. Suddenly the little aircraft whipped into a sharp turn on the tarmac and gunned its way back to the camera.

"Hey," Frank called out, "I just remembered, my insurance doesn't cover me if I don't have a co-pilot."

And Frank Sinatra, actor, swinger, and businessman, got out of the plane and made way for his double.

The next sequence was to be shot at night, which was one of our larger mistakes. By nightfall, all the stars, in a manful effort to out-Sinatra Sinatra, had been drinking toasts to each other in 180-proof Slivovitz. They showed up on the runway, where we had lit oil flares to illuminate a night landing, happy as a rabbi with a *minyan.* Had they all exhaled at the same time, the flares would have ignited a fireball that would have lent credence to the rumors that Israel possesses The Bomb.

It became literally necessary to prop two of the actors up and point them at the camera. Frank—who had probably drunk more toasts than any of them, being a very cordial man—scarcely showed any instability. A lifetime spent entertaining in saloons has certain advantages. While the others were verging on collapse, Mr. Sinatra's evening had scarcely begun. An assistant director came over to me, troubled, and informed me that Frank had told him he was thinking of throwing a little party later on, and would the production supply some Nice Jewish Girls?

The assistant didn't think the item was in the budget, and besides, since he was a married man, his acquaintance with Nice Jewish Girls was limited.

In Israel, when the impossible must be done immediately, you turn it over to the Army. We mentioned the supply problem to an officer who was assigned to the production.

I am pleased to report that the Israeli Army came through with flying colors. Unofficially, of course. I was told the party took place precisely at D-Day, H-Hour, and made the Sinai Campaign look like a weenie roast. Sinatra was pleased, his guests were pleased, and some Nice Jewish Girls learned to sing "Call Me Irresponsible."

TEL AVIV STREET—NIGHT
Crowded with people, cheering, singing, waving flags. An Israeli Army jeep is making its way through the jam-packed humanity. Vince is at the wheel, Mickey beside him, passing out bottles of wine to the celebrants as the hilarity increases.

JEEP—MED. CLOSE
Mickey picks up a couple of bottles of wine and tucks them under his arm. He shouts to Vince so he can be heard above the din.

MICKEY—(*shouting*) *I'm getting off —to see a friend in the neighborhood.*

VINCE—(*shouting back*) *Don't leave me—I'm anti-Semitic!*

A pretty girl leans into the jeep and kisses him.

VINCE—*Propaganda!*

STREET—MED. CLOSE
Mickey is shoving his way through the throng toward an apartment house.

MAGDA'S VOICE—*Mickey! MICKEY!*

He turns, CAMERA PANNING to reveal Magda pushing her way through the crowd to his side.

Sinatra's biggest scene—in the picture, that is—was yet to come. It was to be the reenactment of the celebration of the announcement of Independence in the streets of Tel Aviv. Even now, Independence Day in Israel is observed with the kind of bone-crunching enthusiasm exhibited in Times Square on New Year's Eve. Seemingly everyone in the tiny country crowds into its streets that night, shouting and dancing the *hora*. If Golda Meir should remarry, even *her* Jewish wedding couldn't top it.

We had secured permission to rope off Noah Square, in the center of Ramat Gan, a Tel Aviv suburb, for our restaging of the event. And then we placed a small advertisement in the press, announcing we would supply free entertainment, and Mr. Sinatra and Mr. Kirk Douglas would be involved in the scene

MAGDA—*I heard you were here, but you're so important now, you only have time for cabinet ministers. Maybe if I got elected—*

She suddenly throws herself into his arms.

TWO SHOT—MICKEY AND MAGDA
The crowd surges around them.

MAGDA—*Mickey, Mickey, Mickey!*
She is crying.

MICKEY—*What are you crying about?*

MAGDA—*You came back.*

MICKEY—*It's only supposed to make the Arabs unhappy. If you'll—*

AN AIR RAID SIREN WAILS. Suddenly, the singing ceases as the crowd rushes by them, heading for the shelters. We HEAR AN EXPLOSION. Mickey pulls Magda inside the glass doors of an apartment house which have been half-covered with tape. He tries to pull her toward the shelter, but she suddenly turns and kisses him. ANOTHER EXPLO- SION, and the glass shatters, obscuring our view of the embrace.

we planned to shoot. The advertisement wasn't small enough.

We hoped a thousand people would show up. Instead, everyone in Tel Aviv with nothing better to do jammed into the square. Arab television must have had its clothes on that night, because over twenty thousand shouting —in Hebrew—"fans" completely overwhelmed us. We were treated to the strange spectacle of Jewish mounted police riding horses into a mob that greeted them with cries of "Cossack!" The horses looked a little self-conscious, but the police did their job almost too well. Twelve spectators were hospitalized. Sinatra was supposed to drive the jeep, with Kirk seated beside him, through the heart of that throng. Both men looked a little dubious, but Frank, at least, had faced

louder and more violent admirers in his salad days and said it looked like 45th Street outside the Paramount Theater's stage door.

Before we could get the jeep started, a shower of leaflets fell from one of the crowded rooftops around the square onto the mob below. The Communist Party of Israel had decided to get into the act. The leaflets advised everyone that these Americans were here to make a movie which desecrated Israel's national heroes and every effort must be made to stop them. Sinatra was a symbol of Fascist oppression, despite his transparent attempts to confuse the issue by fraternizing with Nice Jewish Girls. The Communist Party recommended the following revolutionary action:

    a. Shine flashlights into the cameras.
    b. If you can't afford a flashlight, light matches.
    c. If you can't afford matches, join the Party.
    d. If the camera points at you, make faces and look directly into the lens.
    e. Whatever they tell you to do, do the opposite.

This last, apparently, infuriated the crowd, who felt that, being Israeli, they didn't have to be told *that*. Instead of obeying the leaflets, most of them, to whom the Communists were old and slightly *meshugga* friends, kept shouting, "Mendel, come down, you could fall off!" The conspirators on the roof seemed offended by this consideration for their welfare, and the whole episode would have been a complete failure if it hadn't been for the police, who charged up on the roof and arrested everybody, restoring their faith in Marx.

Meanwhile, Sinatra was attempting to drive the jeep and Kirk Douglas through a jam-up of twenty thousand autograph seekers. The jeep was almost turned over. Somehow a portion of the street was cleared and Frank made the run again. Eight of our brawny stunt men fought their way to the side of our stars and managed to extricate them at the end of the shot. Kirk climbed out and made a brave attempt to play the next scene, with Senta Berger, in the middle of the happy mob. The Communists were shouting on their way to jail, pausing only to inquire from the police if they could stop for some autographs. The police agreed it might be a good idea if they *all* got some autographs. The mounted police felt neglected and charged into the crowd again. It became necessary to call the whole thing off and restage the meeting of Kirk and Senta at Cinecitta in Rome, where things were quieter.

The Ramat Gan incident was nicely rounded out in Tel Aviv some weeks later, when the government held a formal reception and presented us with little bronze medals for having made a picture in Israel. I felt a purple heart would have been more appropriate, but the medals were accepted with warm thanks. To my surprise, one of the gentlemen congratulating me on my work was one of the Communists I had last seen on the roof, hurling pamphlets and imprecations on my head. He, too, had been invited to the reception, along with several of his co-revolutionists. They all told me how pleased they were that I had changed the entire story of the picture to conform with their objections. We shook hands. I am still trying to puzzle the whole thing out.

I was also puzzling out why Mr. Sinatra would have interrupted his schedule to travel twelve thousand miles to be trampled on by a howling mob of Jewish autograph seekers, when he could have had the same pleasure in Las Vegas. *This* mystery was finally solved.

Sinatra is a highly complex individual, whose public image is only a fraction of the man. I'm sure I don't understand him; neither have three wives; and I have a suspicion Frank himself is a little confused. When we were trying to arrange our shooting schedule, I suggested we might be able to postpone shooting Sinatra's segments until our arrival in Rome. Word came back that unless he was to work in Israel, Sinatra wasn't interested.

The reason became clear when arrangements were made for the payment of his salary. It was all assigned to the Frank Sinatra Arab-Israeli Youth Center in the ancient city of Nazareth. Neither I nor any of my Hollywood acquaintances had ever heard of it before. We were a little amazed that Frank had heard of Nazareth.

But he had, apparently some time ago. He invited us all proudly to the dedication of the Youth Center. Nazareth, where Jesus spent his boyhood, is a largely Arabic city. Camels still parade through the center of town, stopping gravely for traffic lights. The tiny streets through the crowded, colorful, noisy, smelly bazaar, with their shops and donkey traffic and Arab porters carrying their burdens on their heads, have remained unchanged through the centuries, except for a slight increase in prices for television repairs. Here can be found unchanged the synagogue which Christ attended as a young man, when He could not escape the lunges of His *minyan*-hunting rabbi. The Youth Center, established by the Histadrut, the Israeli Labor Union, is a sort of YMHA for both Arab and Israeli children. It is an experiment in unlikely togetherness.

Sinatra, in a little speech before the audience of shirtsleeved Arabs and their Jewish neighbors in the Center's auditorium, said simply, "I never grew up enough to really understand adults, but I think I understand kids. If we can get them together when they're young enough, maybe when they get big they'll be smarter than we have been."

It was translated into Hebrew and Arabic for an audience that was touched and appreciative. Sinatra sat down, and the children started to present an entertainment they had prepared for the occasion. Immediately Frank was back in his own bag. Amateur night he doesn't need. Amateur night in Hebrew he needs even less. He squirmed in his seat for a few minutes, then got to his feet and slipped out of the building where he was being honored.

He left the City of Christ and flew back in his Lear Jet to Tel Aviv. And some Nice Jewish Girls.

Dov Airfield. Frank Sinatra and the author looking for some Nice Jewish Girls.

The author and Sinatra, who has just remembered he has an insurance problem.

Sinatra fighting a war with two cents plain.

Frank Sinatra, The Kid from Texas.

The night everybody got too happy. Kirk, the director, and the pilot who flew the transport plane in the picture—as he had actually done in the War of Liberation.

There was a canard circulated that if the two gentlemen shaking hands should let go, they would both fall down.

Noah Square, Ramat Gan, just before the crowd broke through the barricades and mobbed Douglas and Sinatra. The building on the right is the one from which the Communist Party dropped its leaflets.

CHAPTER XX

WORLD'S CHUBBIEST BELLY DANCER—CLOSE SHOT
To the accompaniment of typically mournful Arab MUSIC, she is performing the ritualistic dance in a manner that would have been provocative ten years and forty pounds ago. CAMERA PANS to reveal:

A BEDOUIN CHIEF—CLOSE SHOT
Abou Ibn Kadir (Haym Topol) is close to seventy, his lined face a mask of impassivity, as he watches the Dancer and digs his hands into a massive bowl of cous-cous, *set in the center of what was once a beautiful oriental rug.*

INT. TENT—MED. CLOSE
Mickey and Ram are trying to eat, politely, from the same unappetizing bowl, as the Dancer continues her gyrations. Kadir is flanked by two fierce-looking TRIBESMEN.

INT. TENT—ANOTHER ANGLE
The Dancer, provoked by their inattention, redoubles her efforts, dancing closer to the old Berber Chief, who promptly slaps her on her considerable rear and shouts something in Arabic, clapping his hands. The

The scene detailed at the left made it necessary for us to conduct auditions at the Avia Hotel for a suitably-muscled young lady. I am not certain Arab chieftains go in much for belly dancers, their pleasures usually being more direct, but we decided it might divert Western audiences and went ahead with our search.

For days we studied a succession of navels which vibrated in every direction known to man, if he were lucky. We had not informed the ladies that we were searching for a belly which had gone somewhat to pot, so they went at their task with enthusiasm, not realizing talent was the least important requisite.

We finally selected an amazingly overendowed young woman who could make a muscle with any part of her body on demand. When

*Arab musicians make a hasty exit,
dragging the Dancer with them. Ibn
Kadir shouts another command and
TWO ARABS enter, carrying the
world's oldest phonograph. Kadir
selects a record, places it on the
phonograph, turns the crank, and sets
the needle in place. We HEAR a
rendition so scratchy, it has obviously
been played over and over during the
years. We HEAR THE VOICE OF
RUDY VALLEE, singing "The
Shiek of Araby." Kadir smiles, closes
his eyes, and hums the melody along
with Vallee.*

MICKEY—(*to Ram*) *The mysterious
East.*

she shook her ample central district, windows rattled for blocks. Any Arab chieftain would have been happy to welcome her to his tent, if it were securely anchored to the ground.

When the time came to shoot the scene, however, a serious religious problem arose. Playing the parts of two of the subsidiary Arabs in the tent were two Jewish actors who were members of the Hassidic sect. Their belief, they informed me, forbade them to remain in the same room with a naked woman. I pointed out that they were not in a room but a tent. And the naked woman was not entirely naked. They insisted that her belly was naked, and since this was some 85 percent of her total area, the difference was academic.

For those of you who are unacquainted with the Hassidim, let me fill this unfortunate void in your experience. They are a sect of ultra-religious Jews who walk around in the middle of the heat of the Israeli summer wearing long black overcoats and black fur hats. When you ask them why they do not take them off, they reply that if they took them off they would not be Hassidim.

There is a further-out group of the ultra-Orthodox called the Neturey Karta, who do not recognize the government of Israel. It is written in the Holy Books that the Jews will get back the Promised Land only when the Messiah returns. If the Messiah had returned, would Israel be in such trouble? Obviously, he hasn't shown up yet.

So the Neturey Karta refuse to use Israeli money, they refuse to serve in the Army, and they refuse to vote. Furthermore, when they come from America to visit Palestine, as they still call it, they will not fly in El Al planes, because El Al is owned by a government that doesn't exist. Would *you* fly on a mythical airline? Even if the pilot wore a long black overcoat and black fur hat?

The Hassidim and similar sects have been in the forefront of the campaign to make Jewish women unattractive. I didn't know that it took a *campaign* until I got to Israel. It seems that hidden somewhere in the aforementioned Holy Books is the admonition that fornication is a necessary evil which should only be indulged in to prevent the extinction of the race. While this may be a blow to Hugh Hefner, it didn't bother the Hassidim much. It takes a long time to get out of those long black overcoats, anyway. But just so they shouldn't be tempted, they had their women shave their heads as soon as they got married, to make them less desirable.

The women, of course, didn't take that lying down (oops). They immediately invented the sheitel, the wig that all Orthodox married women wear, and the men were back where they started. Except that sex couldn't be the wild, carefree, uninhibited romp it had been before, unless the wig was glued on pretty well.

So the rabbis came up with another rule. In essence, they moved the goalposts back an extra ten yards. The rule was: in the sexual act, there should be *no bodily contact.* Pretty good one-upmanship, you should excuse the expression.

But the Hassidim are a hardy, determined lot. They found a way. After the candlelight and wine, the stereo records and the *halvah,* the couple retires to bed, disrobes, and a sheet is thrown over the female.

But there is one hole in it.

So that this nation, under God, shall not perish from the earth.

But wait. Not so fast. Not so simple. Back another ten yards: the male must think only *religious thoughts* while in action.

When I asked Haym Topol how this was possible, he answered solemnly, "Fortunately, there are some parts of the Bible that are very dirty."

Amen.

You can understand, then, the problem of our two Hassidic actors. Since I could not throw a sheet over our belly dancer and retain the essence of the scene, there was nothing to do but excuse them from their duties.

In their place, two of the Arab truck drivers on the production were pressed into service, albeit willingly. They could act about as well as they drove a truck, but as long as they were willing to stay in a room with a naked woman, I wasn't going to complain. Never in my wildest imagination had I dreamed I would run into that sort of problem with members of the acting profession. We learn something new every day.

I certainly did, on the day that followed, when I attempted to continue shooting the scene. The two Arabs didn't show up. They were driving a truck to Jerusalem. When they were finally rounded up and returned, they didn't seem too happy about resuming a career in the drama. I gathered from them that, in the Moslem world, a belly dancer is a creature of grace and beauty, who studies her difficult art for years, until she can bring joy and desire to the eyes of men, and make them homesick for the gazelle-eyed *houri* promised all Muslims in Paradise.

Our belly dancer made them homesick for their truck. We had to pay them time-and-a-half to get them to stay in the tent with her.

I had another experience with the Arab mind shortly afterward. We had found, in the Arab section of Lod near Lydda Airport, a low, round-domed Arab home that was ideal for the focal point of a battle sequence in which Israeli forces invaded a small Jordanian town. There was even a mosque picturesquely situated in the background. Lod itself has a great many Arab inhabitants, who are allowed to live this close to the airport because they did not oppose the Israelis in 1947. Their opinion may have changed since then, because I noted a number of hostile stares from under picturesque burnooses when we scouted the area. But I felt that the section was ideal for the scene and asked our Israeli production manager to secure the use of the exterior of the picturesque home.

He stared at me as if I were insane.

"Don't you know," he demanded as if speaking to a child, "that the man who owns that house is the chief of the Arab underground in Israel? Don't you know that he is the one who blew up the train to Jerusalem only last week?"

"Don't you know," I demanded as if speaking to a child, "that you ought to arrest him then?"

The Israeli production manager looked horrified.

"Never!" he cried. "Why would we want to do that?"

"But if he blew up the train—"

He explained slowly, so I would comprehend, "This fellow has been chief of the underground for a long time. We know him. We understand him. If we put him in jail, they will elect another chief. We won't know him. We will have to find him. That takes time. This one, at least we know where he lives!"

I digested this information, then told him I still wanted to use that house.

Impossible, was the answer.

"Why don't we ask him?" I inquired. "What have we got to lose? He knows you know him, you know he knows you know him, what difference will it make to him if he lets us use his house, knowing you asked him because you know he knows you know he knows you know him?"

The production manager threw up his hands, and we went over to the house.

The chief of the Arab underground listened gravely, and finally nodded his approval on one condition: that he be allowed to sit outside his house and watch us make movies. After all, he said, what difference did it make to anyone, since everyone knew he knew we knew he knew we knew him?

I will never forget the day we shot that battle. The chief of the Arab underground, dressed formally in silken robes and a magnificent red fez, had his wife carry a rug and some pillows into his front yard. He sat on one, and I sat on another. Then his wife brought us, in a magnificent old copper pot, some deliciously sweet Turkish coffee. With *hel* on it, *hel* being an aromatic herb.

The chief of the Arab underground ceremoniously poured me a drink. We raised our cups and drank. And then he sat back happily and watched the Israeli Army, firing dummy machine gun bullets from his back yard, absolutely annihilate a group of Arab soldiers near his front yard.

At the conclusion, he turned to me.

"Well done," he said and shook my hand.

Next week he was in jail for blowing up one train too many.
But he knew he would be out soon.
And the Israelis knew he knew it.

Haym Topol, age thirty, playing an old Arab; the author playing an old director.

Our belly dancer breaking the Hassidic laws for Stathis Giallelis as the young Palmach commander trying to look old enough to watch, Douglas, and Haym Topol as the old Berber chieftain.

CHAPTER XXI

*FULL SHOT—SHIP'S BOATS—
DAWN*
*A group of large rowboats, jammed
with passengers, is heading toward
shore; in B.G., we can make out the
dim outlines of a merchant ship. The
sea seems to be filled with the small
boats. As the lead boat comes to
Camera, we see it is commanded by
a Palmach officer, ANDRÉ SIMON,
who is Magda's husband.*

BEACH—FULL SHOT
*A group of the Haganah, rifles in
hand, appears over a sand dune. They
are led by Asher Gonen (Yul
Brynner). Among them we see Mickey
(Kirk Douglas) and Magda (Senta
Berger). CAMERA RISES to reveal,
in the distance, a column of British
armored cars and lorries heading for
the beach.*

*FLASHES—PASSENGERS AND
HAGANAH*
*This is a series of HAND-HELD
SHOTS in which we see the
passengers—men, women, and children
—being helped from the boats by
the Haganah as they reach the surf.
André is the last one out of his boat.*

The time had come for us to
shoot our Landing of the
Immigrants Scene. No American ever makes a picture in
Israel without including one
sequence depicting the Landing of the Immigrants. I think
it is because there is nothing
that induces as much sym-
pathy in a movie audience as
the sight of a seasick Jewish
extra.

By this time, we all knew
the picture was in trouble.
We were running far behind
our schedule and were already
half a million dollars over
our budget estimates. There
was no official wringing of
hands by the Mirisches, who
were somewhat inured to
this by now, but I could
detect a slight note of
anguish in some of their
cables. They had been
courageous, helpful, and
considerate, and felt they
were entitled to a little profit
as well.

Magda hurries to meet him. The refugees are laughing and shouting.

BRITISH OFFICER'S VOICE—(*on loudspeaker*) *No one is to leave this beach.*

All action FREEZES.

BEACH—REVERSE ANGLE
The British armor has taken up its position. Troops move out of the lorries and draw up in a single line. A YOUNG BRITISH OFFICER stands by a loudspeaker truck, speaking into a microphone.

BRITISH OFFICER—(*on loudspeaker*) *We are not the Gestapo, ladies and gentlemen, but there are laws of entry to this country which we are under orders to enforce. You there—you civilians moving down to the beach area—you are to stop and go back.*

GROUP SHOT—MICKEY, MAGDA, AND ANDRÉ
They wait, watching.

BEACH—FULL SHOT

A GROUP OF CIVILIANS carrying blankets and food has paused on their way down to the beach.

CLOSE SHOT—BRITISH OFFICER
He is young and worried.

BRITISH OFFICER—(*on loudspeaker*) *Please do not make it necessary for us to use our arms. But those entering illegally must go back to await their permits.*

CLOSE SHOT—ASHER
He steps forward. His gun has been hidden.

Tempers were getting short. Kirk and I were having daily differences of opinion. Yul was taking out his frustrations in other ways. Once he showed me a cigarette burn on the palm of his right hand and told me he had stepped on a lighted cigarette the night before, walking on Dizengoff Street. When I looked confused, Yul explained impatiently that he had, of course, been walking on his hands.

Only Senta Berger remained happy and contented. Her Romantic Interest had flown in from Vienna, bringing with him half a ton of Sacher Torte. And, in this scene on the beach, she would have an opportunity to take off her clothes and display another side of her talent.

But our real difficulty came from an area we never anticipated. As our location, we had chosen Palmahim Beach, a desolate stretch of shoreline on the outskirts of Tel Aviv. There was a road leading to it down which the British Army trucks could arrive, and sand dunes over which the people of

ASHER—*No one goes back ever.*

BEACH—FULL SHOT

Slowly, the civilians resume their advance to the beach.

CLOSE SHOT—BRITISH OFFICER
He is perspiring now.

BRITISH OFFICER—(*on loudspeaker*)
Halt!

A JUNIOR OFFICER touches him on the shoulder.

JUNIOR OFFICER—*Look over there, sir. Looks like Wembley Stadium letting out.*

THE SAND DUNES—FULL SHOT
A line of people has appeared over the crest of the dunes, filling the screen from side to side. CAMERA BOOMS HIGHER to reveal they are only the avant-garde of the people of Tel Aviv, pouring down onto the beach—men, women, and children by the hundreds.

BEACH—ANOTHER ANGLE
Now it has become a flood of people, running directly over Camera, shouting and cheering, surrounding the immigrants and the Haganah.

BRITISH OFFICER'S VOICE—(*on loudspeaker*) *Those landing from the sea are warned to remain separated from the others.*

GROUP—MED. SHOT
Mickey and Magda are in the midst of the throng.

MICKEY—(*to Magda*) *Take off your clothes.*

Tel Aviv could storm for the confrontation indicated in the screenplay. We had four cameras, one extra camera-man—Israeli—eight hundred extras, and five Israeli assistant directors. These assistants were knowledgeable, willing, hard-working, and had all been directors themselves. Among the eight hundred extras, six hundred and fifty had also been directors in the Old Country. The other one hundred and fifty had been film critics.

The problem was that what we had here in Tel Aviv was a failure to communicate. In Israel, where at that time the entire labor force was employed, to find eight hundred people with nothing better to do than lie around on a beach and watch us perspire, we had to go to the newly arrived immigrants who had not yet been assigned jobs. Our assistant directors spoke perfect Hebrew. Our extras spoke perfect Hungarian, Rumanian, Russian, Polish, and Czechoslovakian. It became necessary to repeat all directions in at least four languages, which took

She looks at him, not comprehending. He grabs her and tears her skirt off, yanks off his own jacket and exchanges it with an IMMIGRANT. Magda understands his purpose, calls in Hebrew to the others; all start exchanging clothes to make it impossible for the British to tell the new arrivals from the others.

TWO SHOT—THE BRITISH OFFICERS

The Junior Officer is smiling. The other Officer glares at him and he wipes it off.

BRITISH OFFICER—(*on loudspeaker*) *All passengers from the Ashkelon will step forward immediately or I will be forced to order my men to open fire.*

THE PEOPLE—MOVING CAMERA

CAMERA PANS over the faces. No one makes a move.

THE TROOPS—FULL SHOT

They are lined up on the beach, rifles at the ready.

BRITISH OFFICER'S VOICE—(*on loudspeaker*) *The first volley will be a warning. If you do not move, the second volley will follow in exactly ten seconds.* (*a pause*) *Prepare to fire. Fire!*

The troops fire a volley in the air.

THE BEACH—MOVING CAMERA
Everyone has turned to face the British.

BRITISH OFFICER'S VOICE—(*on loudspeaker*) *One . . . two . . .*

from 5:00 A.M. until one in the afternoon—and at four o'clock the Sabbath started. I was already lighting candles for what was left of our budget.

In addition, while we started out with eight hundred extras at 5:00 A.M., by midday their curiosity about movie stars had been adequately satisfied. They had seen—and touched—in person, Kirk Douglas and Yul Brynner and Senta Berger, and assured themselves they weren't so much. Also, they had had lunch. They had informed me, through various interpreters, that most of my cameras had been placed incorrectly, Senta's make-up was poor, and the extras playing the arriving immigrants didn't look seasick enough. Thereafter, they started retiring from the motion picture industry in large numbers. By late afternoon, we had no more than four hundred directors left.

There were other irritations. In rehearsal, the crowd mobbed Kirk and Yul boisterously, autograph pads at the ready. Sometimes they

CAMERA STARTS TO MOVE DOWN THE LINE of waiting faces.

BRITISH OFFICER'S VOICE—(*on loudspeaker*) *Three . . . four . . .*

CAMERA PASSES Mickey, Magda and André.

BRITISH OFFICER'S VOICE—(*on loudspeaker*) *Five . . . six . . . seven . . .*

CAMERA CONTINUES DOWN THE LINE of silent people, past Asher Gonen. A BABY CRIES.

BRITISH OFFICER'S VOICE—(*on loudspeaker*) *Eight . . . nine . . .*

No one has budged an inch.

TWO SHOT—BRITISH OFFICERS Tense and watchful.

BRITISH OFFICER—(*on loudspeaker*) *Ten!*

He pauses, takes a deep breath, hesitates.

JUNIOR OFFICER—*I suppose now's the time to find out if we're bloody Nazis or not, isn't it?*

BRITISH OFFICER—*Such a stubborn people.*

(*he turns to his soldiers*)

At rest.

BEACH—FULL SHOT

A ROAR goes up from the crowd as the troops lower their rifles. They are shouting and talking and laughing and singing, Mickey, Magda

came close to trampling the stars into the sand, and once Senta Berger was knocked down. Kirk finally got up on a box and made a stirring speech to the crowd in Yiddish, urging them to be orderly and take directions. They applauded him vociferously, the Hungarians believing he had addressed them in Rumanian, the Rumanians certain he had been speaking Czechoslovakian. Then they cheerfully trampled everybody into the sand again.

We ran through a rehearsal, more or less. The arriving "refugees" climbed out of the boats after their hazardous journey through the British blockade wearing dark glasses, bikinis, and one or two Beethoven sweatshirts. It took a few more hours to straighten them out historically.

The ship from which they had landed was supposed to be lying on the horizon, forming the background for the shot. But the only ship large enough for the role was in the port of Haifa, and its owners had asked $4,000 to have it sit offshore *and Asher in their midst, as they start off the beach.*

TWO SHOT—BRITISH OFFICERS Watching.

BRITISH OFFICER—*Now I suppose they'll start dancing.*

CLOSE SHOT—MICKEY
In the middle of the incredible throng. He has found the Israeli Army.

for us. While we were mulling this generous offer, Aldo Tonti had come up with a brilliant suggestion. One of his spaghetti chefs was also a talented artist, having once forged the Mona Lisa for the label of a leading Italian tomato paste; this chef-artist was also

capable of painting a "glass shot," a highly technical arrangement in which a portion of a setting is painted on a sheet of glass, through which the camera then photographs a scene. The chef painted for us the vessel we needed, carefully positioned on the glass to make it appear, through the camera lens, that is was lying offshore, thus saving us approximately $3,950.

When it came time to make the shot, however, we discovered he had overenthusiastically painted smoke billowing from the ship's funnels. A wind was blowing, visibly whipping up the real whitecaps offshore, but having absolutely no effect on this extremely sturdy Italian smoke painted on the glass billowing in the wrong direction. The entire shot was useless.

Aldo, however, urged us not to worry. The smoke could be made to billow properly by some simple double-exposure work in the film laboratory in London.

He was right. This work later cost us $3,950.

In spite of all these difficulties, by late in the afternoon we were ready to make our first shot of the day. Hundreds of extras had been coaxed to remain, by the simple process of refusing to pay them until *after* we had made the scene. Four cameras were set up at various sections of the beach, but the most important, with its Israeli cameraman, was buried in the sand to catch the entire wave of people racing onto the beach and over the camera position.

Finally we shouted "Action!" in five different languages and, wonder of wonders, *everybody* moved. They came charging onto the beach over the sand dunes, shouting and cheering and crying just as they were supposed to—they had all been actors in the Old Country before they started to direct.

When, at last, it was all over and we were congratulating ourselves, as a matter of routine I called down to the operator of the buried camera, "How was it?"

If I had an Old Testament handy at this moment, I would swear on it; but you must believe me that his answer, in perfect English, was, "Wasn't that a *rehearsal?*"

There is an old story about Cecil B. De Mille in exactly the same situation—"Ready when you are, C.B.!"—and if I had been certain the Israeli cameraman had heard it, I would have had him stood up in front of our British firing squad. While I was mulling this possibility, a nameless Israeli journalist, one of a group of several dozen newspapermen watching us work, tapped me on the shoulder.

"You're the Director?" he asked, as if daring me to deny it.

I nodded.

"I don't like to mix in," he said, mixing in, "but you're making a terrible mistake."

I already knew that; in fact, I had known it for several months, but it was impossible for me to back out without being sued, so I had continued. I motioned the nameless Israeli journalist to continue. He didn't need any encouragement.

"In the first place, look at the trucks you have the British Army driving! *American Chevrolets!* In the second place, no Landing of the Immigrants would ever take place in broad daylight, and especially, in the third place, so close to Tel Aviv; also, in the fourth place, if the British were so close, everybody would have been killed. The whole scene is impossible and ridiculous. You understand, of course, I'm just trying to be helpful."

I motioned wearily to Gershon, who happened to be nearby.

"I would like to introduce you to Sgan Aluf Gershon Rivlin," I said to the nameless Israeli journalist, "the Official Historian of the Israeli Army."

The journalist eyed him suspiciously, but there is nothing suspicious about Gershon Rivlin.

"Gershon," I asked, "what kind of trucks did the British Occupying Forces in Palestine drive in 1947?"

"Chevrolets," said Gershon.

"How come?"

"What do you mean, how come? Lend-Lease!"

"Were any immigrant landings ever made in broad daylight?"

"Sometimes. It's a lot easier seeing where you're going, especially when you're landing women and babies."

"But surely they wouldn't land this close to Tel Aviv?"

"That's what the British thought. That's why we did it."

"What beach did you use?"

"Palmahim. *This* beach."

"Were the British soliders this close?"

"Closer!"

"How do *you* know?"

"I was the Commander of the Palmach unit that covered the landings."

I looked at the nameless Israeli jouralist. He shrugged.

"I was only eight years old at the time," he said.

It was a short-lived victory. The journalist apparently had had some sort of run-in with Yul Brynner before our encounter. Yul is a professional; when he is working, he concentrates on his role and has no time to be pleasant to those who interrupt him. In Israel, where everyone, from Premier to bagel-baker is supposed to be *haimish*—one of the family—any hint of stand-offishness is taken as an affront to the nation. The journalist immediately charged with his *shochet's* knife at the ready. I quote from a free translation we received of his story in *Ma'ariv*, the Tel Aviv daily newspaper:

> *And here is Yul Brynner, who personifies the Commander of the Haganah in the film. A Commander with such a sour face the Haganah had never seen. . . . One of his admirers comes near and asks for an autograph. The star pushes him rudely, "What is it here?" They are disturbing his rest (!). His secretary comes to his help, brings a large parasol, smiles to him and throws out the admirers. . . .*

*The same portrait of a "sour face" is seen at the Herzlia
Studios. Brynner sits with an outrageous face on the shooting
stage. And he keeps silent, silent, silent. . . . At one point in
the scene, Topol as the Arab points to Brynner and asks
Douglas, "Who is this idiot?" Brynner fights hard—to no
avail—to take out this phrase from the script.*

I learned long ago no one ever wins an argument with a news-
paperman—or woman—who is working. Yul apparently doesn't care.
He is still something of an enigma to me. He can be a warm friend,
a good father, a happy companion; or he can be glacially calm, cold
as ice, aloof from everything; and the next moment he can be shouting in anger. I still don't know which part is acting, which part is
real, and which part is Brooklyn gypsy.

Yul had his ultimate encounter with the Israeli temperament at a
party where he was introduced to David Ben Gurion. It swiftly became
apparent that Ben Gurion had never heard of him. Yul, bleeding
internally, explained at great length that he was a movie star. The
old man seemed mildly interested. Yul pressed his advantage. Certainly the white-haired patriarch had seen Brynner's magnificent
starring performance in *The King and I?*

"*The King and I,*" mused Ben Gurion, "which one were you?"

Palmahim Beach. The landing of the immigrants from Hollywood. At the right is Michael Shillo, playing the part of André, Senta's movie husband.

The King and I.

Cast and director taking a break from the heat. Note Yul Brynner, of whom the unnamed Israeli journalist wrote, "Such a sour face the Haganah had never seen."

Photographed, unfortunately, *after* Senta took her clothes off.

When we thought the camera was rolling. Ready when you are, C.B.

CHAPTER XXII

A motion picture is a living thing. It has its birth pains and its growing pains, infancy, adolescence, middle age; it becomes an individual, for better or worse, and then comes inevitably to its end. The good pictures become immortal. The rest of them lie, unmourned, in the vast cemetery of the Late, Late Show.

Cast a Giant Shadow was assuming, on celluloid, its own identity. In the banquet hall of the Avia Hotel, where we set up a screen and a projector to view our dailies, run by My Son, The Projectionist, we could see it taking form. It was not what I had put on paper. All of the pressures that were forming it, pressures of time and money and actors and jealousy and hope, were turning it into a series of visual and audible images that had only scant relationship to the actual life of a man named David Marcus. At this stage, as in a child, the seed of the future had already taken root; only much later, when the music and the sound and the editing had been completed, would the child be introduced to the world, and would the proud father learn whether or not it should have been strangled in the womb.

The best pictures are greater than the sum of their parts; when the painstaking job of putting the tiny photographs together has been completed, they can become something much more than was ever intended. Make-believe becomes a new kind of reality, and the absorption of an audience breathes life into what is, after all, only shadow. We share images and insights from our own experience with the people on the screen whom we come to know in ninety-five or one hundred and twenty minutes better than most of our friends and some of our children. Then it is all worthwhile.

I had no intimation, at that time, that there was any chance of failure. Of course, we were spending too much money; of course, the problems of shooting in Israel were mushrooming daily; of course, there was friction between the cast and the director and the crew and the country. But I had been in Rome when William Wyler was directing *Ben Hur*. Everyone was complaining about the waste on the picture, and about Wyler's alleged heartlessness to his crew and his performers. The grumbling grew to such proportions that, the story goes, Wyler lined them all up at Cinecitta one day and spoke to them over a loudspeaker. "I know you all call me a son-of-a-bitch," he said, "but when the picture's a hit, you'll call me 'Daddy.' "

When the picture's a hit.

I can recall the last day of shooting on *Yours, Mine, and Ours*, a film I directed, starring Lucille Ball and Henry Fonda. It concerned a widow with eight children who married a widower with ten, a true story of the eighteen offspring in the Beardsley clan. Lucy, a consummate comedienne and a fine actress, is also a tycoon and president of her own considerable corporation. On her television series, she is quite rightly in control of every element, because her talent, her money, and her knowledge qualify her. She could not quite understand why I chose to rely upon my own knowledge and instinct in directing the motion picture instead of doing things her way. While I agreed her way might have been better, I insisted on making my own mistakes. As one who had directed eighteen hundred Jews, I was not going to be ruled by one red-headed Protestant. The clashes were frequent and bitter, and the production was almost closed down on several occasions. But when we had shot that last closeup, Lucy turned those wonderful eyes in my direction and asked, "Well . . . how did you really like working with me?"

And I answered foolishly, "Lucy, this is the first time I ever made a picture with nineteen children."

She burst into tears. For months after the film was completed, she barely spoke to me.

And then it was released and became a tremendous hit. Now we are friends.

My relations with Kirk Douglas did not quite approach the traumatic depths of my experience with Miss Ball. But *our* picture was not a hit, and I have seen little of Mr. Douglas since.

But we are, I think, friends in a different way. Kirk had made a picture in Israel before, *The Juggler*, from Michael Blankfort's novel, directed by Edward Dmytryk, so his discovery of the meaning of his heritage had preceded mine. But making a movie about a man with the character and force of David Marcus, involved in a war of extinction that is still being fought, left its mark on both of us. Kirk is very much a movie star; he has been one as long as anybody except the Old

INT. KINDERGARTEN—DAY

Mickey (Kirk Douglas) and Asher (Yul Brynner) enter from the hospital area outside.

ASHER—*I must think of my men. You saw yourself. They are worn out.*

They sit in the tiny chairs

MICKEY—*We're all worn out, but we'll do it. We made it across the Red Sea, didn't we?*

ASHER—*Mickey . . . this is the first time I ever heard you say "we."*

MICKEY—*Yeah . . . You people and your pipsqueak nation. Your tin can army that fights with seltzer bottles. All my life I've been looking for where I belong . . . and it turns out it's here, the Catskill Mountains with Arabs. I've been angry at the world ever since I was circumcised without my permission . . . and all of a sudden I've found out I'm not so special after all. Everybody around me here is in the same boat and nobody's bellyaching. Okay. Stand up and be counted, the man said. Grow up is more like it. I'm not fighting any more because I'm ashamed and trying to prove something. I'm fighting because I'm stiff-necked and proud of it. Next week, Asher. Next week in Jerusalem!*

Man of the Eyepatch, Duke Wayne. He has the arrogance of the old Hollywood, born of money and luxury and the rapt attention of his agents, and the reaction to the poverty he came from in Amsterdam, New York. In those pre-Barbra Streisand days, when he battled his way to recognition, being openly Jewish in Hollywood was frowned upon by the Image Makers. The very stage name he picked for himself is an indication of the care with which he planned his future. "Kirk Douglas" does not sound like a fellow who wore a *talis* at his Bar Mitzvah. But in tearing the screenplay apart, we both discovered similarities between ourselves and Mickey—or the character I had written for Mickey. The scene at the left was written after one of our lengthy knock-down-drag-out conferences, and it had as much of the two of us in it as it did of Colonel Marcus. Up until that time, we had both been playacting; we would do our bit for Little Israel and go home, cleansed. But after months of involvement with the place and the time and the people, I think we both realized where home was.

Our *Gemütlichkeit* didn't last very long. Soon we were up in the hills of the Martyr's Forest, where six million trees have been planted to symbolize the six million souls destroyed in Hitler's gas chambers; all night long we were shooting scenes depicting the building of the fantastic Marcus Road by the civilians from Tel Aviv and Jerusalem.

ROAD FROM HULDA—NIGHT

Four bulldozers lead a strange parade of men and women, old and young, in their work clothes, a few children among them, carrying shovels, picks, rakes, baskets.

COMMAND CAR—MED. CLOSE

Mickey (Kirk Douglas) and Ram (Stathis Giallelis) watch them.

MICKEY—*Do they know if the Arab Legion pushes a patrol through and finds out what they're doing, they'll come under artillery fire . . . and worse?*

RAM—*They know.*

MICKEY—*Then why do they come?*

RAM—*I'm still trying to figure out why you came.*

DISSOLVE TO:

BASE OF CLIFF—NIGHT

A weird convoy is on the newly completed section of the Marcus Road being dug out of the mountain, camels, mules, oxcarts, jeeps, loaded with flour

By that time, all the pressures on all of us had taken effect. Kirk and I were bone-weary and tired of the whole thing. Hundreds of extras had to be housed and fed and directed in the darkness and cold of a mountain night. Our inadequate generators and arc lights could not be depended upon to illuminate the scene properly. Our crew, which had worked all day and was now being called upon to work through the night, was near another mutiny. We had bulldozers, camels, donkeys, mules, guns, dynamite charges, pneumatic drills and aerial flares to coordinate. Even Moishe, at my elbow with hot coffee and *knishes,* could not make life bearable. Nate Edwards was frowning at me as the night wore on and we were getting little accomplished. The trees

sacks, canned goods, guns for Jerusa-
lem. The workers make room for them
as they pass. The cargo is transferred
to the backs of half-naked men,
CAMERA PANNING WITH THEM
as they fight their way up the cliffside.
CAMERA PANS to Mickey, watching,
standing outside his tent. He is weary,
dirty, and uncomfortable. He crosses to
one of the camels being unloaded,
stares at it, shaking his head, then con-
tinues to join MacAfee (Gordon
Jackson) who is supervising the trans-
fer of the cargo.

cast eerie shadows, each a
reminder of a lost soul. I was
beginning to feel that I
deserved a tree of my own,
when the group of young
extras who were to climb the
cliffs bearing the supplies
for Jerusalem sent a representative to me to ask for
more money. It seems they
had been told by the extras
who had worked for us the
night before that it was

simple, easy, restful work, and that they would be home by eight o'clock. True, we had finished the preceding night by 7:30, but that was an entirely different scene, and this night we might very well have to work through until dawn. On receiving this information, they went on a sit-down strike.

At the same time, the camels were becoming obstreperous, and Kirk was losing his temper. One of the beasts took a nip at him and Kirk took it as a personal affront. I walked with him into the tent we had set up as part of the scene, and all his pent-up frustration about the picture boiled over. His character was wrong, the dialogue was wrong, and I was wrong. I explained to him a few things that were wrong with *him,* and in our state of nervous exhaustion we were on the verge of going a fast five rounds—an exaggeration, of course; I figured on taking a dive as quickly as possible, because as far as I was concerned, Kirk Douglas was still Middleweight Champion of the World. I was saved from having my blood spilled all over the Martyr's Forest by the entrance of one of our assistant directors, who informed me that our two opposing technical advisers—Colonel Gershon Rivlin and Colonel Shmuel Mohr—had disagreed again. Mohr said they didn't use camels on the road, Rivlin said they did. The camel driver agreed with Mohr and wanted to go home. His camels were freezing. Another representative arrived from the striking climbers and told me their price had now doubled.

I took a deep breath and informed everyone that we were closing down. There would be no more photography that night. Kirk could go home, so could the camels, and the extras could go home and stay there. We would find others to take their place tomorrow night to reenact this triumphant moment in Israel's history.

We folded our tents and started, not too silently, to slip away. Lights sputtered out along the mountain. The road that had been built in reality under the threat of gunfire would not be completed in make-believe because the commander couldn't control his troops. Moishe was opening the door of our car when the representative of the striking climbers rushed to me and said his men had changed their minds: they were willing to work all night at the old prices, for the glory of Israel. I thanked him and said I had been unable to convince the camels. And one stubborn mule.

The next day, I received a handwritten note from Kirk. It was not an apology, it was a note of understanding. And of doubt. He didn't know how we had drifted into opposition, and it was bad for both of us to continue that way. So we made up, in our own fashion, and for the rest of the production we were both kind and cooperative, for the good of the picture.

We might have done better angry.

We had one more contretemps on the mountain before we shot the climactic scene that would end the film. According to the script and history, two United Nations observers were to inspect the road and certify that trucks could actually move along its entire length and that the siege of Jerusalem had indeed been broken. When the two actors playing the roles arrived in a khaki jeep driven by an actor in the role of a Haganah soldier, a storm of protest broke forth, led by one of our two adviser-colonels. Colonel Mohr protested that we must be out of our minds, the two officers weren't wearing United Nations uniforms! Furthermore, the jeep they were driving must be painted white and bear the UN insignia. He was backed up by every expert lined up on the mountain. It looked like a long delay while we located new uniforms and painted the jeep white. Since, the night before, the jeep *had* been painted white and Colonel Rivlin had ordered me to paint it khaki, you can understand my impatience. My two advisers were getting us into the auto-painting business.

Gershon stood by quietly until the shouting had subsided. Then he said, "There were no United Nations uniforms in Jerusalem in those days. The United Nations was too new. The two officers were from the Norwegian Army and wore Norwegian uniforms. There was no United Nations insignia on the jeep because no one knew what the United Nations insignia was."

Everyone turned to look at him, including Colonel Mohr. Gershon looked apologetic.

"I'm sorry," he said, "but you see, *I* was the Haganah man who drove the jeep."

I digested the incredible news that Gershon could drive; furthermore, that he would dare to drive up the side of a cliff that must have been almost impassable.

Gershon sighed about this and explained. They *couldn't* drive up that cliff. The road hadn't been finished in time. There was one short stretch where they had to haul the trucks up by cable for a few days. This was the Israeli Army's final bluff. The United Nations had to be kept from learning the truth; so Gershon, who looked so kind and so innocent, was employed to hoodwink them. They drove to the base of the cliff. They saw trucks coming *down* from Jerusalem. Obviously, the road was completed. They had lunch inside a tent; then they started from the *top* of the cliff, where the jeep had been pulled while they were eating, and continued their journey.

It had been a very nice lunch, Gershon told us. During which he personally had lifted the siege of Jerusalem.

My autographed photo of Lieutenant Colonel Gershon Rivlin describing the day
he drove the jeep on the Marcus Road.

Between two fires in the Martyr's Forest. The director in the middle of his technical advisors. At the left, Lieutenant Colonel Shmuel Mohr; at the right, Lieutenant Colonel Gershon Rivlin. Left center, Stathis Giallelis.

CHAPTER XXIII

A SECTION OF THE ROAD—DAY
Work is going on as usual as some
battered trucks make their way through
the dust. A formation of the Haganah
marches along the roadside, Safir
(James Donald) at the head. Suddenly
the trucks pull to a halt, the workers
straighten up and turn to look. Safir
stops and follows their gaze.

THE CLIFF—FULL SHOT
A line of trucks winding up the pre-
cipitous road chiseled into the cliffside
has halted. To one side of the road, a
jeep is being lowered down the steep
slope by ropes. In the rear of the jeep
is a plain wooden coffin. Asher Gonen
(Yul Brynner) is walking behind it,
with an Honor Guard of the Haganah.

CLOSE SHOT—SAFIR
As he watches.

THE JEEP—CLOSE SHOT

CAMERA MOVES WITH THE JEEP
down the cliffside, passing the halted,
silent trucks and workers. We reach an
open truck loaded with boys and girls
of the Palmach, Ram (Stathis Giallelis)
seated beside the driver. Ram climbs
out of the truck and runs toward the
jeep. He unpins the colored ribbons on

Every available old truck in
the Tel Aviv area had been
put at our disposal; the army
supplied us with hundreds of
men and we had hired
hundreds of extras. This was
it, the finale of the picture,
our last big outdoor scene
in Israel, the one in which
the convoys moved tri-
umphantly up the road to
Jerusalem hacked out of the
sides of mountains, paused
while the trucks were hauled
up that one uncompleted
sheer drop, and continued on
to the Holy City; the morning
after Colonel David Marcus
had been shot through the
head at the tiny, picturesque
monastery of Notre Dame
at the top of the mountain.

As Mickey's plain coffin,
in the back of a jeep, descended the makeshift road
against the traffic, inside it
should have been about one
million dollars of our budget.
That's how much more than

*his shoulder and places them on the
coffin, then turns quickly back to the
truck.*

*NEAR TRUCK—MED. SHOT
Ram shouts something in Hebrew as he
climbs back on the truck. He motions
everyone forward and the column starts
to move. Ram stands on the running
board. One of the girls starts to sing the
hora we heard earlier, in a clear
soprano voice. But now the melody is
heard andante, sadly, the bright song
now a lament. Ram shouts at her in
Hebrew, and in a moment the others
take up the song, increasing the tempo,
clapping out the rhythm, changing the
mood until it becomes a melody of
triumph, echoing throughout the wadi.
It is taken up by some of the workers
as the CAMERA PANS to reveal:*

*THE CONVOY—FULL SHOT
It winds down and down the mountain
below us and far back along the incredible road from Kibbutz Hulda, the
trucks loaded with supplies, many of
them painted with one word:*

JERUSALEM!

*Only one vehicle is moving in the
opposite direction: Mickey's jeep. But
the song of triumph continues. Over
this we hear the SOUND of a
telegraph key and:*

BEN GURION'S VOICE—(*Luther Adler*)
*Mrs. David Marcus, Westminster
Road, Brooklyn, New York. Your husband fell last night at his post in the
hills of Jerusalem, the last casualty*

planned we had now buried
in the production. Never send
to know for whom the bell
tolls; it is usually for United
Artists.

The genesis of the scene
that was being enacted had
occurred all those months ago
when Rivlin had introduced
me to General Vivyan
Herzog. Herzog had recalled
the nights of tension while
the people of Israel were carv-
ing the road out of the cliffs
under the noses of the Arab
Legion—and the moment of
triumph when it was
announced that it had been
completed and the way
opened to Jerusalem.

Herzog was trudging up
that road, whose counter-
part our crew had counter-
feited for the film, carrying
in his hand a sack of four
chickens for his father.
These were a gift from nine
men who had been saved
from prison by the Chief
Rabbi, and at the time
were worth their weight in
gold. All about him were
soldiers and civilians and
supplies on their way to
the newly liberated city. The
atmosphere was one of
happiness and victory.

before the truce. As a man and a commander he endeared himself to all those who came into personal contact with him. His name will live forever in the annals of our people.

There is a change in Ben Gurion's voice now; he is no longer the Prime Minister.

BEN GURION'S VOICE—*Emma. He was the best man we had.*

The trucks continue up Mickey's mountain. Mickey's jeep disappears in the distance. The SONG RISES TO A DRIVING CRESCENDO.

FADE OUT.

SHALOM

As he rounded a bend, Herzog saw a jeep being lowered by ropes down the side of a cliff, the only vehicle moving away from Jerusalem. It contained Mickey's plain board coffin.

The General wept.

I attempted, in some measure, to reconstruct that moment for the finale of *Cast a Giant Shadow*. Perhaps, in the midst of all our trucks and extras and crew and kibitzers and Elmer Bernstein's wonderful but overpowering music,

what had moved Herzog, and what had moved me when I heard him tell of it, had somehow gotten lost, fallen off the mountain, and all that was left were those four chickens, busily laying an egg.

As I stood on top of the mountain in the Martyr's Forest that day, I looked down at the hundreds of men and dozens of trucks which could not move because one of the trucks had just broken an axle; Aldo Tonti, behind me, was berating one of his sons for having ruined the last take by the hackneyed method of forgetting to put film in the camera; and one of the assistant directors brought me the happy tidings that there was a mutiny in the crew again because something was moving inside the box lunches. I knew then how much more I could have accomplished had I attempted to do much less; and I reflected that Colonel David Marcus would be alive today if he had taken enough time from his other tasks to learn Hebrew.

Neither he nor I had understood the lesson which had created a nation—all that matters is Survival.

CHAPTER XXIV

We were coming to the close of our Hebraic odyssey, and some of our crew members were already leaving to prepare for the resumption of shooting in Italy when I was honored by a visit from My Son, The Assistant Director. Pardon me. By now he was My Son, The Photographer, having discovered that assistant directing took too much out of him for him to fully enjoy the pleasures of the Avia Hotel. At the height of the season, new stewardesses were arriving every hour on the hour, and he was falling behind schedule. So he wangled himself a job with Eliot Elisofon, the *Life* Magazine genius, herring-lover, and salad-maker. While my son never learned much about photography, he did learn how to chill lettuce. Also, his knowledge of Israel and Judaism, skimpy when he arrived, had grown by leaps and bounds, especially after he got himself promoted to Chief Escort for Miss Israel when she visited our production. He kept telling me how happy he was he had escaped the clutches of an American girl and been enabled to broaden his horizons. American girls expect the world on a platter, he informed me, while a European or Israeli young lady knows how to cherish, pamper, and cater to her man in every way, obviously the correct attitude.

The reason for the visit from My Son, The Assistant Film Editor— by this time, needless to say, having learned to make Roquefort dressing, he had no further need of Mr. Elisofon—was to tell me that, at last, he had found his *métier*, his *raison d'être*. For the last few weeks he had been working in our cutting room, aiding in the splicing and editing of the film, and had decided this was the ideal way to spend the rest of his life. I pointed out to him that the other two assistants with whom he labored in a narrow and darkened room, were enjoyably young and extremely female. I suspected his relationship with both of them had somehow influenced his decision. Some day he would see them out in the light and decide he had picked the wrong future.

I had no firm opposition to anyone seeking a career in the motion picture industry as long as he had another career to fall back on in the event the film business decided it might be chic to commit suicide as it has many times in the past. So I suggested, in clear Anglo-Saxon terminology, that it was time for him to return to the United States and pick up the threads of his academic career, which he had abandoned after four long weeks in law school.

Reluctantly, he left for home when we finished production and applied for admission to graduate school for the study of psychology, for which he was eminently prepared after three months with the Israelis. We received a smug letter from him, telling us that he had met the young lady with whom he had had his falling out before leaving for Israel, explained to her how his eyes had been opened by his acquaintance with other, more international females, and told her, as gently as possible, that he could never be satisfied with a narrow-minded American girl again.

The next week we received another letter, in which he stated that anyone is entitled to make a mistake, and could we be home in time for the wedding?

After twelve weeks of basic training in the land of my fathers, he married the most beautiful, determined, red-headed, lovable *shiksa* you ever saw. It was a civil ceremony, my son not wishing to run the risk of having to face a Bad Rabbi, who might insist on a Hassidic honeymoon.

From then on his wife took over his career, which rapidly resulted in his becoming an expert on lunar simulation, his employment on the Apollo Project, and his securing a Ph.D. from Stanford University and a post on its distinguished faculty. I take no credit for any of his achievements now, except for his ability to make salad dressing. After all his strenuous efforts to find the proper exotic sphere for his talents, he has become, prosaically, My Son, The Doctor.

My Son the Arab and Miss Israel. (*Zinn Arthur*)

Luther Adler at the Herzlia Studio delivering Ben Gurion's declaration of the independence of the State of Israel to twenty or thirty dropouts from the Screen Extras Guild of Israel pretending to be two hundred.

CHAPTER XXV

It was time to leave Israel. Not that we had finished shooting the picture. Far from it. It was time to leave Israel because we had run over our shooting schedule, and the Avia Hotel was throwing us out of our rooms. No entreaties, no pleading with the government could hold back the solid stream of tourists who had booked our accommodations months in advance. One room unvacated would back up a line of irate Americans through the waiting rooms at Fiumicino, Orly, London, and Kennedy airports. Boeing 707s would be stacked, wing tip to wing tip, halfway around the globe.

Frantic arrangements were made to build the fortress of Iraq Suidan at Cinecitta so we could finish shooting our battle scenes there, with the Alban Hills above Rome substituting for the hills of Jerusalem. Italian extras were being recruited to battle to the death as Jews and Arabs.

Our friends in the Israeli Defense Forces had arranged a little going-away present for us. They had reserved the right to review all of our film before it was shipped out of Israel. However, since, as I have mentioned, color negative could not be processed in their country, we were allowed to ship it to Rome, where it happily remained, and only the positive film was shipped back into Israel for Army censorship. This is obviously akin to closing the barn door after the horse is stolen, but it preserved face on both sides.

The Army insisted on screening every foot of film shipped back, a process which required, to their horror, some seven dreary hours in a projection room.

After due military deliberation, the Israeli Defense Forces commanded us to correct the following, and I quote:

> *In Scene 327, the girl with a flowery skirt doing the Hora is completely out of step. Change this.*

In Scene 634, the men are running too fast.
In Reel 60, Magda's fingernails, as she is standing by the car, are too neatly done.
Reel 59, the whole theme of chasing a chicken under fire is unreal.

I suppose if you are running an army, no detail is too small to escape military scrutiny. The girl in the *hora* who was out of step might have been tapping out a message to a co-conspirator. The men who were running too fast were, obviously, guilty of something. Running too fast is liable to get you shot almost anywhere in the world. The fingernails were a dead giveaway that Magda had microfilm concealed under them. And an Israeli chicken, when chased, does not flee. Our chicken was obviously an infiltrator.

The remainder of the Army's criticisms were a little less amusing. They concerned obvious flaws in the film's concept that none of us were prepared to face, any more than the fleeing chicken had been prepared to face enemy fire. We brushed them aside. Let the Israeli Army fight its wars, let *us* win our Academy Awards.

The rest is history.

We had one final scene for the Army to find fault with before we left the country—the reenactment of David Ben Gurion's dramatic announcement of the creation of the State of Israel on May 15, 1948. This had taken place before a meeting of the People's Council in the Rothschild Museum, while Arab forces were already on the attack.

For this scene we built a set representing the interior of the museum, on the only sound stage in Israel. That is, we were told it was a sound stage; although it had been completed years before, with all the equipment installed, no one had ever had the temerity to shoot sound on it. I stood on the stage and clapped my hands together and listened critically to the reverberations, but I was assured that it had been pronounced perfect for the recording of sound by a professor from the University of Jerusalem, who had also applauded on that same spot.

When I inquired why no one had ever used it for recording, the answer was a shrug. What Israeli director would listen to a professor from the University of Jerusalem? If he was so smart, why wasn't he making movies?

We decided to risk it, but not before we had pointed out two slight flaws in the construction of the studio. In an effort to keep out sound, the huge doors of the stage closed on hinges like those of a bank vault. It took a safe-cracker to get them open, and when they *were* open, it was necessary to lay planks over the somewhat corrugated entrance to get equipment in and out. I explained that, in Hollywood, the doors were counterbalanced, and slid vertically up and down with the touch of a hand. The owners of the studio promised to look into that. It might work.

Furthermore, while the temperature in Herzlia, where the studio is located, was running close to 100 degrees, the only way to ventilate the stage was to leave the doors open and wave newspapers. This is not a wise thing to do when recording, unless you want to include on the sound track the noise of traffic, the local chickens, and the screams from the budget department next door.

It was explained to me that the stage had been designed very care-fully for the installation of air-conditioning equipment, but the owners had spent so much money on the design they didn't have any left for the equipment. No one had yet dropped dead from heat prostration during shooting, but, of course, no one had yet closed the doors.

It took considerable argument from us and a little coercion from the government before a hole was chopped in one wall and a fan in-stalled. The fan made so much noise it could not be run while record-ing sound. The temperature on the stage kept climbing.

We had created an indoor Negev.

And something more. In Hollywood, the hiring of extras is done wholesale. There is a fixed price for human beings on the hoof, set by the Screen Extras Guild. A producer merely sends in an order for two dozen effete, intellectual types for cocktail party sequence, forty careless-type girls with zippers for orgy scene, or one gross of falling-off-horse-type Indians for John Wayne picture. Several times this num-ber show up, the producer or director or their assistants select the ones they want, and the job is done. In Israel there was no Guild. Each extra had to be met with, bargained with, and contracted for indi-vidually.

The time it took to hire, at retail, two hundred highly individual-istic intellectual-type Hebrew extras to play the members of the

People's Council was astronomical. It was finally done; they crowded onto the baking sound stage to take their places in their seats as we prepared to film one of the truly climactic moments in the history of a people who would just as soon not have any more climaxes, thank you.

Everyone in our crew was affected by the moment. Here was our final scene in Israel, and there on the stage was that talented actor, Luther Adler, delivering Ben Gurion's ringing words:

> *We have been told that if we go through with our plan, this city of Tel Aviv will be bombed tonight by an enemy air force. They might come over in great strength and as yet we are not equipped to meet such an attack. We have also received word that the United Nations would like to revise its decision granting us independence. We consider their original decision to be irrevocable.*

Our two hundred individual contractors applauded and cheered wildly. Luther continued:

> *Accordingly, we, members of the People's Council, here assembled on the day of the termination of the British Mandate and by virtue of our national and historic right and on the strength of the resolution of the United Nations General Assembly, hereby declare the establishment of the State of Israel.*

Pandemonium. Our extras sprang to their feet and cheered again wildly, happily, as the orchestra struck up *Hatikvah*, the national anthem. They pounded each other on the back as they sang. Tears streamed down their faces; the reality of the moment touched all of us.

When the cameras had stopped rolling, I thanked the extras for their work, and informed them they could wait outside where it was cooler—night had fallen, we were shooting late to complete the last sequence—while the set was turned around. This, technically, meant that the lights and cameras were to be moved to photograph the scene from another angle.

Half an hour later, Aldo and the technicians had completed their labors and we were ready to begin again. I sent word for our intelligent extras to return.

No one showed up.

A few minutes later, I was approached by a committee, one of whose members introduced himself as the President of the Israeli Screen Extras Guild.

"But there is no Israeli Screen Extras Guild!" I informed him.

"That was half an hour ago," he told me intelligently. "There is now."

I felt as if I were back in the Martyr's Forest. I probably was. But *this* mutiny was no haphazard affair. The Israeli Screen Extras Guild had not only organized itself in thirty minutes and elected a president, it had also set up a scale of prices; these, needless to say, were triple what they had contracted for as individuals, but what good is a union if it can't improve the lot of the downtrodden? They also felt that this was a particularly good time to form a union, as they had already been photographed in half the scene, and we would obviously need the same faces for the other half. Besides, wasn't this our last night in Israel?

It was then that I delivered to them my own Declaration of Independence. While I admired their initiative, I disapproved of their timing. No one who was unwilling to work at the scale negotiated in good faith would be allowed on the sound stage. If this meant that the People's Council of the State of Israel would be reduced to two members, so be it. Someone would have to rewrite history.

And then I ordered the bank vault doors—which had now become somewhat symbolic—firmly closed.

About twenty members of the new Screen Extras Guild decided they had been members too long, and declared their willingness to resign and work. Having already had the experience of making four tanks resemble the Israeli tank corps, I arranged them and the camera as artfully as possible to hide the fact that one hundred and eighty members of the group that had earlier affirmed the independence of Israel were missing. The twenty remaining couldn't weep as effectively, but I felt my own tears would make up the deficit.

We finished the scene and our production in the Holy Land.

Immediately afterward, we had arranged for a farewell party to be held on the set for our cast and crew, an American-style party with Arab watermelon and Israeli beer. It was a gay and festive occasion, albeit underlined with sadness at leaving this frustrating, brave little country. There was a ceremony during which the owners of the studio presented me with a silver chalice with the inspired inscription:

TO M. SH.
OUR FIRST PRODUCER IN THE HERTZLIA
FILM STUDIOS
JULY, '65

I was a little startled as the implication of that inscription hit me. The studios had been built in 1963. That meant that no one had ever shot a picture there, sound *or* silent, until we had risked our necks. Guess who had paid for that lovely silver chalice.

After recovering from this shock, I noted that the festivities were a little more festive than we had planned. People were everywhere, drinking beer, laughing, congratulating each other, celebrating happily. Too many people. It dawned on me that we had been honored by the presence of the entire 180 remaining members of the newly created Israeli Screen Extras Guild. The president came over and told me what a fine party it was, all his constituents were enjoying it hugely, but the beer was a little warm. Also, some of the watermelon was overripe.

There is a Hebrew word called *chutzpah,* which for centuries has been explained thusly to the Gentile world: if a fellow should murder his mother and father and then claim the mercy of the court because he is an orphan, *that,* ladies and gentlemen, is *chutzpah.*

And that, ladies and gentlemen, is Israel.

Without it, this tiny nation would be beneath the waters of the Red Sea.

Without a Screen Extras Guild.

CHAPTER XXVI

The little house in Savyon was closed up, the huge antenna leaning sadly against the roof with the patch in the shape of a unit manager. The antenna had been donated to the Electronics Department at Bar-Elan University, which showed up promptly six months later to claim it. The green Volkswagen camper had been shipped to Rome to await our arrival, redolent with salad dressing and rye bread and memories. Yaakov the Electrician had kicked the fuse box, turning off the electricity. Moishe had arrived in the company car, washed and combed and wearing, for the first time in his life, a tie he had borrowed from a friend.

The Israelis are an extremely sentimental people who make a business of denying it. But even Moishe had been openly touched at the party the previous night, when Nate Edwards, ten-gallon hat firmly emplaced on his head, had risen to his feet and, in a voice choked with emotion, mumbled something unintelligible to the assembled crew. After considerable argument, it was finally agreed that what he had been attempting to say was "Shalom." To this day, Israel has won no more difficult victory.

Moishe drove us to Lydda Airport, past the home of the chief of the Arab underground, who had just blown up the train to Haifa. I waved at him sentimentally. As we passed the Avia Hotel, the Arab watermelon guard was folding his tent and preparing to silently steal away to his next job as a cantaloupe guard; twenty or thirty stewardesses in bikinis were wandering about, obviously desolated since the departure of my son; the Bad Rabbi was on duty, shouting commands in the kitchen and breaking ketchup bottles; three cars, whose owners had bought the road, tried to hit us at an intersection and ran into a ditch as Moishe deftly avoided them.

It was a touching moment.

At the airport was Lieutenant Colonel Gershon Rivlin, bloodthirsty hero of the underground; he had brought flowers. Nehemia was there with Menehama, who had brought a *kugel.* Asher Hirschberg was driving to meet us from Jerusalem, and was due to be towed in any minute. Actors were there, and actresses, and the cameraman who had forgotten to start the camera at Palmahim Beach. And our maid was there.

I haven't mentioned her before, because she showed up late in our stay. She was an old woman who spoke only Ladino. This language is the Yiddish of the Mediterranean, spoken mainly by descendants of refugees from the Spanish Inquisition. Our maid, whose name I never learned, had apparently come to Israel from Turkey, and she was cheerful and capable and completely confused. My wife, of course, spoke Ladino to her immediately and they got along famously. But our maid was too shy to mention that she wanted to come to the airport to see us off. So she had walked the four-and-a-half miles in the blazing heat. Unsentimentally, of course.

Moishe fought off a swarm of porters and hoisted our considerable luggage to his broad shoulders as if they were filled with duck feathers. He swore colorfully in Hebrew at a few passengers who got in his way and battled his way to the baggage counter. He inquired if I wanted some ice cream, or somebody slugged, or if my wife would like a cold drink. Gently, we turned him down. Then he looked around carefully, to be certain that no one could witness his breaking the code of the Sabra, and said, very quietly, "Never in my whole life have I known love before," and turned quickly away and left us.

The 707 rose swiftly from the airstrip, and in three minutes we could see below us from border to border and coast to coast. To be honest, you could see *that* from the Lydda Control Tower, but it is more impressive from the air—the green of the fields where the desert once stood; the row upon row of kosher hotels; the Happy Hassidim, no doubt still in their black coats and fur hats in the middle of July; the *kibbutzim* with their *metapeleths;* people shoving their neighbors out of their way in the queues at the meat markets; the arguments and the shouting and the Overseas Operator quoting the latest delay;

the mailmen rushing to their brokers' offices; the Army that includes Aunt Becky—in short, the entire unworkable, unmanageable, incredible, defiant nation which refuses to disappear.

Even when you make a bad picture about it.

I had learned many things about the country and about my family; but mainly about myself. For the picture was a financial disaster, into which I poured almost three years of my life. But I would gladly do it again, if I ever found anyone courageous enough to give me another $5 million, for I had been given an insight and a pride in my own people, their history and their aspirations, their stubbornness and their gentleness, their kindness and their irritating aggressiveness; and this had come, finally, to one who had been only vaguely conscious—and resentful—of his heritage.

I had failed. But I had had the *chutzpah* to try.

I was one of Them.

Hey, Rabbi, wait for Baby!

POSTSCRIPT

Ａnd so we arrived in Rome, the lovely city on the Tiber from which had come the Legions which had torn down the Temple of Solomon, dispersed my people to the ends of the earth, and made it necessary for them to establish the UJA to get back. Previously, my experiences while shooting films in Italy had seemed reckless adventures; after Israel, the Italians appeared as calm and reasonable people, their penchant for petty larceny the amusing antics of lovable children.

And there was no Bad Rabbi supervising my *lasagna al forno.*

It was to Rome that John Wayne reported, boisterously recovered from his dramatic illness, to wade his way through Italian nightclubs and World War II battle scenes with equal vigor.

AT COMMAND CAR—(FLASH-BACK)
Mickey and General Randolph (John Wayne) climb out of the car. A group of officers and GIs has been waiting for them. There is something almost eerie about the appearance of the area, the unusual silence of the GIs, and the fact that the only sound that can be heard is the distant rumble of the artillery. The group continues toward the barbed wire surrounding the gate. CAMERA PANS to a sign on a wall reading:

DACHAU

TWO SHOT—MICKEY AND RANDOLPH

There are those who will always say that Duke's Academy Award was a sentimental tribute that had nothing to do with Wayne's histrionic ability. Don't you believe it. Look at the army of his imitators, most of whom are pumping gas now. His greatest achievement is making an audience believe that he is not acting, that what they are looking at on the screen is the *real* John Wayne, just being himself. *Himself* happens to be a cheerful, right-wing but

225

CAMERA PRECEDES THEM. We sense rather than see what is going on in B. G. What is in front of them we never see.

MICKEY—*Those that are alive weigh an average of eighty-five pounds . . .*

CAMERA MOVES TO AN EX-TREME CLOSE SHOT OF RAN-DOLPH. All we see are his eyes and the three stars on his helmet.

MICKEY'S VOICE—*And here are three thousand two hundred corpses, as near as we can tell, that they didn't have time to bury . . .*

What is mirrored in Randolph's eyes tells the whole story. After a moment he turns to one of his officers.

RANDOLPH—*McGreedy. Give this insubordinate son-of-a-bitch every god-damn truck and blanket in the Third Army and I don't care who you have to steal them from.*

He turns quickly away.

kind-hearted old actor with nineteen grandchildren. He once told me his most comforting victory was his ten-year-straight-no-options contract with Paramount. "Do you realize," he said, "they'll have to pay me over half a million dollars just to step on a sound stage when I'm seventy-one years old?"

The scene at the left is one that was based on Colonel Marcus's World War II encounter with General George Patton, after Mickey had participated in the liberation of one of the first of the Nazi concentration camps to be exposed to Allied view. It depended for effect entirely on what John Wayne, the actor, could convey to an audience with his eyes. It worked. After

all, he had twice as many eyes to act with as he did in winning the Oscar.

Along with Wayne, Angie Dickinson arrived to play the role of Emma Marcus. Angie was lovely and cooperative and newly married to a songwriter named Burt Bacharach, whom no one but Angie had heard very much about. Her role was relatively minor, compared to Senta Berger's, but Angie took it all in good grace until the matter of billing came up. Then there were considerable fireworks, at the end of which she was not speaking to her agent or to me or to anyone named Mirisch.

Still, in spite of all the problems that developed, shooting in Italy didn't have the *tam*—a Hebrew word inadequately translated as "flavor"—of our Israeli saga, although the Italians tried hard. First of all, to complete the battle sequence at the rebuilt Latrun fortress, the Italian Army had promised to supply us with flamethrowers and tanks. Suddenly, the promise was rescinded. The rumor was that, again, Arab diplomacy and the Italian need for Arabian oil to keep all those Ferraris running had something to do with it.

The tanks we could build out of plywood and old Fiats, but the flamethrowers were an absolute necessity, and all appeared lost until one of our Italian aides revealed that he knew the secret *amore* of the owner of the flamethrower factory. It seemed odd to me that love and flamethrowers had any connection, but a brief reflection on the heat of Italian passion convinced me I might be wrong. The *amore* convinced the factory owner—by what means, I did not inquire—that the honor of Italy was at stake. At any rate, the flamethrowers, flamethrower experts, and protective equipment showed up promptly on the back lot at Cinecitta. It seems that each flamethrower must be tested adequately before delivery to the Italian army, and the owner of the factory had merely decided it would be convenient to test them on our set. They worked beautifully. I was sorely tempted to write a testimonial and mail it to the Italian General Staff, but cooler heads prevailed.

The final, climactic night of shooting took place in the Alban Hills, where we staged an Arab-Israeli battle that shook the heavens with the explosions of Italian fireworks, which we had purchased from a factory nearby. The shouts of Italian "Arabs" cursing at Italian "Israelis," who cursed back, echoed through the olive groves and pimiento fields. Four cameras turned simultaneously as the Arab armies tried to overwhelm the tiny Israeli force protecting Mickey's secret "Burma Road," only to be thrown back time and again on command of the director. The last shot was concluded at 3:00 A.M., after which we all drove back to Rome in a cloudburst which turned into the worst flood in a century, almost isolating the city for days. We didn't mind. The picture was finished.

It was only then that we discovered that all the film from the main camera photographing the battle sequence had disappeared. I recalled ominously a story Danny Kaye had once told me of the last day's shooting in Marseilles of *Me and the Colonel*. Following the conclusion of photography, all the stars had left for their various countries;

the producer, William Goetz, was awakened in his room at the George V in Paris by a voice which informed him that the truck carrying the negative of the last day's shooting had been hijacked, and that it would be returned for the paltry sum of $250,000. The late Mr. Goetz, not a man to be trifled with, rose up in righteous wrath, refused to pay a penny, recalled, at tremendous expense, every actor in the sequence, and returned to Marseilles and reshot the scene in its entirety, carrying the exposed negative back to Paris clutched to his breast. It was, as Mr. Kaye proudly explained to me, a truly noble and courageous gesture. The fact that the sequence they reshot was the first to be cut from the picture after the preview was inconsequential.

I had visions of some similar expensive stratagem. We waited expectantly for the ransom call. It never came. The Rome police were called in, and went to work diligently, with absolutely no result, although we did get the addresses of some good Italian restaurants.

Then, one day, we received an irate telephone call from a movie studio that specialized in short subjects.

There were Jews chasing Arabs through their cartoons!

What had actually happened took several days and considerable Chianti to unravel. Some influential official in Rome had a relative who was unemployed. He had persuaded our production staff to hire him as a fourth assistant camera loader, a position equivalent to being Secretary of Mental Health under Adolf Hitler. It was assumed he would be called upon to perform no duty more strenuous than reaching for his weekly check. But the relative had reckoned without the *pazzo* American director, who had decided to use *four* cameras simultaneously, requiring even the fourth assistant camera loader to load a movie camera. Since he had never seen one before, this proved somewhat of a challenge. He almost strangled himself in 35mm film before one of the other assistants helped him out. But, through some oversight, he was allowed to *un*load the camera all by his little lonesome. Now, a reel of film is not always run completely through the camera. It is necessary to open the camera, send the exposed film on the back reel to the laboratory to be developed, and place the unexposed film from the front reel in a box so it might be used later.

Only someone so incredibly foolish he could not tell the front of a camera from the back could make a mistake.

Enter the relative.

The unexposed film had been sent to the laboratory to be developed. The exposed film had been labeled "unexposed short end." Nate Edwards, watching every dime, had sold all our unexposed film after the picture was completed to an Italian cartoon studio. But this unexposed film wasn't exactly unexposed; it was in a condition similar to being a little bit pregnant. The studio had photographed their animated drawings on negative that had already been at our Battle for Jerusalem. Ergo: live Jews chasing live Arabs through Italian cartoons.

Although photography on the film had been completed—or so we thought—there still remained the months of editing, dubbing, and scoring that always become the interminable anticlimax to the weeks of intensive pressure before the cameras. The difference, of course, is that it no longer costs $12,000 a minute for the director to change his mind. But anticlimax in Rome, with an apartment on the Via Marguta and a car and chauffeur on the tab of the production, is more than tolerable. After several pleasurable anticlimactic months, we brought the film and the sound track back to America and ran it at the Samuel Goldwyn Studios—and discovered that almost everything we had recorded in Israel was unusable. Our American sound equipment had been in the hands of a British sound crew who swore they were familiar with its operation; the only way I had been able to hear the results of the recording was on a pair of headphones, or on our inadequate speakers at the Avia Hotel. Played back on the huge theater speakers in Hollywood, it was quite evident that something was wrong.

It was necessary to record most of the dialogue all over again. Frank Sinatra and Kirk Douglas relived the Israeli war on a recording stage in Hollywood; Yul Brynner and Senta Berger did the same in London. But even the background sounds and the crowd noises had to be done over—and in Hebrew. Fortunately, in Hollywood there is a large colony of young Israelis, attending the various universities and, at the same time, attempting to break into the film industry. Some of them, I understand, have been trying to break in for eight or nine years. We recruited dozens of them to help recreate the sounds of home. I would stand on the recording stage, headset to my ears, and listen as they shouted and harangued each other in their native tongue; it was like being back in the wheat fields at Iraq Suidan or the blistering sands of the Negev. I would often turn involuntarily, expecting to see Moishe at my elbow with a glass of seltzer.

All of us still had our hopes high; whatever little faults we could find with the film would soon be cured by intelligent editing and by reshooting a few little scenes—in London, this time, where Elmer Bernstein also recorded the music.

Then we were ready for a few private showings. Harold Mirisch sat beside me at the first running, squeezing my arm approvingly, forgetting how I had been squeezing his bankroll. There was a special showing in Palm Springs for some of his close friends, and another in New York for the close friends of the president of United Artists. Everyone seemed pleased.

We even arranged to have Haym Topol fly over from Tel Aviv to promote our film, appearing on the television show Danny Kaye had on CBS at the time. Haym came over eagerly, moved into my house, and then inquired if Danny Kaye knew who he was.

I thought this was a little matter of ego, so I assured him Danny knew his work well. Haym shook his head. His *work,* that was one thing, but would Danny punch him in the nose?

What for?

Well, Haym explained, there was a little thing that had happened in Israel a long time ago. A very little thing. Kaye had come there to entertain the Israeli Army after the Sinai campaign. At that time, Haym was in the army, with a little theatrical troupe which put on satirical sketches for the soldiers. Word spread that Danny was a smashing success, which naturally troubled Haym's sensitive Israeli soul. He sent scouts to preview Danny's act at another army camp, then spent a frantic twenty-four hours writing and rehearsing a routine of his own satirizing Danny as a performer and including a considerable amount of Mr. Kaye's own precious material.

When Danny arrived at the camp, Haym went on ahead of him and killed the audience, in Hebrew, with some of Danny's best jokes. Then out stepped Mr. Kaye, who had not been paying close attention. He laid a bomb so large it would have supported the Israeli military effort for a war and a half. He was startled, hurt, and, when he learned the truth, homicidal. He was prepared to recircumcise Mr. Topol at both ends. But Mr. Topol had prudently left camp, and had not planned to see Mr. Kaye again, ever. Until today.

Disturbed, I inquired why Haym hadn't informed me of all this before accepting his round trip ticket.

It was, Haym declared, because of his intense desire to do all he could to help our wonderful picture succeed. And to get a free trip to America.

Underwhelmed by his honesty, I accompanied him hesitantly to the studio where the show was to go into rehearsal. Danny was waiting. He took one look at Haym and threw his arms around him. Why hadn't Haym told him who he really was? Seeing him in the film, made up as an old Arab, Kaye had no idea Topol was the talented performer he had met in Israel while entertaining the army! They became bosom friends. Kaye invited Topol to his house where he cooked, with his own hands, one of his fabulous Chinese dinners, which Haym was afraid to touch for fear it contained strychnine gai pan. It gradually dawned on Haym that either Danny Kaye was the most forgiving comedian in the world, or he had only the vaguest notion of *which* Israeli soldier Haym had been. He must have met hundreds who were also performers. Haym never enlightened him, and their friendship bloomed.

Then, when it was time for Haym to go on the air on Danny's television show, he found that all his best lines had been switched to Mr. Kaye.

To this day, Haym is not certain if this was revenge or just show biz.

Shortly after the television show broadcast, *Cast a Giant Shadow* opened on Broadway at the De Mille Theater. The advertising department, evidently having come to the startling conclusion that nobody wanted to see a picture about a Jewish general, eliminated from national advertising all mention of the nation of Israel, the War of Liberation, the Jews, or Colonel Mickey Marcus.

In spite of that, at the end of the film opening night, the audience in the theater stood up and cheered. I believed them, forgetting they had all bought Israel Bonds to get in. The New York *Daily News* gave it **** and called it a rousing adventure story, a drama of historical significance. The *World Telegram* shouted, "This is a searing, almost hysterically partisan drama . . . Kirk Douglas overwhelms role and opponents with sheer, magnetic force of personality . . . This picture is like that widely advertised rye bread. You don't have to be Jewish to enjoy it and be swept into its seething frenzy." But, the critic might have added, it helps.

As the movie opened around the country, the Chicago *Daily News* reviewed it as, "A crackling, first-rate drama . . . a model of intelligent evaluation . . . crisp, intelligent screenplay . . . as producer, director, and writer, Shavelson has shown he is a gifted filmmaker who can be trusted with modern history." I almost moved to Chicago. And Arthur Knight wrote in the *Saturday Review* that it ". . . manages to convey more of the complexities and crosscurrents attendant upon the birth of Israel . . . than do most conventional histories or the even more conventional historical novels on the subject. . . . Most remarkable of all . . . is its constant, and fascinating, explication of military tactics, so that the deployment of men, guns, and tanks is never merely pictorial, but part of the working out of a grand strategy whose logic and necessity have already been grasped. . . . While these are all virtues of script, Shavelson has also distinguished himself as a director. His big action scenes have not only scope, but focus; one is never at a loss to understand what is going on . . . Even better, however, is the restraint of his vignettes. . . ." But why go on? After that, he only mentions the actors.

You might wonder, in the light of the above, why the movie did not earn a fortune and a trunkful of Oscars for everyone concerned. The truth is that a motion picture is a highly subjective experience, a mirror which each of us sees from a different angle, depending upon what we have brought to it. There were other critics, small, venal men who were swayed by such low considerations as honesty and integrity and their measured artistic judgment. They tore the picture to shreds, and the public, the final arbiter, agreed with them by staying away in droves.

Next time, gentlemen. Next time. But not in Jerusalem.

The director and Angie Dickinson discussing her billing at an airfield near Rome.

Kirk and Angie in bed again between love scenes. If every wife had a make-up man beside the nuptial couch, the divorce rate would take a sharp drop.

At Coney Island on the Tiber. Lucille is driving.

Cinecitta. Angie and director in our Coney Island set that never reached the
screen.

Near Rome. John Wayne playing John Wayne.

John Wayne and Aldo Tonti. Aldo is the one on the right.

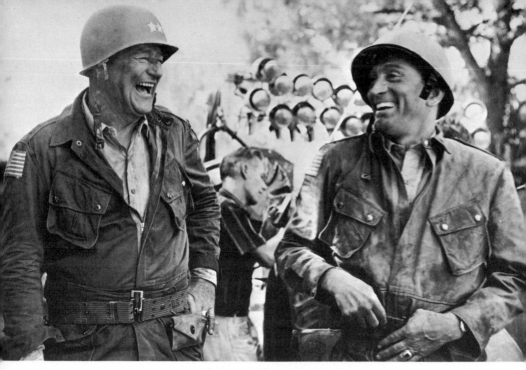

Wayne and Douglas discussing their salaries.

Dachau, constructed at Cinecitta. Wayne, as a counterpart of General George Patton, being given his first view of the concentration camp by Kirk, as Colonel Marcus.

Shortly after the Six Day War, I returned to the scene of the crime, mainly to see if they would let me in. No antiaircraft guns fired at the plane, and I realized that, by that time, Nasser must have taken my place in Israeli hearts.

Nothing seemed to have changed very much. Gershon Rivlin was there to greet my wife and me, wearing the same uniform. His nephew, who in 1965 had accompanied us on a location trip to the Dead Sea lugging his tommy gun, had been killed scaling the Golan Heights. Two or three others whom we knew slightly had been victims of the battles, but for the most part our friends had come through unscathed.

The food had improved. Colorful restaurants and efficient hotels had sprung up all over Tel Aviv. But the maids still tore up the toilet paper in the Deborah on Fridays.

Haym Topol took us for a drive to Jerusalem, and exulted in the fact that he could now give us a choice of *four* highways to that city. We drove right by the fortress of Latrun, where the infant Army had been baptized in blood by the Arab Legion. Now it was in Israel, and the monks in the monastery nearby were selling Latrun Wine.

In Jerusalem we went directly to the sacred Wailing Wall, which had been denied us before. We even had lunch in an Arab hotel in what had been Jordanian Jerusalem; and the Arab maître d'hotel selected the proper delicacies for us from the menu. We wandered about the narrow, strident streets of the Old City, to the twelve Stations of the Cross, and drank Turkish coffee at one of the coffee houses, amid a hundred men who all looked like—and for all we knew might well have been—chiefs of the Arab underground.

We went to Bethlehem and stood in the Manger, or at least, what the travel folders said was the Manger.

We did all the things Colonel David Marcus had hoped some day to do. But all of it seemed unreal.

Until we got a call from Moishe. He insisted on showing us around; he would come down from Nahariya and meet us in Akko, the ancient Arab city of Acre.

How would we find him?

"Easy," said Moishe, "just ask for Moishe with the white Moostang."

"Moishe!" I cried, "you've got a car! You're working for your father!"

Somewhat sadly, he admitted he had switched from the arts to the salami business. But the white Mustang from his father had apparently healed all wounds.

We met him on a corner of the fabled city, the Mustang shining like the Holy Grail, and he gave us the tour, not only of the new Israel, but of Moishe.

Had he been in the fighting? So who wasn't? Moishe had been in the paratroops, he was called up by a secret word on the radio to his unit, everyone on the block had knocked on his door to make sure he had heard it. He was immediately taken to the Secret Air Base near Tel Aviv. This is the same Secret Air Base where Danny Kaye and Jack Benny and other American show business personalities have entertained the troops. I had, on occasion, picked up soldiers hitchhiking there, who had carefully instructed me in the shortest route to their hidden headquarters.

Moishe and his unit had been told to stand by; they were to be dropped onto Egyptian airfields to destroy enemy planes on the ground. About midnight came word to forget it. The Israeli Air Force hadn't left any planes for them to destroy.

The paratroopers were told to get some rest. At 3:00 A.M. they would be dropped into the desert to knock out an Egyptian fortress blocking the path of the Israeli Armored Forces. Moishe was furnished with his pack, a tommy gun, a bazooka, ammunition, hand grenades, and a parachute.

"When they hoisted it on my back," he said, "already I could fall down. I made up my mind if I should jump, I wouldn't bother wearing the parachute, it wouldn't help. With that weight I'd hit so hard, I'd go right into the ground anyway."

At three o'clock in the morning the boys were awakened to be told that a message had been received from the Israeli Armored Forces; they were already twenty miles beyond the fortress. The paratroopers could go back to sleep.

At 5:00 A.M. they were awakened again and told they were to be loaded into busses. Moishe protested he had never been taught to parachute from a bus. No one listened; since their presence was not required in Egypt, the paratroopers were heading for the Old City of Jerusalem.

So, like the refugees of 1948, they arrived at the scene of battle in a Tel Aviv bus. The difference was that these were tough, battle-trained experts. And they all spoke one language.

Moishe's unit was given the honor of being the first to attempt to breach the wall of the Old City. The paratroopers were also told that, because this was holy ground, they would not be accompanied by tanks or covered by artillery. Nothing must be destroyed except the Jordanian Army, which, however, *would* be using tanks and artillery. To Moishe, the whole bus ride seemed a mistake. He should have asked for a transfer.

They were to use a tank only to batter in the Dung Gates, so called because they were at the rear and used in ancient times for the removal of offal. But Moishe's commander refused. If his men were to be the first Hebrew troops into old Jerusalem, they would enter by the historic, heavily guarded Lion's Gate, not sneak around the back way. Moishe implied that he was not thrilled by his commander's sense of history.

At any rate, the paratroop battalion smashed through the Lion's Gate on foot and poured into the Old City. Moishe charged through with the rest of them and, he told us, it all seemed like a game, like something that was happening to someone else, until he came around a corner and there, in the street, lay four of his comrades without their heads. A Jordanian tank was turning its turret toward him.

"For the first time," Moishe remarked, "I say to myself, 'Moishe, maybe you don't go home. Maybe you don't go home to the white Mustang. Ever.' All the time they were shooting, but they missed. So I knocked out the tank and I kept running, all the time running."

"Moishe," I said, "just a minute. You knocked out the tank? How?"

"How should I know?" he asked, surprised that I should be so foolish. "I'm here, so I know I knocked it out. I ran, I shot, I ran, I don't remember what I did. All of a sudden I couldn't run any more, there was a big wall in front of me. All the soldiers were crying. I couldn't understand. Then I understood. This wall was The Wall. I couldn't believe. I sat down at the bottom of the Wall.

"Next thing, somebody comes over to me, pushes in my face a microphone. 'You are the first unit to reach the Wall of the Temple,' this somebody says. 'Say something for Kol Yisrael, the Voice of Israel.' So I said something, I don't know what, I was crying, too, and you know? My parents, they were listening, on the radio they heard my voice, all of a sudden they know I'm not dead."

Possibly, I thought, if Moishe had written my script for me, and if I had driven the car for him, things would have worked out better.

"So my commander comes over, I figure he is going to say, 'Moishe, here is a medal, you are now an *Aluf,* go home, have a good rest, first you should give me your autograph.' But you know what he says? 'Moishe, get back on the bus!' For what, I want to know? What am I, a Bus Trooper? So he says it's because they need me in Syria, I'm such a great hero. Believe me, I live in Nahariya, right next to Syria, all my life, I'm not in such a hurry to see it. I get on the bus, it drives us back to the Secret Air Base, they put us into helicopters, when I jump out I can see Nahariya, but I don't bother to look, because we are landing on the Golan Heights."

By this time, as I have neglected to mention, we and Moishe and the white Mustang had driven to these same cliffs inside which the Syrian Army had dug tremendous underground emplacements for their artillery. The paratroopers hit them from behind, and the guns, being in caves, could not be turned around. The Israeli tanks, Moishe told us, climbed the almost perpendicular heights so fast they were running over their own engineers, who were attempting to build a road for them.

We got out of the Mustang and Moishe took us over to one of the gun emplacements. All about us, burned-out tanks and trucks, the rubble of war, lay undisturbed, months after the battle. A Syrian jeep hung from the top of a telephone pole, where jubilant Israeli soldiers had somehow placed it. We went into the deserted bunker. There were still traces of the last occupants, some clothes, cigarettes, an air of desolation; this must have been a grim place to be unless you had something terribly important to fight for. Moishe motioned and led us to the slit opening in the concrete. Through it we could see, below us, the entire valley of the Galilee and the Sea of Galilee itself. An incredible field of fire, an impregnable position; but the men within it had not been impregnable within themselves.

Moishe spoke in quieter tones now. About how the paratroopers triumphantly took the town of Kuneitra, toward which we were now driving. And two of his friends, searching through an empty house, had came upon a beautiful 21-inch television set, a prize among prizes. They picked it up and disappeared forever from this world. It had been expertly booby-trapped.

The fighting had continued. The advance units pushed on into Syria. And Moishe had been approached by an Israeli officer who had taken him to a group of wounded Syrian soldiers. He was a little reluctant to tell us this last, but, finally, decided his friends were entitled to know how it was, how it *all* was.

There were no drugs to spare, the Syrians were dying anyway. He was ordered to shoot them.

"It happened over there," Moishe said, pointing out a field. "You know how it is, I talk Arab, since a boy I talk it. And so I pick up my gun, this Syrian soldier holds up a picture and says, 'My wife! My children! Please!' " Moishe turned to me. "Like a movie, you know? Only believe me, it's not a camera in my hand. I shoot. If only I don't talk Arab, maybe it wouldn't be so bad. But I shoot anyway. I'm crying but I shoot. It's a war. But now I'm tired of it. I am very tired of this war."

We didn't talk much after that. He took us to Nahariya and we met his parents, and had a wonderful dinner—ham and pork. And Moishe gave my wife the pictures of the pigs the Orthodox developer had once refused to print.

I couldn't get this story out of my mind, so I asked some friends in the Army about the incident later. It was true. Some soldiers had refused to obey the order and had been sentenced by a military court.

The sentences had been commuted. And then the officer who gave the order had been court-martialed. He is in prison.

I tell the story because some of us, sometimes, find ourselves rejoicing in the triumphs of a tiny nation beset upon all sides.

And forget that war is not a cause for rejoicing, ever.